INCLUDING PARENTS?

INCLUSIVE EDUCATION

Series Editors:

Gary Thomas, Professor of Education, Oxford Brookes University, and Christine O'Hanlon, School of Education, University of East Anglia

The movement towards inclusive education is gathering momentum throughout the world. But how is it realized in practice? The volumes within this series will examine the arguments for inclusive schools and the evidence for the success of inclusion. The intention behind the series is to fuse a discussion about the ideals behind inclusion with pictures of inclusion in practice. The aim is to straddle the theory/practice divide, keeping in mind the strong social and political principles behind the move to inclusion whilst observing and noting the practical challenges to be met.

Current and forthcoming titles:

INCLUDING PARENTS?

Education, citizenship and parental agency

Carol Vincent

Open University Press
Buckingham · Philadelphia

Open University Press
Celtic Court
22 Ballmoor
Buckingham
MK18 1XW

email: enquiries@openup.co.uk
world wide web: www.openup.co.uk

and
325 Chestnut Street
Philadelphia, PA 19106, USA

First Published 2000

A catalogue record of this book is available from the British Library

ISBN   0 335 20442 2 (pb)   0 335 20443 0 (hb)

Library of Congress Cataloging-in-Publication Data Available

Typeset by Graphicaft Limited, Hong Kong
Printed in Great Britain by Biddles Limited, Guildford and King's Lynn

For Madi,
with love

Contents

Series editors' preface

'Inclusion' has become something of a buzz-word. It's difficult to trace its provenance or the growth in its use over the last two decades, but what is certain is that it is now de rigeur for mission statements, political speeches and policy documents of all kinds. It has become a cliché – obligatory in the discourse of all right-thinking people.

The making of 'inclusion' into a cliché, inevitable as it perhaps is, is nevertheless disappointing, since it means that the word is often merely a filler in the conversation. It means that people can talk about 'inclusion' without really thinking about what they mean, merely to add a progressive gloss to what they are saying. Politicians who talk casually about the need for a more inclusive society know that they will be seen as open-minded and enlightened, and will be confident in the knowledge that all sorts of difficult practical questions can be circumvented. If this happens, and if there is insufficient thought about the nitty gritty mechanics (what the Fabians called 'gas and water' matters), those who do work hard for inclusion can easily be dismissed as peddling empty promises.

This series is dedicated to examining in detail some of the ideas which lie behind inclusive education. Inclusion, much more than 'integration' or 'mainstreaming', is embedded in a range of contexts – political and social as well as psychological and educational – and our aim in this series is to make some examination of these contexts. In providing a forum for discussion and critique we hope to provide the basis for a wider intellectual and practical foundation for more inclusive practice in schools and elsewhere.

In noting that inclusive education is indeed about more than simply 'integration', it is important to stress that inclusive education is really about extending the comprehensive ideal in education. Those who talk about it are therefore less concerned with children's supposed 'special educational needs' (and it is becoming increasingly difficult meaningfully to define what such needs are) and more concerned with developing an education system in which tolerance, diversity and equity are striven for. To aim for such developments is surely uncontentious; what is perhaps more controversial is the means by which this is done. There are many and varied ways of helping to develop more inclusive schools and the authors of this series look at some of these. While one focus in this has to be on the place and role of the special school, it is by no means the only focus: the thinking and practice which go on inside and outside schools may do much to exclude or marginalize children and the authors of this series try to give serious attention to such thinking and practice.

The books in this series therefore examine a range of matters: the knowledge of special education; the frames of analysis which have given legitimacy to such knowledge; the changing political mood which inspires a move to inclusion. In the context of all this, they also examine some new developments in inclusive thinking and practice inside and outside schools.

Carol Vincent's book is an important contribution to the literature on inclusion for it looks at some of the stereotypes which surround parenting as it is seen by schools in particular and by society more generally. Far from enabling inclusion, the constructs used to frame parents' place in education often in fact marginalize and exclude. Drawing on the notion that 'reservoirs of citizenship' exist in what she calls 'parent-centred organizations' (PCOs) she makes a powerful argument for the case that these organizations can help to enable participation. Following her in-depth research on different kinds of such organization, she concludes that while these PCOs and similar organizations are fragile in nature, they are nevertheless an important new development in enabling more active participation by parents in education.

The development of such small scale associational initiatives is indeed important in civic life, for there are many dilemmas which face those who value the idea of an inclusive society. A contradiction in the voice of government disturbs the dialogue both of this book and that in the rest of the series. It is that while one voice speaks of making society in general and schools in particular more inclusive, another maintains a vigorous agenda of competition and performativity. If choice, selection and the comparison of schools on the basis of their pupils' attainment hold the foreground in educational policy it is difficult to see how real progress toward a more inclusive education system can be made. Perhaps part of the answer lies in precisely the kind of organization which Carol Vincent analyses with such perspicacity in this book: the setting up of collectives of ordinary people who can ensure that issues important to them and to their children are discussed.

Gary Thomas
Christine O'Hanlon

Preface

This book is about parents and parental action around education. At its
centre is a consideration of parents' varied relationships with the education
system. An understanding of these relationships and the different roles played
by parents and professionals is vital in illuminating the hierarchies, procedures and balances of power that construct professional–lay relations in
education. Additionally, as I argue in this book, these interactions shed some
light on a wider set of relationships – those between citizens and welfare
state institutions in general. That is to say, parents' experiences of their
children's schools are one aspect of their wider experiences with welfare state
institutions. Clearly, a discussion of parents as citizens requires a broader
focus on parental activity within the education system than simply a consideration of their relationships with their own child's school. A relevant, but
often neglected, phenomenon is the growth of local groups around educational issues, and the experiences of those parents involved. A study of such
groups is at the heart of this book. A second key issue is the way in which
relationships between parents and education professionals are mediated by
ethnicity, class and gender. My third concern is to consider the different
ways in which parents become involved with educational issues. While parents
are often written and spoken about as one group, in order to differentiate
them from other social actors (such as teachers, for example), the wide
diversity within the parent body and the ways in which this influences
parental actions and reactions requires careful exploration. This book reports
and analyses my research with parents of varied backgrounds and their experiences of involvement with the education system, in particular through campaigns and mobilizations, but also through individual schools.

Chapter 1 discusses the subject positions usually open to parents: *parent
as consumer* and *parent as partner*. I then suggest that a focus on *parent as
citizen* can reveal aspects of the home–school relationship, which are obscured
and overlooked by the other two subject positions. In addition, such a focus
can prove revealing as to the state of citizenship in Britain today, particularly

concerning the degree of passivity which describes the relationship of most citizens to the public sphere. I argue that explanations for this inactivity centre on traditional notions of citizenship which despite, or rather because of, their claims to universalism and unity operate to exclude or marginalize particular sectors of the population. The formation of 'counterpublics' appears to offer a solution – arenas where people can, through deliberation, formulate their own agendas and critiques. I ask whether parent groups, referred to by the more specific terminology of 'parent-centred organizations' (PCOs) could be understood as fulfilling this purpose. Before the empirical interrogation of this proposal, Chapter 2 examines other relevant discourses around parenting. In this chapter I argue that the normative concept of a 'good' parent is highly classed and gendered, and it is working class women who are the target of the greatest attention through state-sponsored tutelage. Using Gramsci's work, I also pick up the themes from Chapter 1 and consider the extent to which the case study PCOs disseminate hegemonic discourses about parenting. I ask whether their professional staff or parent members or clients wish to and are able to challenge such discourses. Chapter 2 also introduces the four case study groups, and briefly describes the research design. Chapter 3 focuses, in particular, on the parent–professional relationship with regard to a special education advice centre. I discuss how the workers attempted, through the development of parent support groups, to extend the traditional mode of advice work, namely individual problem solving. Chapter 4, written in conjunction with Simon Warren, is concerned with the work of a parent education group, and discusses, in this context, the ideas and practices of 'sensitive mothering' (Walkerdine and Lucey 1989). We argue that such discourses appear oppressive, and try to reconcile this viewpoint with the women students' enjoyment of the course, and the benefits they felt they received from it. Chapter 5 contrasts two parent-run groups, a campaigning group and a self-help support group, and locates their actions and members' accounts of their experiences in relation to the literature on social movements. I suggest that the social class profile of the membership of both groups was crucial in understanding the largely conservative trajectory which they took. However, I also argue that the members of the black parents' support group came closest of all the four case study groups to providing a 'counterpublic', through members' emphasis on challenging aspects of the education system they believed to be discriminatory. Chapter 6, written by myself and Simon Warren, switches the focus from PCOs to schools and considers how refugee and asylum-seeking families, those for whom formal citizenship rights cannot be taken for granted, fare in a competitive, increasingly managerial education system. We argue that the pressure generated for teachers by these forces create situations in which pupils are increasingly abstracted from their home lives, and viewed as disembodied. The opportunity for parents and teachers to engage in a debate concerning the children's welfare and educational progress, and, moreover, one which is not constructed solely according to the school's agenda, is therefore marginalized. Chapter 7, the concluding chapter, considers the wider implications of the empirical data emerging from this study of PCOs in relation to citizenship, public participation and agency.

I conclude that the PCOs are limited, fragile and partial in their scope and their impact. However, despite this, they do offer a space in which lay voices can be injected into debates on educational issues. Additionally, PCOs can identify areas and formulate discussion on issues normally overlooked or understood only in particular ways. Their limitations are very real, but in contrast to the passivity which currently defines citizenship, they go some way towards the creation of a language and several arenas in which (at least some) parents acting as citizens can participate in shaping educational opportunities for all children.

Acknowledgements

I started planning the research on which this book is based in 1995. In the intervening five years I have accumulated a long, long list of debts. I owe thanks to the following.

First of all, I owe thanks to those people who feature in these pages, who kindly gave up their time to talk to me about parenting, education, and their experiences of agency and activity. I learnt a great deal from them, more than can be expressed in one book. Particular thanks go to Sarah, Diana, Maggie, Paul, and Vjollca. I hope I have given some idea of the conflicts, tensions, pressure and opportunities with which they all engage.

I am grateful to the Economic and Social Research Council for funding the research project on parents' groups (R000221634) and to the Nuffield Foundation for funding the study of refugee parents and schools.

Simon Warren, who has co-authored two chapters here, played an invaluable role in the conduct and completion of the two projects, especially the refugee study. He also maintained his good humour and calm throughout the various crises and impossible deadlines that beset us. My grateful thanks for everything he contributed. Barry Troyna discussed my plans for this research and gave me, as ever, invaluable advice. In the years that I knew him, he played a major role in shaping and developing my approach to research, and I owe him – and still miss him – a great deal.

A large number of people made time (some at very short notice) to read parts of this book and gave me helpful and constructive feedback. Thanks to the series editors Gary Thomas and Christine O'Hanlon for being very supportive of this project since its inception. In particular, thanks to Gary Thomas for valiantly struggling through the entire manuscript. Thanks also to Stephen Ball, Sarah Gale, Sharon Gewirtz, Sue Heath, Ian Loveland, Jane Martin, Sarah Neal, Stewart Ranson, Diane Reay, Sheila Riddell, Simon Warren, Geoff Whitty and Philip Woods. Members of the Kings College 'Parental Choice and Market Forces' seminar group have read and commented on earlier versions of the material presented here and, as usual, I have learnt a lot from these interchanges.

During the writing of this book, I moved jobs. I would like to thank Jim Campbell, Donna Jay (also for the excellent transcribing), Ann Lewis, Pat Sikes, Wendy Robinson and Simon Warren for their encouragement during my time at Warwick. However, the lure of life without the M1 was great, and I would also like to thank Dave Gillborn and Geoff Whitty for their support since I have been at the Institute of Education, as well as to members of Policy Studies for making it such a congenial place to work.

There is yet another list of people whose friendship I have enjoyed over the last five years, and from whose conversation I have learnt. I am indebted to Sarah, Diane, Stephen, Dave, Sharon, Sheila, Sue and Simon in this respect.

Finally – and fundamentally – my family. The greatest of thanks go to my mum for just being there, and to Ian in particular, for his steadfastness, his 'wit', his calm and his 'new man-ness'. I would be lost without him. This book is dedicated to our daughter, Madi – for managing to make even 6 o'clock in the morning an (almost) enjoyable time!

List of abbreviations

ACE   Advisory Centre for Education
ACES   African/Caribbean Education Support (pseudonym for a case study group)
APM   Annual Parents' Meeting
CASE   Campaign for the Advancement of State Education
DfEE   Department for Education and Employment
IPPR   Institute for Public Policy Research
LEA   Local education authority
NSM   New social movement
OFSTED   Office for Standards in Education
PCO   Parent-centred organization
PIE   Participating in Education (pseudonym for a case study group)
SEAC   Special education advice centre (pseudonym for a case study group)
SEN   Special educational needs
SENCo   Special educational needs coordinator

Parents and education: consumers, partners or citizens?

> There is an intermediary sphere between private matters and the affairs of state which is perhaps the most strategic. This is the sphere of altruistic participation in voluntary associations; although the latter are not directly political in character, they are nevertheless 'reservoirs of citizenship'.
>
> (Leca 1992: 21)

This book considers the roles and relationships open to parents in their dealings with the state education system. For the most part, my focus is not on parent–teacher relationships within individual schools, but rather on the role of locally based, parent-centred groups and organizations. The workings of these groups, and the roles they play in contributing to the wider education system, are largely overlooked in recent literature; the dominant 'gaze' within educational research focuses on the operations and interactions within classrooms, schools and/or local education authorities, rather than those pertaining to locally based educationally oriented organizations. Yet it is my contention that such groups deserve attention and appreciation in any discussion of moves towards a more inclusive education system.

In order to substantiate that statement, this introductory chapter looks at the 'subject positions' (Apple 1996) that are open to parents in the current education system; by that I mean the ways in which understandings of 'appropriate' parental behaviour and relationships with other parents and teachers are reached, disseminated, accepted, challenged and/or subverted. In my first book (Vincent 1996), I suggested that these subject positions numbered four: *parent as supporter/learner, parent as consumer, parent as independent* and *parent as participant* (see Table 1.1).

What I want to do here is to consider the three main categories of activity (the fourth, *parent as independent* involves a minimal relationship with the

Table 1.1 Parents' subject positions

Parents' role	Supporter/learner	Consumer	Independent	Participant
Function	To support professionals and adopt their concerns and approaches	To encourage school accountability and high standards	To maintain minimal contact with the school	To be involved in governance of the school as well as the education of their own child
Mechanisms	• Curriculum support via professionally run schemes • Attending school educational events • Supporting/ organizing school social and fund-raising events	• Choosing a school using 'league tables' and provisions for open enrolment • Receiving information as detailed in government guidelines	Little home–school communication or interaction. Parent may provide alternative forms of education e.g. supplementary classes	• Parent governors • Statutorily based parents' groups • Membership of local/ national education groups and organizations
Focus	For attainment issues – individual child. For extra-curricular activities and fundraising – whole class/ school	For attainment issues – individual child. Limited involvement in management issues – e.g. voting for changes in school's status	Individual child	Potential focus on all aspects of education on range of levels: • individual child • whole school • local and national educational issues

Source: Adapted from Vincent (1996)

school), not so much at the level of practices as I did previously but at a conceptual level. I suggest that there are two dominant common-sense understandings of parents' relations to state education: *parent as consumer* and *parent as partner* with education professionals ('partner' is a more general widely used term for what I previously termed 'parent as supporter/learner'). I will posit an alternative understanding of the relationship between parents and the education system: *parent as citizen* (developing my earlier understanding of this category). Following on from this, I critique traditional readings of citizenship, and develop a conceptualization, based on ideas of deliberative democracy, which can begin to account for collective action among a population marked by heterogeneity and difference. Finally in this chapter, I suggest how such a conceptualization could be usefully employed to think about parents in relation to educational institutions.

Consumerism (parent as consumer)

The symbolic establishment of consumer sovereignty was a key feature of the restructuring of education that started in the late 1980s under a Conservative government. A decade later, it seems equally clear that, in policy terms, consumer use of exit as a sanction against aberrant producer behaviour is still in place. In actuality the situation is more complex. The imperfections of parental choice policies in practice have been well documented (e.g. Gewirtz *et al*. 1995, Whitty *et al*. 1998; Woods *et al*. 1998). These researchers have emphasized the processes by which popular schools are themselves in a position to do the choosing. Motivated by their wish to attract particular groups of 'desirable' pupils, many schools have implemented similar traditionally based organizational and pedagogical regimes, which they think might be popular with parents (Fitz *et al*. 1993; Halpin *et al*. 1997). The research of Philip Woods and his colleagues (1998) develops this argument. They suggest that the schools in their study were poor at 'consumer scanning', that is gathering the views and opinions of actual and prospective parents and pupils. They explain this in terms of a reliance by teachers upon their own professional expertise as being the best guide to practice, decision making and innovation. In addition, schools are encouraged into certain modes of behaviour by two other sets of influences: central government policies and legislation (the literacy and numeracy hours in primary schools for example), and the behaviour of other local competitors. Thus there appears to be a degree of commonality in the initiatives adopted by schools and little scope for parents to affect change directly, although it is important to note that there have been documented instances of middle class parents exerting a direct pressure upon schools to modify some aspect of their curriculum, pedagogy or organization (see below). Most notable among initiatives are the proliferation of examples of 'symbolic' (Woods *et al*. 1998) or 'reinvented' (Halpin *et al*. 1997) traditionalism (e.g. uniform, an emphasis upon discipline and academic standards), which suggests that this is what schools think parents (or to be more accurate, a particular type of parent whom they wish to attract) want from their child's school. Yet there are indications that many parents consider the personal and social outcomes of schooling to be as important as the academic ones despite schools' increasing tendency to privilege the latter (Gewirtz *et al*. 1995; Vincent and Warren 1998; Woods *et al*. 1998).

Research analysing the effects of choice policies in Britain and in other Western states suggests that allowing parents to choose a school does not necessarily result in greater parental involvement with that school (Goldring 1997; Whitty *et al*. 1998; Woods *et al*. 1998; Vincent and Martin 2000). Consumerism rests on the power of 'exit', an economic mechanism that has no necessary nor inevitable relationship with 'voice', a political mechanism. The terms *exit* and *voice* are taken from Hirschman's (1970) seminal work, *Exit, Voice and Loyalty*, and are described thus:

> The availability to consumers of the exit option and their frequent resort to it are characteristic of 'normal' competition . . . the exit option is widely held to be uniquely powerful by inflicting revenue losses on delinquent management.
>
> (1970: 21)

> To resort to voice, rather than exit, is for the customer or member to make an attempt at changing the practices, policies and outputs of the firm from which one buys or the organisation to which one belongs. Voice is here defined as any attempt at all to change, rather than escape from, an objectionable state of affairs, whether through individual or collective petition.
>
> (1970: 30)

Yet the opportunities for the exercise of individual or collective parental voice *within* a school appear limited.[1] 'Voice' is also a more unfamiliar response than 'exit' for many clients and more 'messy', more uncertain in its outcome (Hirschman 1970; Larabee 1999). Instances of parental lobbying on behalf of their own child are known to every school, but whether parents possess an effective individual voice (i.e. in the sense of a dialogue leading to school activity and change) is largely determined by two sets of factors. The first is the differential possession and employment of individual parents' social, cultural and material resources, and the second, the school's view of the aspects of their children's education with which parents should be concerned (Vincent *et al.* 1999). There have been recent attempts to formalize the latter with the mandatory introduction of home–school agreements (see Chapter 2).

The exercise of collective voice is an unfamiliar concept for many parents and the legislation of the late 1980s predicated on an individual market model was clearly at odds with collective action (Adler *et al.* 1989; Westoby 1989). Indeed, it is possible to argue that the concept of collective voice is marginalized under the consumer model. Although this model does encompass the powers parents have to elect several of their number as parent governors, to attend Annual Parents' Meetings (APMs), and to vote for changes in the status of the school, the role of parent-as-manager is normally limited in effect. When parents vote in a ballot for status alteration, for instance, their 'voice' lasts only for a moment, the involvement does not continue after the vote, and research on the ballots on grant maintained status indicated that in that case at least, parents were often enacting the wishes of the headteacher and/or governing body (Fitz *et al.* 1993). It is possible that ballots on grammar school retention may provoke significant local mobilization. As was seen over 20 years ago, this is one subject around which local groups are likely to campaign (e.g. in London, the Barnet Parents' Federation).

The 'voice' of parents through Annual Parents' Meetings or school-based Parents' Associations is muted. APMs are often poorly attended (Martin *et al.*

1995), and the activities of Parents' Associations tend to be focused on arranging fundraising and social events. Even in cases where parental activity and involvement in the running of a school is high, that activity is often carefully channelled and controlled by teachers (Martin and Vincent 1999). Thus parental 'voice' rarely impinges upon the operation of the school as an educational institution. High-profile exceptions to this have been documented, involving parents being instrumental in causing schools to change their policies (see Ball and Vincent 2000 for overview), but these appear to be uncommon occurrences in the UK. The representation of parents' interests apparently put in place by the installation of parent governors on the governing body is also weak. Parent governors, a tiny minority of the parent body (and one in which ethnic minority and working class governors are still under-represented; Deem *et al.* 1995), are instructed to see themselves as integral parts of the governing body (Hatcher *et al.* 1993; Deem *et al.* 1995), rather than as representatives of particular interest groups – representative parents, rather than parent representatives. In recent years some LEAs have made moves towards placing parent governors on education committees as parent representatives (usually with observer status only). However the position of these parents after the introduction of the new 'cabinet'-style forms of local government (part of the Local Government Bill) is unclear. Thus, with the possible exception of activity around the future of grammar schools, there appear to be few instances of and opportunities for collective parental participation at any level of the UK education system, and even the exercise of individual 'voice' is dependent to some extent upon local circumstances.

Partnership (parent as supporter/learner)

Partnership is the common term used, especially by professionals but also by some parents, to describe the actual, intended or, more often, ideal relationship between parents and teachers. It elides parental involvement and support for the school as an institution (its policies, its events, its fundraising) with parental support for children's education (e.g. participating in home reading schemes). I have commented elsewhere that such 'partnerships', with the connotations of equality inherent in the term, are often legitimating devices used by schools to encourage parental support for their aims and objectives. It is because of this that I have previously used the term *parent as supporter/learner* to describe the incorporation of those parents undertaking particular activities and practices suggested by the school as appropriate and useful tasks, both in support of the institution itself and the child's education (Vincent 1996; Vincent and Tomlinson 1997). This does not mean that these parents are necessarily passive conductors of the school's agenda; indeed qualitative studies of parents of primary school children reveal the extensive amount of educational work, in the broadest sense, which mothers carry out in support of their children, not all of which follows the school's agenda and priorities (David *et al.* 1993; Vincent 1996; Reay 1998). I refer to 'mother' here because the parent who most commonly assumes responsibility for the child's education, across social class groups and ethnicities, appears to be the woman – an issue further discussed below. All forms of parental involvement in education are not, in any case, sanctioned by mainstream schools. The thriving supplementary school movement is one form of provision, sometimes organized and delivered by parents, which has little connection with the mainstream and about which many mainstream teachers know little.

Parental support is by no means homogeneous in its nature. I have already alluded to its gendered nature, and there is some research exploring its racialized dimension (e.g. Bhatti 1999). Social class is another crucial aspect. In my earlier study (Vincent 1996) I found evidence that some teachers still maintained deficit views of the abilities and interests of working class parents in relation to education, and that such deficiencies were often read off from cultural differences, poverty or non-traditional family organization. On the same point, the shaping of parental involvement by social class differentials, Diane Reay concludes the following from her study of parent–teacher relationships in a middle and working class school in London:

> Women across the sample [i.e. from different class groups] were engaged in practical, educational and emotional work in support of their children's education. They were monitoring their children's progress and attempting to repair any educational deficits they discovered (Griffith and Smith 1990) . . . What made a difference was not women's activities but the context in which they took place and the resources underpinning them. Although many of the working class women had fewer cultural resources than middle class mothers, including far lower incomes, fewer educational qualifications, less educational knowledge and information about the system, this did not indicate lower levels of involvement in children's education. What it did mean was less effective practices, as working class women found it difficult to assume the role of educational expert, were less likely to persuade the teachers to act on their complaints and were ill-equipped financially, socially and psychologically to compensate for the deficits they perceived in their children's education.
>
> (Reay 1998: 163; see also Lareau 1989)

In addition, as Reay points out, different schools will look for and encourage different sorts of involvement, some sticking within traditional models, others experimenting with more participative innovations (Martin and Vincent 1999). Nor is it the case that all parents at all times are positioned as subordinate in their relationships with teachers (Todd and Higgins 1998). While their location within an institution gives teachers a measure of security and status, this can be challenged by parents. I noted earlier that the literature in this area contains examples of middle class parents affecting change in school policies and procedures, but more common forms of interaction also allow some opportunities for contestation and challenge. MacLure and Walker's (1999) work on parents' evenings, for instance, shows parents introducing their own agendas into consultations, and also challenging teachers' judgements of their children or their practices. However, teachers maintained overall control of the exchanges, with parents largely consenting to and collaborating in an exchange which positioned them as 'clients'. Thus the involvement of parents in their children's education is a differentiated and complex phenomenon, and one hardly done justice by the use of a simplistic, blanket term such as 'partnership'.

Citizenship (parent as participant)

> Society is pluralising in front of our eyes . . . we are sleepwalking into diversity.
>
> (Hall 2000)

The terms of reference which posit consumerism and partnership as viable and valid options for framing parents' relations with the education system leave out, I believe, a broader angle. That is, that some interesting aspects of the relationship, previously obscured and overlooked, can be brought into the picture through a consideration of parent–school relationships as an exemplar of relations between citizens and state institutions. In addition, a focus on parental relationships with educational institutions can prove revealing as to the state of citizenship in Britain today; its differentiated nature for particular groups and individuals; the degree of passivity which infuses modern citizenship; and the trajectories and experiences of citizen agency and activity.

There is some confusion over how well developed 'citizenship practices' are in the UK. The more formal the practice, the less practised it appears to be. The 1999 *British Social Attitudes Survey* (Jowell *et al.* 1999) reveals a very low level of interest and participation (even at the level of voting) in local government. Less than 5 per cent of people could correctly name their local councillor for example. However, a remarkably high 87 per cent of the sample said they had undertaken some voluntary activity in the last year or were members of some sort of local organization. The report also suggests that strong social ties of this sort are more common among the relatively affluent (see also Hall 1997; Halpern 1999).

The discussions of citizenship rights and responsibilities, proffered periodically by politicians, tend to be somewhat muted and conducted within limited terms of reference. In the last two decades, two Conservative Home Secretaries (Douglas Hurd and Michael Howard) exhorted the public to 'active citizenship' which in their definition meant an emphasis on citizens' duties towards their communities, particularly where the prevention of crime was concerned. The definition of the Labour Prime Minister, Tony Blair, as offered in early 1999, also concentrated on individual responsibility within local communities, his emphasis being on volunteering (Brindle 1999). For many people, citizenship comprises little more than voting in elections (and turnouts in local and European elections are notoriously low, often under 30 per cent) and a vague and somewhat ill-defined sense of rights against the state (Stewart 1997). We live, in short, within a passive polity. As Benhabib notes, 'the development of the modern state in Western industrial societies created a specific kind of politics; a politics of domestication, containment and boundary drawing' (1996a: 7). Efforts to explain this passivity can centre on two key points: first, the growth of the welfare state and its restructuring by neo-liberalism, and second, the limitations of traditional understandings of citizenship.

Citizenship and the rise and fall of the welfare state

The growth of the social democratic welfare state in Britain was tightly bound up with a rich and productive concept of citizenship, as epitomized by the work of T. H. Marshall. His conception of citizenship had three component parts: political (e.g. the right to vote), civil (e.g. individual freedoms, of speech, right to hold property, access to courts, etc.) and social. The latter referred to access to welfare rights which would protect citizens from poverty, and allow them to participate fully in society. Marshall viewed the welfare state as the guarantor of these social rights. As Turner notes,

> The merit of T. H. Marshall's approach to class and citizenship was that it presented a promising response to the relationship between scarcity and solidarity within the context of a modern industrial society (Marshall 1981). For Marshall citizenship was a set of institutions which protected individuals and families from the full impact of the market place . . . Citizenship represented a social response to the inequalities of opportunity and condition which are typical of capitalist societies.
>
> (Turner 1996: 261)

Later analyses of citizenship within welfare state societies, including criticisms of Marshall's own work, were less optimistic. Such state-centred perspectives on citizenship derived from a social and political context in which the state seemed to offer, through its welfare functions, a role as benign provider and protector. More critical analyses sought to question this understanding of the state and to demonstrate ways in which this seemingly benevolent paternalism obscured the continuing existence of major class inequalities (Ellison 1997: 700).

Anna Yeatman (1994) presents a detailed and specific description of postwar citizenship in social democratic societies, drawing on the work of Donzelot (1979) to suggest that the welfare state understanding of citizenship is informed by social class distinctions and divisions. Citizens able to gain economic independence can *contract* particular services. Those who cannot, can in theory gain access to state-provided welfare services but, in doing so, come under the *tutelage* of professionals 'who determine whether you fit the criteria for eligibility . . . what your real needs are, and how and whether they can be fulfilled' (Yeatman 1994: 77). It is arguable that in the case of state education, a certain blurring of the boundaries between contract and tutelage is apparent. Middle class parents who in many other spheres of life (such as private health care or housing) have straightforwardly contractual relationships with providers may find themselves in a more complex relationship with the providers of state education. As noted above, the nature and extent of the home–school relationship is normally determined by the school on its own terms. Thus all parents may be offered tutelage by the school in order to encourage appropriate parental behaviour in support of the school's educational project (Martin and Vincent 1999), although it is important to remember that within this some may be positioned as more valued and valuable clients than others.

The distinction between contract and tutelage is echoed by Leonard in his description of the modern welfare state and the division drawn within that between *dependent* and *independent* social actors. The discursive construction of welfare dependency stigmatizes welfare recipients, and unfavourably contrasts them with those who can live independently of benefits, the term 'independence' signifying 'autonomy, industriousness and self-reliance' (1997: 52) (although as Leonard points out, the 'independent' are actually market dependent). The former, in return for benefits, are subject to a more intensive, detailed and regulatory gaze by welfare state professionals than the latter receive (although no subjects are immune from state-sponsored regulatory discourses). Similarly, Fraser and Gordon (1997) outline a genealogy of 'dependency', examining changes in the term's usage in economic, sociological, political and moral/psychological registers. They conclude that shifting semantics mirror wider socio-historical and psychological discourses which increasingly portray 'independence' as the norm, 'dependency' as pathological, while overlooking the potential of interdependent relations.

The influence of neo-liberalism is easily discernible in these semantic shifts. Operating in opposition to Marshall's collective citizenship of entitlement, neo-liberal restructuring of the welfare state has led to an emphasis on 'the individual persona and private autonomy of the individual' (Oliver 1991: 160). This minimalist version of citizenship constructs individuals as 'homo economicus' (Peters 1994), as self-interested, self-sufficient, independent, rational utility maximizers (also Dunleavy 1991). Thus the focus for political activity around citizenship under the Conservative governments of the 1980s and 1990s, as exemplified by the proliferation of charters, was individual citizen's rights as consumers of public services. This was interwoven with a neo-conservative emphasis on citizens' duties towards their communities (such as crime prevention referred to earlier). The two strands are bound together by a common thread – that citizens want and need only a minimal relationship with the state and the public sector institutions within it.

The 'Third Way' of New Labour promises a radical departure from the passivity of the 'old left' social democratic citizenship and the minimalism of new right versions (Blair 1998; Giddens 1998). The Third Way lays stress on the importance of self-determination and individual agency within a framework which emphasizes 'no rights without responsibilities' (Giddens 1998: 65). I briefly consider below this, as yet broadly sketched, programme for renewed social democracy and its implications for generating active citizenship (see Chapter 7).

Citizenship and difference

Jane Martin and I (Martin and Vincent 1999) recently set out the following conceptualization to suggest that there are two main political traditions through which citizenship can be interpreted and practised – liberalism and civic republicanism. These two understandings are ideal types, and one can see hints and echoes of both informing postwar political discourse and practice in the UK, although clearly liberalism has had the more weighty impact.

Advocates of *liberalism* (see especially the work of John Rawls) understand citizenship as a political community of individuals; a universal citizenship of free and equal persons who have protection against undue interference in the form of the rights they hold against the state.

> Citizenship is the capacity for each person to form, revise and rationally pursue his/her definition of the good. Citizens are seen as using their rights to promote their self-interest within certain constraints imposed by the exigency to respect the rights of others.
>
> (Mouffe 1993a: 61)

Individuals are posited, as in Michael Sandel's (1982) term, as 'unencumbered'; separate and self-contained, motivated by the pursuit of private desires. Attaining and maintaining this condition requires a certain amount of inter-action with others. However, the process and procedures for achieving this, liberalism's 'formalistic ethic of rights' (Young 1990: 229), has been criticized for imposing a common framework of rights, and thereby assuming a mono-cultural rationality. Moreover, feminist critics have argued that liberalism is defined by the way in which private and particular aspects of individual life are ruled out of court (e.g. Pateman 1989; Yeatman 1994: 84). The notions of a common good, a public spirit and civic activity are viewed as equally irrelevant, hence Barber's (1984) use of the term 'thin democracy' to describe liberal democracy.

Civic republicanism is based on a belief in a civic community which is sustained by rational consensus. It is primarily distinguished from liberalism by its commitment to the practice of citizenship, as opposed to the passive bearing of rights. Political participation is fundamental to the concept, and accorded an ideal and virtuous status. In traditional understandings of civic republicanism, the public good is understood as something existing independ-ently of, and indeed gaining priority over, individual wishes, an understanding which as Mouffe (1993a: 62) points out is not tenable in late twentieth-century democracies with their emphasis on individual liberty. There are two further points to be made here: one is the austere nature of civic republicanism, the importance of duty and obligation (Marquand 1994), what Hegel termed 'civic virtue'. The second is that the ideal of a substantive 'common good' and shared moral values assumes a homogeneous reason and rationality. Such a stance fails to centre, indeed to acknowledge, the plurality of perspect-ives that postmodern analyses foreground (Young 1990; Yeatman 1994).

The traditions of civic republicanism have been revived by communitarians arguing the need for a rebuilding of social solidarity in the face of anomie and atomization caused by the dominance of liberalism and more recently neo-liberalism (Mouffe 1993b). However, in response, Young (1990) for example criticizes communitarian writers for laying too heavy and too utopian a stress on imagined communities infused by social unity and transparency where power relations, antagonism and difference disappear in rational debate and discussion in search of the 'common good'.

An increasing number of commentators in recent years have highlighted the way in which traditional understandings of citizenship, as outlined above, are exclusionary in practice despite the rhetoric and signifiers of inclusion: terms and practices such as participation in the public sphere, 'universal rights', 'common good', and 'consensus'. This blanket signifying of inclusion ignores structural inequalities of power which act to marginalize particular individuals and groups. Thus some will feel themselves excluded in effect from 'universal rights' or will present radically different readings of the 'common good' from that presumed to be the majority view.

The relationship between independence and interdependency, the individual and the group, is to a certain extent elided in traditional understandings of citizenship. While liberalism privileges individual rights, it suggests that when decisions affecting the collectivity do have to be taken, democratic politics involves public deliberation focused on the common good (Rawls 1971; Cohen 1997: 69). As Benhabib says, summing up Habermas's reading of liberalism, 'the task of politics is the co-ordination of divergent interests amongst private persons' (Benhabib 1996a: 6). Civic republicanism goes further by suggesting that political participation and debate require members to subordinate aspects of their individual subjectivity (e.g. affiliation to a particular ethnic group) to a shared identity as citizens. 'The good of politics is the creation of solidarity amongst citizens' (Benhabib1996a: 6). Thus in liberalism and civic republicanism, the crucial relationship between the individual and the wider societal group is masked by pretensions to homogeneity, assumptions of a common culture and rationality. This leads to a denial of difference and diversity, based on different ways of 'seeing'; differences which derive from social positionings and subjectivities based on (although not exclusively) social class, gender and ethnicity. Iris Young uses a similar argument, in relation to 'individualism' and 'community', to the one that I have laid out concerning liberalism and civic republicanism. She states that although the two are often posited as opposites, both are informed by the same logic, each denying difference although in opposing ways:

> Liberal individualism denies difference by positing the self as a solid, self-sufficient unity, not defined by anything or anyone other than itself ... Proponents of community, on the other hand, deny difference by ... conceiv[ing] of the social subject as a relation of unity or mutuality composed by identification and symmetry among individuals within a totality. Communitarianism represents an urge to see persons in unity with one another in a shared whole.
>
> (Young 1990: 229)

Thus the seemingly abstract nature of citizenship is exposed as a chimera; the apparent universalism and equality look very different when considered through the lens of social class, gender or ethnicity. Several theorists develop this argument further, pointing to the mistaken illusion of a unified polity, a universal citizenry and civic public, which is required to shed particularity and difference in order to participate in the public domain (Young 1990; Phillips 1995). Traditional models of citizenship impose a univocal understanding of what counts as universal values; one that denies and therefore excludes and silences other voices.

Women and citizenship

I have already commented on the ways in which social class can shape experiences of citizenship. Apart from class, one of the most commonly noted axes of exclusion from the seemingly inclusive discourse of traditional citizenship is gender.[2]

Carole Pateman's work (1989) has shown how the Enlightenment philosophy has equated virtues deemed necessary for operating in the public sphere – such as rationality, order and objectivity – with men, and emotion, disorder and subjectivity with women who are therefore deemed unsuitable for public and political participation. Nancy Fraser (1997a), discussing the gendered understanding of the public sphere, cites the work of Landes (1988) and Eley (1992) on this point. Landes describes the growth of the republican public sphere in eighteenth-century France as deliberately opposed to the more woman-friendly but aristocratic salon culture. Eley notes that in the growing bourgeois public sphere of eighteenth- and nineteenth-century England, France and Germany, a network of philosophical, civic, professional and cultural societies and groups developed that were not open to women or working class men. As a result of such cultural traditions, women's presence and activity within the private sphere of the home and the family is positioned as low-status in comparison to men's public deliberations. But this is not to say that women's roles are not loaded with responsibility. Caring, whether for the old or young, is still not generally perceived as high-status work, yet mothering for example requires the shouldering of responsibility for all aspects of a child's development including their development as a 'good citizen'. As some feminists argue, the home, family and motherhood are key to the reproduction of labour power relations, massively important, massively oppressed (Walkerdine and Lucey 1989; Lister 1990, 1996; Yuval Davis 1997 cited in Arnot and Dillabough 1999) (see Chapter 2).

However, Fraser (1997a) continues by pointing to historical examples of alternative public spheres constructed by women and black people in the nineteenth and early twentieth centuries in response to their exclusion from the bourgeois public sphere. From these examples, Fraser notes the risks of assuming the existence of a single public sphere, and suggests that there has always been a 'plurality of competing publics' (1997a: 75; see also Keane 1998). Similarly Eley, in his historical study, notes:

Consequently, the public sphere [as a concept] makes more sense as the structured setting where cultural and ideological contest or negotiation amongst a variety of publics takes place, rather than as the spontaneous and class-specific achievement of the bourgeoisie.

(Eley 1992: 306)

Deliberations and dialogue

Thus the notion of a 'single comprehensive public' (Fraser 1997a: 80) can be discredited, for ignoring both the fractures and cleavages existing among different groups in society, and also the disparities in power and resources that imbue these stratifications.

Yeatman (1994) and others (Young 1990; Phillips 1993, 1995) argue that a conception of citizenship is needed which is rooted in the contested nature of public purposes, and enables different voices to present their cultural identities and material class interests in an enlarged public space in conditions of open dialogue. Within this, identities are respected and compromises, if not consensus, reached between rival traditions (Vincent and Martin 2000). Theorists have variously described this process as 'dialogic democracy' (Giddens 1994), 'dialogic communitarianism' (Frazer and Lacey 1993), 'deliberative democracy' (Benhabib 1992), 'double democratization' (Held 1987).[3]

This broad approach, emphasizing as it does difference and diversity, has been criticized for its potential to result in nothing more than a multiplicity, a splintering of interest groups, 'a cacophony of particular claims for recognition and redress' (Young 1997a: 384). However, Iris Young claims that such misgivings are based on the confusion of essentialist notions of identity with difference. Everyone, she argues, relates to a plurality of social groups; identities are not fixed with uniform subject positions bifurcating them. We all have multiple positionings arising from gender, class, ethnicity, religion, sexuality, language, age, and so on. These social groupings have particular meanings ascribed to them as a result of social forces and structures, and as individuals we have little choice but to engage with those meanings. That engagement, Young argues, is the very source of our individuality; our sense of our own identity arises from the different ways in which we attempt this engagement. Therefore since personal identity cannot be read off at the level of the group, social groups should not be defined in terms of essential attributes that all members share. Rather, individuals associated with a particular group may share an orientation, a sense of *perspective* on particular aspects of social life, but differ and diverge on other aspects (this issue is more fully explored in Chapter 2). As a result, the availability of multiple perspectives arising from the different understandings and allegiances to which we all have access provides a resource through which we can communicate with others (Young 1997a).

If differently positioned citizens engage in public discussion with the aim of solving problems with a spirit of openness and mutual accountability, then these conditions are sufficient for transformative deliberation. They need not be committed to a common interest or a common good; indeed their stance of openness and mutual accountability requires them to attend to their particular differences in order to understand the situation and perspective of others ... If citizens participate in public discussion that includes all social perspectives in their partiality and gives them a hearing, they are most likely to arrive at just and wise solutions to their shared problems.

(Young 1997a: 400)

Stuart Hall (2000: 47) has argued that the principle underlying our approach to each other should not be difference, which is too unstable a category to allow organization, but *'différance'*, a term he feels captures a mixture of commonalties and similarities as well as shifting points of difference.

The approaches laid out by these theorists all require a broadening of the normative concept of public participation, both in terms of arena and activity; a breaking down of divisions between private and public which would allow for the multiplication of both spaces and concerns in which and about which public dialogue is possible. Many theorists then point to the importance of citizenship activity at a local level, as this seems to promise immediacy, directness, accessibility and the potential for agency which are not offered by traditional forms of representational democracy (Gould 1988: 185). As Mouffe points out, such a conception not only replenishes the inadequate liberal notion of citizenship as little more than legal status, but also offers an alternative to the bureaucratic and statist approach to politics of the traditional 'old' Left (Mouffe 1992: 5). Local activity may also offer fragmentation and limitation. A plurality and multiplicity of associative sites and potential activity is therefore necessary; not only sites which operate at the local level but those which span a range including political parties, social movements, voluntary groups and so on, operating at national and regional as well as local level (Held 1987; Keane 1988, 1998; Melucci 1989; Benhabib 1996a):

It is through the interlocking net of these multiple forms of associations, networks and organisations that an anonymous 'public conversation' results. It is central to the model of deliberative democracy that it privileges such a public sphere of mutually interlocking and overlapping networks and associations of deliberation, contestation and argumentation.

(Benhabib 1996b: 73–4)

Citizenship activity can no longer be considered as exclusively taking place within the boundaries of the nation state. Tassin's (1992) work (quoted in Ellison 1997) suggests that with regard to Europe, the political institutions that cut across nation states provide new pluralistic public spaces for dialogue (also Mouffe 1992). In an optimistic analysis, this can be seen as a potentially liberating development for minority groups.[4] As Jean Leca (1992: 21) argues, citizenship of nation states is tightly interwoven with ideas of nationality and cultural community resulting in powerful discourses of inclusion or exclusion (see Chapter 6 on refugee parents).

Social capital and deliberative democracy

Social capital is a concept currently very much in vogue. It describes the social networks, the shared norms and trust between members of a group and the sanctions that act to deter aberrant behaviour. Measuring social capital – seen as an index of a nation's well-being – can be attempted on a number of dimensions, such as measuring social trust, voluntary activity and/ or associational membership. It is the literature's emphasis on assocational activity that links it with the concerns of theorists of deliberative demo-cracy (see, e.g., Putnam 1993, 1995). Synthesizing two internally differentiated literatures is never an easy task. In addition, in this case, the literatures employ two different registers. Social capital literature speaks to and with policy makers' concerns and is focused upon the generation of social capital through planned intervention (see Bentley 1998; Halpern 1999; Hatcher 1999; and in relation to lifelong learning, Schuller and Field 1998; Field 1999), whereas deliberative democracy texts, inhabiting the rather more rarefied air of polit-ical philosophy, mostly assume organic association. There are other points of tension and also some intersection. Some (but not all) approaches to social capital theory articulate closely with communitarian thinking, and minimize the exclusionary potential of close-knit, traditional community networks (Schuller and Field 1998; Halpern 1999). Most versions of deliberative demo-cracy are, of course, premised on the centrality of diversity and difference as underpinning associational life. However, it is with reference to potential outcomes that the two literatures seem to find common (if somewhat fuzzy) ground.

The aims of deliberative democracy are contested by theorists. Benhabib (1996a) gets to the heart of the tension in the introduction to her edited collection on *Democracy and Difference* where she highlights the difference between authors. There are those (including Cohen and Young and her-self, all cited here) who defend versions of deliberative democracy as first developed by Habermas (1987) (although with considerable reservations and individual developments; see for example Young's reworked 'communicative democracy'; Young 1996). These writers generally understand deliberative procedures as meaning the creation of a public dialogue about collective problems, the aim being to reach a consensus, after the airing of many different views and a shared and careful examination of these views. Another strand of thinking is what Benhabib calls the 'agonistic model of democratic politics' which affirms the inescapability of conflict and contestation over values. Richard Hatcher (1999) quotes Perry Anderson on this point: 'Politics remains eminently strategic: not an exchange of opinion, but a contest for power . . . The danger of conceiving democratic life as dialogue is that we may forget that its primary reality is strife' (Anderson 1994: 43, cited in Hatcher 1999: 46). As a result, 'the experience of a radical and plural demo-cracy can only consist in the recognition of the multiplicity of social logics and the necessity of their articulation. But this articulation should always be recreated and renegotiated and there is no hope of a final reconciliation' (Mouffe 1992: 14, also Mouffe 1993a). Various writers coalesce, however, around the fragile ground of temporary solutions, agreements, the development of shared understanding where possible, combined with the procedural guarantees of liberalism (the rule of law, respect for individual rights, value pluralism, etc.) (Benhabib 1996a). It is here that some writers on social capital also see potential areas for development. David Halpern (1999), for instance, argues that policy makers' efforts are best directed at generating 'shared understandings within a society of what constitutes acceptable behaviour' (p. 36). The question that remains is, Where do these accounts and critiques lead? What version of citizenship emerges?

A reworking of citizenship? The implications of deliberative democracy

Nick Ellison (1997) suggests that having (theoretically at least) overturned universalistic notions of the common good, having expanded the range of institutions and sites in which citizenship activity and public conversation can take place, and having accepted that such a conversation will be shaped by different and diverse 'ways of seeing', what emerges for him is citizenship as 'defensive engagement'. By this Ellison means that citizens should be understood as integrated social subjects (cf. Young 1997a) pursuing a range of different interests and claims which require different forms of participation at different times in an increasingly fragmented and complex public realm (1997: 710–11). This would include local and often temporary attempts to establish and maintain grassroots alliances around particular issues. Ellison notes that these forms of engagement are often tightly bound up with anxiety arising from the collapse of former social, political and economic certainties.

> Citizenship no longer conveys a universalistic sense of inclusion or participation in a stable political community . . . instead we are left with a restless desire for social engagement, citizenship becomes a form of social and political practice borne out of the need to establish new solidarities across a range of putative 'communities' as a defence against social changes which continually threaten to frustrate such ambitions.
>
> (Ellison 1997: 714)

In this conceptualization, Ellison is clearly influenced by the recent work of Giddens and Beck which holds (in a brief and therefore somewhat crude sketch) that in a fractured and global social world individuals can actively create a biography for themselves based on the opportunities and risks created by the breaking down of formerly rigid customs and traditions, economic globalization and the advance of technology (Beck 1992; Giddens 1994). However, Ellison contests the degree to which Giddens in particular appears to assume agency on the part of all individuals. Some individuals and groups, disadvantaged in terms of the resources they possess, will fail to engage successfully with such a demanding form of citizenship:

> Some groups will be more adept than others in adjusting to more fluid social and political forms, constructing and reconstructing solidarities

which further a variety of claims across time and space according to the dictates of social change.

(Ellison 1997: 714)

Placing Ellison's analysis alongside that of Bill Jordan (1996), a more cynical view of Ellison's 'defensive engagements' presents itself. Jordan sees middle class activity as largely directed inward towards the private sphere of home and family and imbued with competitiveness and individualism (see also Jordan et al. 1994). He talks of 'new narrower mutualities and clubs, formed by the choices of those comfortable actors' (1996: 241). This would seem to cast doubt on the likelihood of middle class actors participating in any collectivity outside their individual households, unless it is in direct defence of their class interests (this point is examined in Chapter 5 in relation to PIE (Participating in Education), a campaigning group). Ellison also suggests that forms of disengagement will occur for less advantaged groups. One example is particular social groupings of young people, existing within but not belonging to mainstream society, rejecting or unable to access traditional trajectories of Western European and American adulthood (getting a job, living independently from one's parents and so on) (Jordan 1996; Ball et al. 2000), and very clearly alienated from and cynical towards mainstream politics (Jones 1996).

In response to such disenfranchizement, Nancy Fraser (1997a) posits the idea of 'subaltern counterpublics'. This term describes the meeting places, literature and actions of subordinated social groups who form an alternative public, in the face of dominance by groups who do not recognize their particular interests. Fraser argues that since structural inequalities in wider society will simply reoccur and reproduce in discursive public arenas, members of subordinate groups require their own space and place, an alternative public sphere, in which to conduct deliberative conversation away from the 'gaze' of the dominant group. She gives the examples of lesbian and gay groups, minority ethnic and feminist groups. This process strengthens the group's abilities to engage with others in the public sphere. As an example, she notes the success of feminist groups:

In this public sphere, feminist women have invented new terms for describing social reality, including 'sexism', 'the double shift', 'sexual harassment' and 'marital, date and acquaintance rape'. Armed with such language, we have recast our needs and identities, thereby reducing, although not eliminating the extent of our disadvantage in official public spheres.

(1997a: 81–2)

Likewise, Jayne Mansbridge talks of 'protected enclaves',

in which the relatively like-minded can consult easily with one another . . . [and] in which members legitimately consider in their deliberations not only what is good for the whole polity, but also what is good for themselves individually . . . and for their group.

(Mansbridge 1996: 57)

Alberto Melucci, in his work on social movements, explores similar ideas. He argues that social movements have lengthy latent periods, with bursts of public action. During these latent times the movements consist of 'invisible networks' where activity is not public, but private, where members are conducting conversations between themselves, and are concerned with the 'on-going process of construction of a sense of "we"' (Melucci 1989: 218; see also Chapter 5):

> The submerged networks of social movements are laboratories of experience. New problems and questions are posed. New answers are invented and tested, and reality is perceived and named in different ways.
>
> (1989: 208)

John Keane deploys similar ideas when he writes of 'micro-public spheres', which he defines as 'a wide variety of local spaces in which citizens enter into disputes about who does and who ought to get what, when and how' (1998: 170). In agreement with Melucci he sees such local public spheres (note the plural, a reminder of the existence of many different publics and public arenas) as sites where aspects of 'reality' can be interrogated and different readings constructed.

These theorists are concerned with vertical societal stratification and inequality and pose counterpublics as a response to this. I am suggesting here that they may also address the problems set up by more horizontal forms of differentiation. Parents of course come from all class and ethnic groups, with differing sexualities, (dis)abilities, religions and so on. Some may identify with and be willing to engage with the official public sphere. Others, as a result of different aspects of their subjectivity, will engage in public discourse through a 'subaltern counterpublic'. Still others may have withdrawn from public discourse all together. However, although this differentiation cannot be ignored or overlooked, I suggest that counterpublics, alternative public arenas, may be valuable for these social actors as a *group*, in their role as parents of children educated in the state system. Counterpublics could assist parents in formulating what Moss (1999: 80) refers to as a 'politics of parenthood', agendas and priorities that may ultimately support, engage with, or contest dominant professional interpretations of the purposes and organization of schooling. They could, in short, offer a 'way-in' for lay voices struggling to raise educational issues.

A whole host of objections immediately present themselves. I address two here. The first asks, 'Why would such groupings be inevitably democratic or egalitarian in their practices?' Counterpublics may consist of those with extreme right-wing views, for example. The counterdiscourses they throw up may be racist or excluding in some other way. Surely at the very least, such collectivities will be selfish and individualistic, seeking the advancement of their own children's prospects at the expense of those of others; articulate middle class parents, perhaps, with resources of cultural and material capital arguing against progressive professional interventions such as mixed ability grouping, or non-selective admissions criteria, or alternatively using their skills and networks to obtain for their own children a larger slice of an impoverished resource 'cake'.[5]

Both Mansbridge and Fraser accept that counterpublics will not inevitably be egalitarian or democratic in their practice, but argue that the general principle – the expansion of public discursive space as a result of counterpublic activity – is a worthy one. An example, specifically relating to education, of the interplay of these tensions is provided by the Cleveland case which took place in the early 1990s. Cleveland LEA (reluctantly) conceded to a white mother's request that her child should move schools to attend one where the vast majority of children were white, and not of Asian origin. This was one of several similar instances of racialized school choice on the part of groups and individuals which received publicity in the late 1980s and early 1990s. In a paper I wrote about the case, I argued that the way forward is to bring such issues into a public and political arena for debate (Vincent 1992). The alternative is for fundamental issues, such as apparent shifts towards a more racially segregated school system, to be decided by legal technicalities[6] and an unplanned, undebated aggregate of individual decisions.

The second objection is that encouraging parental 'voice' in relation to educational decision making will simply pit the particularist views of parents concerned with their own child against the universal concerns of teachers. But working with, starting with, particularity is the key to deliberative democracy. Some theorists (in particular those who subscribe to an agonistic version of democracy) emphasize people's commitment to their own interests; this is their source of motivation to enter into a public dialogue. They then suggest debate in search of a position of reconciliation, but argue that alongside this must remain a recognition of the irreconcilable nature of some issues (e.g. Mouffe 1993a; Mansbridge 1996: 47–9). Of course, negotiating such a tension can prove unbearably uncomfortable at the micro level of personal relationships, something often forgotten by the theorists. A reworking of the argument focusing on parental particularity might state that their involvement in educational decision making will simply privilege the views of those parents who have the necessary resources and abilities to state their case with strength and persistence, while silencing other groups. This is of course the very scenario that 'subaltern counterpublics' are designed to avoid, as marginalized voices begin to enter into public debate.

Education, a crucial determinant of individual life chances, would appear to be a highly appropriate field for the formation of 'subaltern counterpublics' – a proposition that the following chapters will test empirically. Who are the parents who become involved in collective action around education? What sort of groups are active on their behalf? What sort of issues are taken up by these groups? And, just as importantly, if we hold these questions up to the light what does the negative image reveal? Who is left out? What issues are excluded from debate? Locating silence and passivity, the absence of activity and agency is, I suggest, also an important task.

Most of the data on which this book is based are drawn from a study of four locally based parent-centred organizations (PCOs) – an advice centre (Chapter 3), a parent education group (Chapter 4), a parent campaigning group and a parent support group (Chapter 5). They are small organizations and groups either run by professionals for parents or run by parent members themselves. Education is their primary concern in all cases. (The project is introduced more fully in Chapter 2.)

It is my contention that PCOs can be understood as 'protected enclaves', the beginnings of the formation of counterpublics. As such they 'function as spaces of withdrawal and regroupment . . . and bases and training grounds for agitational activities directed towards wider publics' (Fraser 1997a: 82). They appear to be, in Leca's (1992) words, potential 'reservoirs of citizenship' – a more active, multifaceted, demanding and immediate conception of citizenship than is made possible by traditional readings of the concept. It now remains for me to interrogate the validity of such a position.

Conclusion

Parental involvement in education is widely assumed to be 'a good thing', for children and schools (although the benefits to individual parents and teachers may be less clear). Yet despite the presumptions of its importance which have persisted over the last 30 years, the key role that educational achievement plays in determining life chances, and the scale of public sector involvement in education, it remains unclear both what kind of involvement, what types of home–school interaction are most desirable and, particularly pertinent to this discussion, what the purposes and aims of such involvement are.

In this chapter, I have argued that the subject positions of 'partner' and 'consumer' channel parental activity with regard to schools into particular limited modes of action, which allow the individuals involved little agency. An understanding of home–school relations as an exemplar of citizen interaction with public sector institutions provides, I suggest, a mode of analysis which highlights some of the complexities involved in encouraging a closer relationship between parent and school. Two commonly mooted problems affecting parental involvement are parents' apparent passivity and inaction, and the diversity of views and opinions among the parent body. By focusing on particularity as a starting point and centring the inevitability of different and diverse subjectivities, the theories cited here, which revolve around issues of citizenship and participation, engage with both these issues.

I have suggested that PCOs can potentially build up networks of parents away from any one school, and the complex relations which exist between individual parents, teachers and children. The hypothesis is that they can form 'protected enclaves' in which groups of parents can meet and discuss their views on the provision of education, locally and nationally and, from this, formulate an agenda to take into the wider public sphere. Chapters 3 to 5 consider this proposition in relation to four different parent groups and organizations. I describe the purpose of the groups and analyse their organization, the underlying principles and values, and their impact. Chapter 6 explores one clearly marginalized group of families – refugee and asylum seekers – and their relationships with schools. This chapter is included because a case study of marginal groups throws the normative assumptions about home–school relations into sharp relief. Before moving on to the research materials, however, Chapter 2 examines some of the discourses which shape ideas around parenting.

Notes

1 I am using 'voice' in the singular here, to contrast parents as a group with education professionals. It should become clear later on in the chapter that I am not overlooking the diversity, the *voices*, within any given parent population.
2 Chapter 6 alludes to ethnicity and citizenship.
3 Differences exist between these understandings. However, for the purposes of this chapter, a broad distinction between these conceptions and more traditional understandings is sufficient.
4 This is not a reference to minority ethnic groups alone. In recent years, the EC has shown more overt support than the British government for, say, moves to end discrimination among women in the workplace.
5 In the field of special education, organized and active voluntary groups such as the British Dyslexia Association and its affiliates have been criticized for this (Vincent and Tomlinson 1997).
6 The case was subject to judicial review, after a challenge from the Commission for Racial Equality. The judge upheld the LEA's decision that it had no alternative but to concede to parental choice.

CHAPTER TWO

Being a 'good' parent

Introduction

In this chapter I will, through a consideration of the discursive construction of 'good' or 'appropriate' parenting, further develop some of the themes identified in the first chapter. First I explore some of the understandings and interpretations of 'good' parenthood found in current policies and state-sponsored discourse. This section is not exhaustive in its examination, but rather recognizes the difficulties of

> develop[ing] one coherent narrative about the relationship between the 'family' and the 'state' . . . While some welfare policies explicitly supported traditional family values, these were undermined in practice; others explicitly supported change while implicitly basing practice on conventional assumptions about male and female roles in family life.
>
> (Arnot *et al.* 1999: 52)

In acknowledgement of the intricate contradictions and tensions which describe this relationship (between family and state), this chapter seeks only to identify those dimensions and aspects of that relationship which seem particularly relevant to the home–school trajectory. Next I draw on the work of Gramsci to consider the process of dissemination, by which hegemonic discourses are relayed to parents by policy makers and education-related professionals, and subsequently the reactions of parents in particular contexts. Do they accept, resist or subvert such messages? The last section of the chapter describes the research project in more detail.

Parenting 'messages'

Parenting and family life has received much attention in recent years as those born in the 'boom' years of the late 1950s and 1960s have themselves had children. Parenting has shifted imperceptibly away from something that was 'natural' towards something that has to be learnt and that can be perfected, or at least improved[1] – witness the plethora of baby and childcare books, the success of such groups as the Parent Company which runs seminars on aspects of parenting, and the development of 'lifestyle journalism' which often deals with parenting issues.

As family relationships, child rearing practices and values, childcare and working parents – issues that were formerly firmly contained within the private sphere – become topics for public conversation and debate, some traditional ideas, assumptions and expectations around family life are contested and challenged. Leonard talks about 'the continuing promulgation, though weakening and disputed, of the "ideology of familialism", a celebration of the virtues of the nuclear family, the nurturing roles of women, the subordination of children and other requirements of the social order' (1997: 38). While changes in the structures of families are becoming more commonplace with the traditional nuclear family in decline, other aspects such as the assumption that domestic and childcare responsibilities are primarily the woman's appear to hold (Gregson and Lowe 1994; Jowell et al. 1998). The idea that families should operate as individual autonomous units is also prominent, and is, I suggest, a major theme within discourses of 'good' parenting. In their study of middle class families, Jordan et al. (1994) referred to the phenomenon of 'individualism-in-action', where adults routinely prioritized family responsibilities over any public issues:

> Interviewees used the repertories of individualism to construct identities that bore the hallmarks of a distinctive culture – one that prioritised the family as a private, self-responsible setting for the pursuit of self-making in clearly gendered roles.
>
> (1994: 5–6)

This familial self-reliance and independence is a key part of 'good' parenting, of providing for and taking responsibility for one's children. However, parental responsibilities multiply as parenting and family life become 'an educational project', something that has to be worked at, rather than simply lived, something which can always be improved (Beck and Beck-Gernsheim 1995: 139). In the media, in the discourse of health professionals and related others, all aspects of parenthood and all stages of childhood are presented as opportunities for constant thinking ahead, gathering information and planning and executing improvements. Beck and Beck-Gernsheim (1995) cite health advice which focuses on the desirable emotional and physical state of the mother *before* conception. From that point onwards, the imperative is to identify and meet a whole range of potential needs and desires on the part of the developing child. Feeding into this intensification of parental roles is the increased commodification of childhood, as consumer goods and services for children diversify and proliferate. There are glossy magazines devoted to children,[2] listings magazines devoted to their entertainment, and a whole host of extra-curricular activities including drama, art, music, linguistic and sporting opportunities. The range of goods and services attend to every facet of baby and child development and entertainment. Taking advantage of these apparent opportunities requires attentiveness and financial resources on the part of parents, and considerable stamina on the part of both child and parent.

The possibility of and potential for becoming a 'better' parent is one open to all, although this process of self-improvement takes different forms for different groups. For 'work-rich' and 'income-rich' (Gorz 1989, cited in Gregson and Lowe 1995) middle class parents, giving their children as many social and educational experiences as possible in the hope that these will be advantageous later in life is an imperative, but one framed as a private, individual concern. For those families 'dependent' on benefits, however, the discharge of their parental responsibilities falls under the gaze of the state. I referred in Chapter 1 to the analyses offered by Fraser and Gordon (1997) and Leonard (1997) concerning the discursive construction of 'dependency'. They note that the term has become infused with a high moral content, what Ruth Levitas (1998) calls a MUD (Moral Underclass Discourse), an 'individualistic and moralistic discourse, using the stigmatising language of the "underclass" and "dependency culture" to construct the socially excluded' (Power and Gewirtz 1999: 5). This serves to draw implicit parallels between 'dependency' and 'liability'. 'Dependent' families are understood to be at risk of dysfunctional relationships, lax parenting, and to need guidance as to their actions (Jetter 1997, et al.; Leonard 1997; Baker 1998).

'Good' parenting is not therefore a class-neutral concept. One recent example of a policy document which makes the discursive construction of good parenting visible is the New Zealand *Code of Social and Family Responsibility*, a discussion document produced by the Department of Social Welfare in 1998.[3] Parental responsibilities are clearly laid out in a series of 'expectations' concerning adults' responsibilities for the health and well-being and good behaviour of children, as well as adults' responsibilities for their own health, employment and finances. The document describes each issue, the current government aid, and the current law, and ends with questions for discussion. As Maureen Baker (1998) points out, the discussion points centre on individual and family responsibility, rather than that of the state, the Code's underlying assumption being that all can be considered alike, as taxpayers, regardless of social class, ethnic or gender differences. Poverty as a context informing and constraining behaviour in many of the situations discussed is rarely mentioned. However, that the poor are the constituency within which the 'problems' lie – non-attendance of children at school, low rates of immunization among infants, poor financial management, long-term unemployment – is clear throughout the discussion document, and many of the suggested 'solutions' include linking the payment of benefits to the desired behaviour (see Baker 1998 for a fuller critique of the Code). I suggest that many of the same ideas concerning family life, parenting and individual responsibility can be found in the public domain in the UK, although the government has not yet taken steps to codify them.

I wish to argue that a similar desire to have all parents behave in an approved fashion underlies the introduction of Home–School Agreements in the UK. This initiative is part of the commitment by the Prime Minister, Tony Blair, to building 'strong communities':

Strong communities depend on shared values and a recognition of the rights and duties of citizenship – not just the duty to pay taxes and obey the law, but the obligation to bring children up as competent responsible citizens, and to support those – such as teachers – who are employed by the state in the task. In the past we have tended to take such duties for granted. But where they are neglected, we should not hesitate to encourage and even enforce . . . as we are seeking to do with initiatives such as our 'home–school contracts' between schools and parents.

(Blair 1998: 12)

This initiative can be viewed as part of a policy ensemble emanating from the restructuring of education in the 1980s and 1990s, which redrew the boundaries between home and school with regard to children's welfare and behaviour. Michael Wyness (1997) argues that the current emphasis on academic performance in schools leaves teachers with little time and few resources to address issues of welfare and socialization (see also Chapter 6). Home–school agreements therefore aim to enforce parental subordination to school for all parents regardless of income level or social class background. The specificity of the contributions to most agreements is most marked with pupils who undertake to fulfil concrete and quantified tasks – being at school on time, bringing particular items of equipment – and least with the school's promises. Many of the latter describe undertakings which should be central to the school's role regardless of the parental circumstances or degree of supportiveness (e.g. trying to ensure that the child achieves his/her full potential, provide a balanced curriculum, and achieve high standards of work and behaviour; see Alexander *et al.* 1995: 52–3; also Blair and Waddington 1997; Vincent and Tomlinson 1997, 1998). Parents too are expected to carry out concrete tasks (e.g. supervising homework, attending school meetings, providing the correct equipment) and to offer unconditional support to the school. Their sense of commitment to the school is assumed. Yet agreements are clearly oriented towards those parents perceived to be failing in their supportive duties with the aim of encouraging their compliance. Commentators have long made the point that many of the clauses of such agreements contain an inherent social class bias as the requirements are considerably easier to fulfil if a family has particular cultural and financial resources (space for the child to do homework, babysitters and transport to attend parent consultation evenings, a fair command of English, given that few schools provide interpretation services and so on; Sallis 1991; Vincent and Tomlinson 1997).

The home–school agreements parents' booklet (DfEE 1998), which seeks to inform parents about the mandatory introduction of home–school agreements in state schools introduced in September 1999, provides an interesting read.[4] It emphasizes that parents have a right to 'have a say' on the content of agreements (although much of this is laid down by central government), but again assumes that this say will not contest in any major way the school's right to define the agenda. Parental support is taken for granted: 'Make sure your child knows that you support the school's policies' (p. 1). The guide also goes into great detail concerning parents' responsibilities for their child's attendance at school, and ensuring that their child behaves well and does their homework. There is no suggestion that parents could engage in a dialogue with the school concerning the purposes of education or the nature of schooling in that particular site (Martin and Vincent 1999). As Blair and Waddington note,

> To date, the system of state education seems to have been unable to decide which model of parent it should respond to. Are parents consumers, or partners or problems? Reflected in the issue of [home–school] 'contracts' we seem to have an unholy and confused amalgamation of all three; the rhetoric of choice and partnership is used as a smoke screen for control and discipline and the imposition of the model of a 'good' parent.
>
> (1997: 301)

A similarly deficit view of families appears in the descriptions of local populations contained in bids produced by some Education Action Zones. In an initial analysis of three successful applications for zone status, Power and Gewirtz (1999) illustrate the way in which parents in these urban areas are described using a moralistic register, and blamed for low academic attainment, disruption in school, and instances of social decay and chaos. 'It is worth noting that in none of the three bids are parents mentioned within the "strengths and opportunities" sections. They always appear under "weaknesses and challenges"' (p. 10).

In September 2000, the government launched a package of measures designed to inform parents about the curriculum, and encourage and direct their involvement with their children's learning. It was claimed that such guidance bridged the gap between those parents who were already familiar with the complexities of the education system and those who were not. Whilst such information is undoubtedly useful in demystifying schools' jargonistic procedures, the materials again promote only an individualistic model of parental involvement, and the guides to learning are open to the charge that parents are required to make their homes function like classrooms.

If 'good' parenting is not a class-neutral concept, neither is it a gender-neutral one. Research on all aspects of parental involvement with school shows that mothers take the responsibility for liaising with the school and also for their child's achievement and progress (choice of school, Gewirtz et al. 1995; contact and communication with school, Lareau 1989; David et al. 1993; Vincent 1996; Reay 1998; Vincent and Martin 2000; and involvement in the curriculum, Merttens and Vass 1993; Hughes et al. 1994). Yet much of this work is invisible (as are many other aspects of mothering work; Smith 1988, 1991; Ribbens 1994; Reay 1998). Diane Reay argues rightly that the wider debate on parental involvement in both policy and research (and I am guilty of this myself) glosses over maternal responsibility. The use of the term 'parental' leaves open the possibility of fathers' involvement, a possibility which in reality fathers may not take up (Reay 1998: 10). Miriam David argues that changes in the structure of families and the increase in maternal employment have in fact led to greater responsibility falling on the mother (David 1993). The mother is expected to take the key role in, and 'total' responsibility for, the development of the child, particularly in his/her early years (Manicom 1984; Wyness 1997). This responsibility appears to hold even in dual earner households where mothers are primarily responsible for finding and choosing care and liaising with carers (Brannen and Moss 1991; Vincent and Ball 1999). Mothers, as Walkerdine and Lucey (1989) argue, are therefore responsible for the social, emotional, moral, intellectual and physical growth of their children. They highlight a powerful discourse of 'good' parenting, that of the 'sensitive mother'. This is the idea that mothers can facilitate their child's play to bring about their better development. Everyday domestic tasks, everyday interactions and conversations could and should become the site for learning for mothers attuned to the needs of their children (see Chapter 4). The desired outcome is not just individual children who are 'ready' for school, children capable of treading the fine line between autonomy and conformity and individuality and uniformity that school demands, but also children who will become reasoning and reasonable citizens.

> The path to democracy begins in the kitchen of the sensitive mother. Here there is supposed to be a nurturant presence which facilitates the development of her child towards natural language and reason. These develop because the sensitive mother is finely tuned to her child's struggle for meaning, extends and elaborates her utterances, transforms her own domestic work into play for her child's cognitive development. All these and more are the ways in which so-called natural development is produced. This development, aimed at getting at the child through the relay point of the mother, aims to produce a reasonable citizen.
>
> (1989: 101)

The mother stands at the junction between the private world of the family and the public world outside. Hers is a mediating role (Ribbens 1994). This mediation often involves issues to do with the regulation of the child. Consequently mothers are judged upon their approach to and effectiveness at both mediation and regulation. Schools are often the first formalized site with which young children come into contact and in which such judgements are made. As Jane Ribbens (1994) further argues, school attendance impacts on family life in a myriad of ways with particular consequences for mothers who must fulfil the school's demands for support. However, policies overlook the implications of this responsibility on family life, the differential resources – both cultural and material – upon which parents can draw, and the fact that in the majority of cases, despite social class and ethnic differences, the responsibility falls disproportionately upon the mother (Griffith and Smith 1991; for a consideration of lone mothers, see Standing 1999). In Chapter 1, I noted Diane Reay's argument that both the middle and working class mothers in her study invested time, effort, money, thought and emotion in their children's education. The investment in terms of its scale held across class boundaries, but what differed was the effectiveness with which middle and working class mothers were able to mould, shape and facilitate the project of their child's educational achievement.

Thus, bringing together class and gender, there have been attempts, through-out this century, to regulate working class mothers, to affect their practices, to make them act more like middle class mothers, although without the accompanying context of relative ease and wealth. An example is offered by Jacques Donzelot (1979) who argued that 'the gigantic hygienic and moral campaign inaugurated amongst the poorer classes at the end of the nineteenth century [in France]' (p. 90) and encompassing not just child rearing but a whole range of behaviours, resulted in the positioning of working class famil-ies as targets for direct state intervention, what he refers to as 'a missionary field' (p. 89). Donzelot's teacher and colleague, Michel Foucault, identifies school as a prime site for marshalling children and parents and extracting desired behaviour. In *Discipline and Punish*, he comments, 'The Christian school must not simply train docile children; it must also make it possible to supervise the parents, to gain information as to their way of life, their resources, their piety and their morals' (1977: 211). This is part of the process Foucault described as 'the swarming of disciplinary mechanisms' (ibid.).

Making a similar point regarding the tutelage given to poor working class parents, Deborah Brennan describes the adoption of the European kindergarten movement in Australia at the turn of the century:

> In Australia as in the United States, the most enthusiastic supporters of the progressive educational ideas embodied in the kindergarten move-ment regarded it as an instrument of social reform. Through kindergartens, these upper and middle class women aimed to reach the families who lived in the unsanitary, over-crowded and poverty stricken suburbs of the major cities, and imbue their children with middle class values such as cleanliness, courtesy, industriousness and thrift.
>
> (Brennan 1998: 16)

As the public sector expanded in Western industrialized nations after the end of the Second World War, so the range of professionals and para-professionals able to offer and, in some cases, impose guidance on families grew (Tomlinson 1982). Social work, medical and educational expertise pro-liferated, and advice became widely available through the media, supported by periodic pronouncements from government.[5] In her study of inner city playgroups, Janet Finch describes 'a slide into cultural imperialism where middle class outsiders step in to take over [playgroups] which working class mothers cannot "manage" on their own. This fits neatly . . . into the process of educating working class women in proper childcare practice' (1984b: 17). I now want to consider the processes by which ideas about 'good' parenting are disseminated, and how and why some ideas attain acceptance and status as 'common-sense' values.

Using (and abusing?) Gramsci

I am interested here in the process by which particular values and beliefs are disseminated, and become hegemonic. The concept of 'hegemony' is of course associated with the work of Antonio Gramsci.[6] Hegemony expresses a process and a phenomenon that goes beyond conscious ideology to embrace common-sense, taken-for-granted understandings and assumptions. Hegemony describes the process by which our perceptions of social 'reality' are formed, and how they then shape our expectations and our sense of 'rightness' about events and situations, actions and beliefs. Hegemony is 'the power to establish authoritative definitions of social situations and social needs, the power to define the universe of legitimate disagreement and the power to shape the political agenda' (Fraser 1992: 53).

Hegemony can therefore operate as a conduit for 'soft oppression' (Giroux 1994), processes which allow forms of social inequality to appear as 'natural' or inevitable. This happens, Giroux argues, as a result of the 'creeping or quiet' infiltration of hegemonic discourses into individual and collective consciousness. Thus particular conceptions such as, in this case, what is involved in the 'correct' upbringing of children become normalized and may encourage the acceptance of inequalities by marginalized groups.

Gramsci made a careful distinction between hegemonic supremacy within society operating through persuasion and consent, and repressive and coercive forms of control (Eley 1992). As hegemony requires the active consent of the population, it is characterized by 'negotiation and change . . . uncertainty, impermanence and contradiction' (Eley 1992: 323). Thus dominant groups within society constantly have to secure the active consent of subordinate groups. Moreover, this task has to be fulfilled within a context of *some* fluidity, as patterns of social relations, domination and subordination shift over time. Thus hegemony involves what Dick Hebdige (1996), quoting Gramsci, calls a 'precarious "moving equilibrium"'. The phrase is a useful one as it suggests a complex and fluctuating interplay of conflict and submission, acceptance and resistance, and contestation and negotiation. The degree of fluctuation and mobility should not of course be overstated, as systemic patterns of inequality prove remarkably resistant to fundamental change (Kenway 1995).

Thus the main theme of this book is the process by which hegemonic discourses concerning appropriate or good parenting (especially mothering) are disseminated through what I have called parent-centred organizations (PCOs), operating within civil society. Civil society is composed of what Gramsci referred to as 'the so-called private' organizations like churches, trade unions and cultural associations which are distinct from processes of production and from the public apparatuses of the state (Gramsci 1971). Today civil society organizations are often defined as non-governmental organizations, in receipt of legal protection from the state (see, e.g., Keane 1998). The relationship between state and civil society is not straightforward, and encompasses tensions, interpenetration, and a degree of mutual reliance. Civil society is understood by Gramsci and later commentators as being a vital arena in which debates and differences concerning how to live are played out.

The importance of civil society for Gramsci is an arena 'where values and meanings are established, where they are debated, contested and changed . . . it is the space that has to be colonised – the famous 'war of position' by any new class seeking to usurp the old.

(Kumar 1993: 383)

John Keane, writing about the 1990s renaissance in interest, thought and comment in the concept of civil society, describes his own focus on the power-sharing potential of state and civil society institutions in a healthy democracy:

Seen from this power-sharing perspective, state actors and institutions within a democracy are constantly forced to respect, protect and share power with civilian actors and institutions – just as civilians living within the state-protected institutions of a civil society are forced to recognise social differences and to share power among themselves.

(Keane 1998: 11)

Keane's emphasis upon the potential of the civil society–state axis as encouraging, indeed compelling, debate, dialogue, participation and accountability has an obvious relevance for the PCOs, themselves (mostly, but see Chapter 3 for an exception) institutions of civil society attempting to foster dialogue with state-sponsored institutions.

Writing from within a very different social, political and cultural framework to our own, Gramsci's work nevertheless highlights themes of relevance to a late modern (or postmodern) audience. Much of Gramsci's writing focused on the interaction of different social groups, and the manner in which power relationships are formed and maintained. He also emphasized the existence of multiple sites for the operation of power, and therefore for subsequent challenges to dominant social groups. One of the focal points of his theory is the role of 'intellectuals', which he described as that of 'deputies' or functionaries to the dominant group (Gramsci 1971: 12). Gramsci argued that, in the course of their work, professionals, such as doctors, priests, lawyers, journalists and teachers, disseminated hegemonic beliefs in order to win the 'active consent' of subaltern social groups (Eley 1992).[7]

Renate Holub (1992) argues that professionals disseminate ideas and values through a shared 'structure of feeling'; a concept she derives from Gramsci's notion of *'esprit de corps'* (see also Williams 1977). The term 'structure of feeling' describes the series of assumptions, ideas and values that structure communication between members of a 'community'. A structure of feeling is the set of affective cultural beliefs and orientations that allow a particular group to make sense of the world around them, to use that understanding to construct and employ what can be called 'mental maps' (Taylor *et al.* 1996) or scripts. A structure of feeling is the distillation of many elements, feelings and assumptions: the elements of place, of history, of economics, feelings of belonging, exclusion or 'ownership', and assumptions of values and beliefs that translate into attitudes informing action (Taylor *et al.* 1996). The term has pluralist connotations, as there are many different communities with varying 'structures of feeling' arising from diverse experiences, understandings and exclusions. Briefly, professionals working in a particular location have *partial* access to that community's 'structure of feeling', and can utilize that access to propose and propound values that support the status quo (Holub 1992). However, Gramsci argued that political counter-hegemony could also be produced through the same structures and on the same terrain (Showstack Sassoon 1980; Femia 1981). Chapters 3, 4 and 5 examine the extent to which the organizers of the PCOs have access to the structures of feeling of clients or fellow members of the group.

As noted in Chapter 1, Iris Young (1997a), although writing from a different perspective, hints at an approach similar to that of 'structures of feeling'. She suggests that members of particular social groups do not have identical interests or identities that can be simply read off from their shared (for example) ethnicity or sexuality. Such an assumption is too simplistic, as it requires one dimension within an individual's subjectivity to be dominant in all situations. As Nancy Hewitt argues (1992), rather than this essentialist understanding, identity can be better conceived of in terms of a chemical compound, as being a compound of race, gender and class (and other elements, sexuality, religion, etc.). 'A compound is a substance of elements that are chemically bonded to each other, the composition of each being transformed, so that the original components can no longer be separated from each other' (p. 318), and each bears the imprint of the other. Different elements of identity or different assemblages of elements may be most salient at particular times depending on context. In this understanding, individuals belong to a range of social groupings. Within any one grouping they are likely to share with others within that group some similar *perspectives* on the social world (examples of the shared perspectives between professionals and clients, and professionals' partial access to clients' structures of feeling, are given in Chapter 3).

Parents and professionals

The role of professionals and the relationships with their clients is therefore an important theme for this book. The literature on professionalism is more fully explored in Chapter 3 but it is worth making the general point here that more recent and critical literature exploring notions of professionalism highlights the difficulties involved in creating an equal partnership between professionals and clients, with a marginal role for the lay 'partner' often the result. The dominating role of the professional has implications for the way in which the client's situation or problem is defined and the solution formulated (Scheurich 1997). The opportunity for the explicit dissemination of particular values is made clear in this quotation from the Gulbenkian Foundation:

> Community workers . . . have a responsibility to make conscious decisions about the social changes and cultural values they wish to encourage, and [to ask] what are the ethical constraints and imperatives in influencing people so as to bring about social change and what constitutes desirable social change.
>
> (1968: 86)

However, as stated earlier, the reaction of the target audience to such a cultural campaign may encompass varying contradictory reactions including accommodation, resistance, challenge, negotiation, and/or rearticulation. It is possible for example that the potential for professional domination in state agencies may not be replicated in those PCOs which operate as a network of parents. Thus it may be the case that parent members of a network – including those who have taken up particular responsibilities within the group – share similar structures of feeling with their fellow members, while in a more formalized professional–client relationship, the professionals can only hope for partial access to the structures of feeling of their client group (see Chapter 5 and Vincent and Warren 1997). As a group, of course, parents could not be expected to subscribe to a common 'structure of feeling'. 'Parent' is too wide a term, incorporating men and women of different social classes and ethnic origins. However, it is possible that the experience of being a parent and interacting with the education system may be enough to ensure some common points of reference (Moss 1999).

Despite the inclusion of this caveat, the tone of this chapter to date risks making the implicit suggestion that the differentiation and heterogeneity of the large body of adults who are also parents can be downplayed in the face of their relationships as a group with professionals, a relationship in which all parent clients are clearly positioned as the subordinate, less powerful group. This presents a distorted picture. As noted in Chapter 1, various ethnographic studies have demonstrated how some middle class groups of parents can marshal their social, economic and cultural capital, and impose their agendas upon schools, successfully resisting professional attempts to define themselves as possessors of expert knowledge requiring lay deference (see Ball and Vincent 2000 for an overview; see also Reay 1998; Birenbaum-Carmeli 1999). The status of teachers is clearly a factor here, with some commentators suggesting that their social position is far from secure, leaving them vulnerable to being overruled by 'prestigious parents' (Lareau 1989; Birenbaum-Carmeli 1999: 62). However, the ability of middle class parents to successfully challenge teacher decisions cannot be assumed. Different sections of the middle class have access to different social resources. In addition, contextual factors have to be considered: the degree of freedom schools in different systems have to determine curricular, pedagogical or budgetary decisions; the legislative rights granted to parents; local traditions and histories of community–school interaction; and so on. As part of a research project of parental voice in school, an in-depth study of a sample of 76 parents in two UK secondary schools was conducted by myself, Jane Martin and Stewart Ranson. We found evidence of attempts by (mainly middle class) parents to challenge the schools on issues such as uniform, mixed ability teaching, and standards of maths teaching. There were, however, no instances of parents succeeding in their challenge in a way that provoked significant policy changes (Vincent et al. 1999).

The next chapters look in more detail at the PCOs and parents' relationships with each other and with professional workers, in an attempt to tease out the dissemination of particular messages about parenting and parents' roles, and to identify and trace parents' reactions and responses to these messages. However, first, in the remainder of this chapter, I briefly discuss the case study sites and give some details of the research design.

The case study PCOs

To reiterate: PCOs are locally based groups and organizations which have parents as their entire or prime focus. In brief, PCOs seek to intervene in the relationship between parents and the education system. They may do this by offering parents information, support and, in some cases, advice and advocacy, on education issues. They may be run by professionals for parent clients or run by parents for other parent members.

The four case studies were:

- A local authority *advice centre* in 'Tate' LEA, staffed by professionals, which offered parents information and support on special education issues. Similar centres appeared in various LEAs in response to the 1993 Education Act on special education, which called for the appointment of a Parent Partnership Officer in each LEA. The parent authority, 'Tate' LEA, is a small, inner urban authority (see Chapter 3 for more details).
- A *parent education group* where parents undertook an accredited practical skills course, involving the completion of educational materials for use with young children (number games, home-made books and so on). This group met in a primary school also in Tate LEA. The group received funding from charitable trusts and not the LEA.
- A *self-help group* which operated as a network, offering mutual support and information on education for African/Caribbean parents. This group was composed of parents in 'Midcity' LEA, a large authority covering inner urban and more suburban areas. The group received funding from an educational organization with charitable status.
- A *pressure group* which campaigned for the enhanced funding of education nationwide. The two local groups studied were in 'Midshire' LEA, an authority covering urban, suburban and rural areas. The group was funded through member subscription, and other fundraising activities.

It can be seen from this brief description that the four case study groups differed considerably in their orientation and their focus of activity. Their variety is indicative of the ways in which parents get involved in educational issues, other than, or in addition to, their relationship with their own child's individual school. Between them the four case studies covered the main purposes and services offered by PCOs at the time the research was conducted, namely advice, education and training, campaigning and self-help.[8] However, this wide scope also presented analytical problems. As will be seen in the following chapters, the groups were just too different – in their focus, their organization, their aims and philosophy – for easy comparisons to be made.

The approach adopted was a qualitative one. The presentation of qualitative research in education has been, and will doubtless remain, a contested

Table 2.1   Number of interviews conducted

PCO	No. of people interviewed	No. of interviews*
Advice centre	26	32
Self-help group	8	9
Pressure group	16	16
Parent education group	13	14
Other parent groups or relevant personnel (e.g. LEA officials)	16**	16
Total	79	87

*   Includes repeat interviews with same respondent
** Includes 6 interviews from generalist parent centre

subject (for recent critiques, see Foster *et al.* 1996 and, for a response, Gillborn 1998; Tooley 1997 and, for a further response, Ball and Gewirtz 1997b). Due to the constraints of space, it is not my intention to contribute to this debate here. A detailed and reflexive portrayal of the research methods employed in this project, which concentrates in particular on ethical issues, is contained within a separate paper (Vincent and Warren forthcoming). Here I shall confine myself to briefly describing the research design.

A qualitative research design was chosen since this gave the most effective access to the perspectives of participants in PCOs, and allowed detailed exploration of the ways in which PCOs are organized and operate, and how they interacted with their clients and other agencies. Data were collected, primarily, through semi-structured interviews, but also through observation and document analysis. Semi-structured interviewing was the most appropriate research tool because of the opportunities it presents for researchers to explore the respondent's perceptions, experiences and beliefs. In addition, semi-structured interviews allow respondents to introduce and develop themes and issues they see as relevant, thus avoiding the imposition of the researcher's agenda.

As groups such as PCOs tend to run on skeleton staffing, or with a small 'core' membership and a larger but fluctuating number of 'paper' members, the numbers interviewed in each site remained relatively small (see Table 2.1). Interviews lasted between 45 minutes and two hours, most continuing for 60–70 minutes. Together with Simon Warren, I also spent time at each PCO in order to develop a sense of the ethos of each organization, and, in particular at the advice centre and parent education group, to observe interactions between workers and clients (see Table 2.2). Direct encounters were obviously critical in terms of the dissemination of particular discourses.

The process of data analysis can be described in two registers (Coffey 1999). One is the impersonal and technical description of how the data were manipulated, coded, reframed and re-presented.[9] The other, more neglected, register engages with the feelings of frustration, depression, self-doubt, optimism and emotional reward that the process of data analysis provokes in the researcher (Coffey 1999). There were indeed moments in this project when

Table 2.2   Observations (A total of 35 observations were conducted)

PCO	Staff meetings	Parent group meetings	Staff–client meetings	Other (e.g. conferences, seminars)	Total
Advice centre	4	3	5	2	14
Self-help group	n/a	3*	0**	2	5
Pressure group	n/a	6	n/a	2	8
Parent education group	0	n/a	6 (course sessions)	2	8
Total	4	12	11	8	35

* The self-help group had a period of over four months when they did not meet due to the illness of the group's convenor
** Contacts between self-help group members and other parents were very informal and ad hoc

coherence, both theoretical and empirical, seemed to emerge from the data, and moments when data remained intractable and 'fuzzy'. Another, often overlooked, point concerns the relationship between theory and data in the research, which as Andrew Brown has recently pointed out, often remains unclear from published accounts.

> The form of presentation of qualitative research frequently renders problematic the relationship between the general statements that result from the analytic process and the use, in presentation and discussion of the research, of high-level concepts drawn from a variety of forms of social theory . . . Does, for instance, the general theoretical orientation predate the analysis (and thus inform the design of the study, the recognition of relevant data and the mode of analysis), or are concepts from social theory drawn upon at a later stage for their resonance with the outcomes of the analytic process?
>
> (Brown 1999: 110)

The set of theoretical and empirical concerns with which I approached this research were closely linked to those expressed in my previous book (Vincent 1996). I was interested in Gramscian theory on the production of hegemonic discourses and how these applied to parent–teacher relationships; in how ideas about being a 'good' parent were disseminated by particular social actors and received by others. In this project, the use of Gramsci's theorizing was intended, for all the reasons cited above to do with specificities of context, as a jumping-off point, a beginning. As the project progressed, the literature on citizenship and difference, on deliberative democracy, became more important as it seemed to address pertinent issues around participation: public passivity and activity, the exclusion from the public sphere experienced by some sections of the population, the fraught relationship between particularity and universality, issues which were emerging from the data (see Chapter 1). In addition, such literature informed another research project on which I was subsequently involved – the layers of empirical meaning and theoretical relevance multiply in such contexts. As Stephen Ball remarks (1991: 167), researchers 'carry over' slices of data, concepts and comparisons in their heads as, over time, they move from one research project to another. Similarly, as the analysis progressed, I found the social movement literature to contain pertinent questions about the experiences for individuals of being in a group or a campaign, and about the impact of such campaigns on hegemonic discourses and understandings (a link back to Gramsci). So I have moved between literatures and the work of other social theorists as appeared appropriate, and as the data seemed to me to demand it (see Ball 1994 for a much fuller elaboration of a conceptual and theoretical 'toolbox'). I have tried to keep an emphasis on the complexities of the data, to avoid clear-cut binaries, by stressing the complications, the subtleties, the shading. Retaining some of the 'fuzziness', a sense of 'messy' data, within the relative order of what follows is an attempt to guard against imposing too tight a regularity of my own upon the thoughts and words of others, a reminder that I am re-presenting their reality through the frame of the research project and the interpretations of the researchers (see also Vincent and Warren forthcoming).

Conclusion

In this chapter, I have drawn attention to the discourse of 'good' parenting. Although the details of such a construction may change and be contested depending on specific contexts,[10] I have suggested that a key feature of the hegemonic or 'official' discourse of 'good' parenting is that of individual responsibility, borne primarily by mothers, residing within self-reliant and self-sufficient family units. 'Good' mothers accept responsibility for all facets of their children's development and work to produce children who will become reasoning and reasonable citizens. Two policy initiatives (the New Zealand Code and the UK's home–school agreements) are offered as examples of the way in which parents are encouraged to take up these normative responsibilities, regardless of their circumstances or their own understanding of what it is to be a good parent (in some cases, for instance, parents may feel that being a 'good' parent may mean supporting the child against the school, a position for which home–school agreements have no room). The remainder of the chapter was taken up with a brief account of research methods and design, and a discussion, drawing on the work of Gramsci, of the way in which particular discourses are disseminated and become hegemonic. I suggest that PCOs may provide sites in which this process can be explored and examined. The next chapter applies this proposition to an account of the work and orientation of a parents' advice centre.

Notes

1 A MORI poll conducted in November 1999 revealed that seven out ten adults questioned said parenting was a skill that had to be learnt, not something that came

naturally. As is made clear later on in this chapter, disadvantaged social groups have historically been the target for programmes of intervention and tutelage concerning mothering practices.

2 *Junior*, for example, is one recent publication which has positioned itself up-market from the more traditional baby magazines that concentrate mostly on pregnancy and caring for the under-3s. In comparison, *Junior* focuses on entertainment, education, health, fashion and travel for the under-8s.

3 The progress of the Code was delayed in the run-up to the General Election in November 1999, which resulted in a change of leadership.

4 Thanks to Laurie Green for the discussion of these issues.

5 New Labour in its first year in office (1997–8) was particularly keen on this, as official guidance on bedtimes, homework, personal and collective responsibility for one's immediate locality, parenting in general and home–school relations issued forth from the Prime Minister's office, the DfEE and the Home Office.

6 Gramsci himself insisted on the importance of historical and spatial specificity for understanding particular events (Gramsci 1971). Therefore it would be perverse to transpose his insights in their entirety to our own historical and social context. Moreover, as John Keane (1998) points out, the complexity and differentiation of power in late modern societies renders Gramsci's emphasis upon the role of the proletariat in achieving fundamental change inappropriate. However, using Gramsci's categories and themes and applying them to the more overtly complex, defused and fractured social entity of today offers the potential for new insights into our own situation (Hall 1988; Holub 1992).

7 Support for the argument that Gramsci's analysis is relevant to the position of public sector professionals today can be found in his criticisms of liberal reformist proposals to expand southern Italy's middle class (1957: 46). The role envisaged for this group contained echoes of the position and function of public sector professionals in the social democracies of the mid- to late twentieth centuries.

8 The original research design was to involve generalist parent centres where advice and information ran alongside a training element for parents themselves. However, two well-known centres of this type were both experiencing serious financial problems in 1996–7 and having to reduce the scope of their activities considerably. Nevertheless, visits were made to one of these centres which provided useful background information.

9 Briefly, in this research, this involved a process of analysis, based on the detailed prescriptions of Strauss (Strauss 1987; Strauss and Corbin 1998), which is reliant on the method of 'constant comparison'. This refers to the way in which the data are broken down and reformed to generate first broad, and then more detailed analytical codes. This sets in train (ideally) a process of increasing precision and 'progressive focusing' whereby the specificity of existing themes are increased, new categories generated and others discarded (Hammersley and Atkinson 1983; Strauss 1987; Ball 1991). A set of codes concerning perceptions of 'community, were eventually discarded, for instance, as other data collected proved more insightful.

10 A current (at the time of writing) example of a contested issue around 'good' parenting is parents' responsibilities with regard to their child's safety outside the home. The NSPCC ran a campaign in the summer of 1999 highlighting the dangers of children playing unsupervized. However, there has equally been concern that today's children are too cosseted and are deprived of opportunities to play freely outside the home.

CHAPTER **THREE**

Seeking advice: the special education advice centre (SEAC)

Introduction

This chapter focuses on one of the four case study PCOs (Parent-centred organizations), a special education advice centre, which I have called SEAC. SEAC was part of the provision offered to parents and schools by Tate LEA,[1] a small inner city authority with pockets of high levels of poverty and deprivation (relative to the national context). It provided information, advice and advocacy (although the last was a contested role) for parents whose children were defined as having special educational needs. The workers provided individual support to parents, accompanied them to meetings with teachers and other LEA staff, and provided interpretation and translation support. They were also involved in the training of classroom assistants and Named Persons (independent individuals who offer parents support during the statutory assessment process), as well as facilitating and encouraging several nascent parent support groups. The data on which this chapter is based are derived from observations of staff meetings and professional–parent meetings, and 26 interviews, 17 with families (seven white families and ten Bangladeshi families). Nineteen individuals – 11 women and eight men – took part in the interviews,[2] all the five members of the SEAC staff and four other individuals from voluntary agencies (see Chapter 2 for more details of the research design).

This chapter is about the role and function of the SEAC, considering the social, political and symbolic location of the Centre, as manifest in the relationships between workers and parent clients. At the heart of questions about the function of such advice centres, whether they operate around education, housing, benefits or the law, is the issue of inclusion. On one level, advice centres seem to be straightforwardly about inclusion – that is, ensuring that people, often from disenfranchised groups, receive the services or provision to which they are entitled (or in the case of legal centres, win the appropriate redress). Workers provide clients with information, advice and sometimes advocacy to help individuals argue their case for particular provision. Clients are to be brought into and helped to operate within the existing system of provision. However, agencies of this kind may often step beyond this role and campaign for changes in existing systems. This may arise from workers coming to believe that problem solving is a limited technique, one which aims to provide remedy for individual cases but which does not affect the client's ability to act on his/her own behalf, and which invariably does not lead to any long-term structural change. Michelle Fine (1997) makes just such an argument in her evaluation of a parent 'empowerment' project in Baltimore in the USA. She identifies the inherent weakness of case work projects – the tendency for workers under pressure to fall in with easy assumptions about where the 'problem' lies.

> What surfaced from the women [mothers] was their need which the staff served responsively. But in that process, systematic change of their schools moved to the back burner. In being responsive, a turn from parental empowerment to crisis intervention may, ironically, feed the impression that the problem lies squarely in the family system . . . Without relentless attention to systemic power and critique, parental involvement projects may simply surface the individual needs of families which will become the vehicle to express, and dilute struggles of power. If unacknowledged, power may hide, cloaked within the 'needs' or 'inadequacies' of disenfranchised mothers, and schools may persist unchallenged, employing practices that damage.
>
> (Fine 1997: 464–5)

Individual case work can allow existing state bureaucracies to function more smoothly by resolving difficult instances and slotting aberrant individuals and families back into the system. In this chapter I explore SEAC's role, and ask whose interests are served through its operation. The first section presents the background to SEAC's establishment. The second considers concepts of professionalism, including the need to 'gender' the work of professionals. This section and the next ask what sort of relationships are possible between professional and client, and emphasize the importance of taking into consideration the boundaries of, and constraints upon, any given context and the individual subjectivities of those professionals involved. The fourth section examines parental responses to the SEAC, and how these are structured by a range of factors, notably social class. The chapter concludes that the parents' groups which the Centre workers helped to establish have the potential to provide a space in which the parents involved can develop a voice of their own, and begin to challenge professional understandings of appropriate service provision for their children. The SEAC groups were embryonic and delicate groupings, the possibility of their withering away ever present. Despite this, I suggest that the formation of such groupings offers a route for development which does not arise from an individual and deficit model of need, but rather one which seeks to subject the special education system to critical scrutiny.

The background

The area covered by Tate LEA has several notable demographic features. Well-established Bangladeshi and white, predominantly working class, communities live in the area. There is a history of considerable tension existing between these two groupings, and some local housing estates have reputations for racist harassment of the Bangladeshi population. Parts of the borough have experienced considerable gentrification over the last decade, which has led to the influx of middle class newcomers, many of whom have opted out of public sector provision and therefore have minimal contact with council services (see also Butler 1996).

The SEAC was established in 1994, funded initially by a three-year GEST (Grants for Education, Support and Training) grant from the DfEE.[3] There were two full-time posts for advice workers, filled for most of the research period by four people: two Bangladeshi workers, Jalal and Amina, one Somali worker, Asha, and one white worker, Sue. The Centre Manager's post was part-time. Jane, the Centre Manager, was a white woman with a history of working on local authority projects designed to encourage parental liaison. With the exception of Jalal, all the workers were female. The Centre came about as a result of a number of different events at local and national level. Nationally, the provision of independent advice to parents relating to special education acquired a certain priority in the 1993 Education Act and LEAs were encouraged to establish Parent-Partnership Initiatives in response. The emphasis on such schemes was continued and reinforced by the Labour Party's 1997 Green Paper on special education and the subsequent Action Plan. Locally, the years immediately preceding SEAC's establishment had witnessed considerable cutbacks to local authority-funded special education support services. Over the same period, there were a number of internal reports that emphasized the difficulty which many Bangladeshi families had in accessing the local education system. These families constituted a sizeable group, comprising 50 per cent of Tate's pupil population, and the authority's awareness of this led to an emphasis in the planning of the Centre on the needs of parents whose first language was not English (there was also a much smaller, but established, Somali community within the local authority's boundaries).

The apparent aim of recent legislation and guidance on special education has been to establish a cooperative framework in which parents are regarded by professionals as essential and equal partners in the assessment. As a consequence, LEAs have to provide information on the identification, assessment and provision for SEN, to inform parents of their rights to representation and independent support (through a Named Person) while their child is undergoing statutory assessment, and their rights of appeal to the Special Education Tribunal against LEA decisions. The language used in both local and national documents is consensual, minimizing conflict and emphasizing 'partnership'. In order to fulfil the GEST criteria, LEAs were expected to develop initiatives which would prevent appeals to the Tribunal. Indeed during the period 1997–8, Tate LEA registered no appeals with the Special Educational Needs Tribunal. Here lies a rather obvious contradiction between encouraging parents to become more aware of processes and procedures around special education in general, and statutory assessment in particular, and yet, at the same time, discouraging them from challenging local authority decisions.

The SEAC workers were aware that the status of the Centre as funded by the local authority and staffed by LEA employees raised questions as to whose interests the workers served: those of the LEA or parent-clients? Tied up with this was the status of the workers: was it possible for local authority special education professionals to develop egalitarian relationships with those parents who came to the Centre, or would the relationships remain within a traditional expert-professional and passive-client mode? Was it possible to inform parents of their rights, while at the same time minimizing conflict between parents and the LEA and, crucially, while succeeding in minimizing the rate of appeals which parents made against the authority? Does not parental 'empowerment' raise the possibility of parents challenging teachers and the authority, and to what extent could the workers, employees of the same authority, encourage them to do that? How effective could the workers be in 'solving' individual problems, when these often had their root in family poverty and/or limited and constrained service provision (access to appropriate public housing, for example, was a major issue within Tate authority)? This conflicting set of demands, expectations and assumptions frames the workload of many public sector professionals working in the caring professions, and before considering the work of SEAC in more detail, I turn now to some broader issues concerning professionalism.

Professionalism and performativity

Professionalism

The immediate postwar period witnessed an expansion of the welfare state and associated occupations. Dominant understandings of the professional role in a social democracy consisted of contradictory impulses. Professionals were to be a force for social amelioration and reform,[4] while also being capable of delivering efficient public services through rational bureaucratic organization (Cole and Furbey 1994). During the late 1960s, the first impulse – that of social amelioration – was strengthened and extended. Professionals employed in welfare state institutions were not only to formulate 'good' policies, but also to encourage the self-development of *individual* clients (see for example, Eric Midwinter's (1972) work on community education). This impulse was given a sharper edge during the 1970s by some professionals, especially 'frontline' workers, who emphasized their potential role as agents of social reform. The task then was to redistribute access to resources and decision-making power to *groups*, not just individuals, seen as disadvantaged (see for example, Bennington's 1977 account of the Community Development Projects).

However, the work of many different groups of public sector professionals, especially those working under the auspices of the welfare state, has been subject to considerable criticism over the last 20 years or so (e.g. Weatherley 1979; Lipsky 1980; Wilding 1982). The critiques have been concerned to expose the 'myth' that these professionals are benign agents involved in relationships with clients unaffected by the structural inequalities which are embedded in wider society, and based on class, ethnicity and/or gender. Welfare state professionals have been castigated for their paternalism, their belief that the services they provided were benign and in the best interests of their clients (McAuslan 1980; Tomlinson 1982; Cole and Furbey 1994), their fierce protection, and where possible expansion, of their own territory, and their focus on individuals. This last, it has been said, induces a de-politicized understanding of the issues involved, casting them as technical problems amenable to 'expert' solution (Wilding 1982; Young 1990).

My intention here is not to refute these criticisms; indeed I have employed this literature in support of earlier arguments (e.g. Troyna and Vincent 1995; Vincent *et al.* 1996). In any case, commentators have also pointed to the limitations on professional power; the constraints and often contradictory demands which they seek to resolve (Lipsky 1980; Young 1990). Johnson (1972) argued that in 'mediated' professions (those in which the state inter-venes in order to define the clients' needs and the ways in which they should be met), the growth of a shared overarching professional identity is unlikely (for more recent developments of this point see Giddens 1991; Hanlon 1998). On the contrary, different and competing professional inter-ests reflect the heterogeneity and conflict which characterize 'the state' itself, and state-sponsored groups. Derek Armstrong (1995) provides an example of this process with his reference to differentiation and competition between special education professionals. He maintains that the struggles taking place between and within professional groups and professional and client groups open up spaces in which new alliances between professional and lay groups can be formed.

However, despite these exceptions, the analytic tendency to focus on the professional–lay person divide remains common, and can risk promoting an essentialist view of 'the professional'; that is, a view that overlooks or minim-izes the differing identities and subjectivities subsumed under that heading and the myriad ways in which individuals negotiate and make sense of contradictory positions and understandings. There is then a need to inter-rogate the fixed and homogeneous conceptualization of a public sector pro-fessional which seems to have persisted in much of the literature. To talk of 'a professional' without making reference to the specificity of a given con-text, and the meanings that make sense in those settings, is to impose an abstraction, to deny the lived experiences of the individuals concerned.

As part of this process, several commentators have drawn attention to the way in which understandings of professional work and the operation of bureaucracies require a gendered analysis (e.g. Crompton 1987; Witz 1990; Davies 1996). Davies, for example, argues that women's inclusion into 'sup-port' roles as semi-professionals allows individuals and organizations to operate in masculinist ways. Impartiality and impersonality are, she main-tains, the hallmarks of professional–client encounters and the workings of bureaucracy. Her examples are mainly drawn from the field of health where many female support roles (nurses, administrators, clerks) are largely unacknowledged and invisible in comparison to the work of senior (and usually male) doctors. This argument will be considered further below, and its application to SEAC assessed.

In addition, it is important to contextualize any analysis. The macro context in which public sector professionals work is changing. The penetration of new managerialist discourses and practices into the public sector has meant that the typical (or stereotypical) Fabian public sector professional has witnessed fundamental restructuring in his or her field, whether it be education, health, housing or social services. These changes do not constitute a 'clean break' with the past, however. Organizational rituals, practices and discourses will retain traces of past ways of working. However, the cumulative effect of the public sector reforms is profound. Hanlon (1998) argues that a new version of 'commercialized' professionalism is being consolidated, and is located in opposition to social democratic professionalism. The tension between the two is, he argues, exacerbating divisions within particular professional groups from both the public and private sectors (see Chapter 6).

Performativity

In education, as in other areas, the Conservative governments of the 1980s and 1990s instituted 'the market' as a disciplinary mechanism. As described in Chapter 1, this has served to reconstitute the various relations within the education system, decentring the position of professionals and apparently privileging others, notably parents and managers (Bowe *et al.* 1992; Ball 1994). On the face of it, the imbalance of professional–client power has changed in two respects. First, the consumer-client has a more active role than previously as s/he makes a rational choice among the various products on offer. Second, the professional's workload is to some degree subject to client demand, in that the professional is also required to assess consumer demands and to change his or her commodities in order to meet these needs (Bowe *et al.* 1992). The resulting outcome of professional responses to, or attempts to direct, consumer demand is deemed by market proponents to be highly efficient.

The elevation of effectiveness and efficiency as the sole criterion of legitimacy (Keane 1992) reflects the increasing dominance of an ethic of managerialism and a concomitant emphasis upon measuring and improving performance (performative strategies). Stephen Ball (1999) argues that managerialism works on the individual from the inside out, overlaying traditional professional values and concerns with those of the entrepreneurial manager working within a competitive market place. Performative regimes, however, drive individuals with the promise and 'terror' (Lyotard 1984) of fulfilling (or not) targets and goals, and succeeding (or not) in rankings and comparisons with others. Performativity therefore has its effects from the outside in (Ball 1999). It thereby becomes a 'regime of truth', '. . . through which people govern themselves and others' (Ball 1994: 22; see also Benhabib 1992).

As Anna Yeatman (1994) argues, performativity can supply a meta-discourse for public policy. It reifies values such as efficiency, silencing questions such as 'efficiency in relation to what ends, whose ends and what time scale (short, medium or long term?)' (1994: 113). Discussion of education therefore focuses not so much on the transformations in people's lives brought about by education, or the quality of their educational experiences, but the *number* of qualified students, the *savings* made in the delivery of services, the *proportion* of students going on into higher education. Furthermore, Robert Funnell (1995) argues that the convergence of 'moral orders' from both private sector corporatism and public sector bureaucracy and the concomitant 'transformation from one order of codes and sets of values to the other' has profound implications for the 'formation of identity and self' for those professionals involved (Funnell 1995: 157; see also Gewirtz 1997; Reay 1996). His analysis emphasizes the ways in which the majority of people in this position reach settlements, and 'centre and orient themselves' to dominant codes and discourses (ibid.). I wish to argue that this process is one of neither subjection nor resistance, but of *active* accommodation, accepting limitations (both practical and conceptual) and employing available resources and opportunities to work towards desired goals.

The demands of performativity impact slightly differently upon our case studies depending on their particular role. Out of the four, as one might expect, it was the local authority SEAC which was subject to the sharpest demands. The workers there were required to keep detailed records of the number of inquiries and cases they dealt with, and in arguing for continued funding they pointed to the cost-effectiveness of their early intervention for the LEA system as a whole.[5] However, these objectives are conceptually limited in that they do not, cannot, describe or encapsulate the potential of an initiative such as the Centre, designed to encourage and increase parental participation in the care and education of children.

Yeatman makes a similar point, when she comments on the apparent contradictions between a performative culture of governance, and one that encourages public participation, 'open dialogue, discussion, dissension and sharing of information' (1994: 113). However, following Lyotard, Yeatman also emphasizes that the performative state can and does make overtures (of a particular kind) in the direction of user groups and clients. In order to improve its own capacities to manage, it is often necessary for a performative state to identify and address emerging demands and issues from particular groups of citizens, and the state cannot therefore insulate itself from politics. Lyotard (1984) makes it quite clear that the state's rationale for this 'openness' is to maintain control. Therefore, although the client may appear to be in a stronger position vis-à-vis the professional under a performative regime, this may not be so. 'Terror' (Lyotard's term) can be used to control clients, marginalizing them just as effectively as their previous passive position did under the welfare state model:

By terror I mean the efficiency gained by eliminating or threatening to eliminate a player from a language game which one shares with him. He

is silenced or consents, not because he has been refuted, but because his
ability to participate has been threatened . . . 'Adapt your aspirations to
our ends or else!'

(Lyotard 1984: 63–4)

One of my concerns in this chapter is to illuminate the ways in which performativity and traditional understandings of social democratic professionalism interact to inscribe particular practices in this local site.

Analysing advice giving

Limitations

It is possible to read the work of the Centre in a number of different ways.
Data could be marshalled with which to accuse the workers of the 'sins' of
professionalism as outlined earlier: paternalism, a belief that service provision
is benign and in the best interests of clients, their fierce protection of their
own territory, and their concentration on individuals. Let us now consider
the evidence for this reading.

Taking the first two criticisms – paternalism and a belief in benign service
provision – together: generally, the workers positioned themselves within a
traditional welfare–professional discourse with all its paternalistic implications. They did not view parents through the guise of market relations, that
is as consumers making complaints about the services with which they are
provided.[6] Instead, the parents were seen as recipients of professional expertise.
Two workers commented that their particular satisfaction came from helping
parents:

> When parents first come in, they're nervous, they didn't know. When
> they leave they have a happy face, they understand. Then you feel good
> that I helped that person . . . done something for someone.
>
> (Amina)

> When you're in a position to offer advice or information that parents
> just didn't realize was there . . . that they're eligible for something or at
> least there's another channel that they can go through.
>
> (Sue)

As will be clear later on, the workers all identified to a considerable degree
with particular groups of their clients, although this identification was not
complete. Most of the parents who came into the Centre remained as clients
in the eyes of the workers, differentiated by their lack of knowledge, confidence and other cultural and material resources:

> A lot of parents, they can't travel, a lot of parents they don't have cars,
> lots of parents they don't feel safe sometimes to ride on the bus by
> themselves, they can't afford taxi services, you know, they need help,
> they need support to get children's education.
>
> (Jalal)

The problems that parents brought to the workers required 'solving' in order that parents and their children could be fitted back into the special education system, thus allowing it to continue operating smoothly and without change. It was readily acknowledged by the workers that there were flaws in that system. Indeed, the relationships between particular schools and parents, the performative constraints of the Code of Practice and the disregarding attitudes of some professionals were seen as particular shortcomings. Jane, the Centre Manager, argued, for instance, that the necessity for schools to complete paperwork related to the Code of Practice led them to engage in an illusory consultation performance with parents, one designed not so much to encourage dialogue, but rather to comply with the requirement that parental viewpoints were recorded. Thus the consultation was different in style but similar in outcome to the superficial consultative mechanisms of the past (see, for example, Booth and Potts 1992). However, despite this articulation of the faults of the special education system, bringing parents within its reach, going through the formal procedures was perceived by the workers to be a benign and worthwhile process. Asha, employed to work with Somali families, described her job in these terms:

> [I was employed] mainly because they did not get the support of the Somali parents. None of the Somali parents used the service, the [SEAC], and therefore for example they could not turn up to medicals when required, they could not turn up for assessments when required, because they didn't know what it was all about. They wouldn't give value to it because they didn't know. They just think, well it's some other bit of paper, and that's it. So by me being here, I'll be able to do the visits, explain to them the importance of it.

It is instructive here to consider the literature on self-advocacy which disseminates a markedly different approach to that taken by the SEAC workers. Dan Goodley (1997), writing about the self-advocacy of people with learning difficulties, suggests that professional advisers may (although this is far from inevitable; see Goodley 1998) detract from and limit the project of self-advocacy. Professionals, he notes, reach their position through specialist training and accreditation. Therefore, their professional identity is based on their control of knowledge of a particular area, which is disability in Goodley's writing, and in the case of SEAC, the related area of special education:

> [There is a] conflict of understandings. That is, a clash between the project of self-advocacy which places independence at the core, and the requirements of a professionalised identity assigned to the staff advisor, which is grounded in dependence. Here then is a conflict between self-advocacy that is potentially striven for by a group, and the limitation of self . . . enforced by paternalistic authority in a professional climate.
>
> (Goodley 1997: 371)

However, as will become clear later, SEAC's Centre Manager was aware of reified professional–client roles arising from conducting individual case work, and tried to mitigate this by developing parent networks.

The second set of criticisms levelled at professionals concerns their vested interests in seeing their 'territory' grow. The Centre workers were certainly concerned to protect their sphere of expertise against a small number of voluntary groups operating in the area. Referring to an independent agency, Jalal commented:

> They're servicing the people in Meer's Green with all types of education, and my understanding is if they want particular advice on special educational needs they should refer to us because we are more equipped and we have more resources, and produce more documents on education, on special needs . . . We are a more sort of mainstream advice centre because we have got the support and backing of Support Learning Services, we are working with other professional bodies such as Speech Therapy and the Hearing Impairment specialist teacher, Vision Impairment specialist teacher . . .

Another agency dealing with education was deemed a threat. Here, Jalal adopted a discourse of performativity in order to defend the position of his own centre. He ignored the potential advantages to clients of the other agency's independence from the LEA, pointing instead to the 'professionalism' of his fellow workers and the benefits of their close links with LEA services.

The third set of criticisms levelled at professionals (or professionalism) concerns their focus on individual need. Indeed, the majority of the SEAC workers' time was spent in relatively short-term individual case work, arising from a large numbers of families.[7] This type of work, with professional and client in 'working pairs' (Goodley 1998) tends to mean that the particular issues and concerns brought up by the case remain the province of private individuals, and are not brought forward into the public arena where they could be used to scrutinize special education procedures and provision as a whole. However, the individual case work was balanced by the SEAC workers' involvement with the other aspect of the Centre's work, the facilitation of parents' groups:

> So far with the parents' groups, we're going to help them with their posters, the mailing and photocopying of material . . . we don't want to be much involved, because we want parents to be more involved than us. If we say at the beginning we are doing everything, then I don't think any parent would come forward; we want them to come forward . . . I wouldn't say I'm involved with them, I couldn't say that.
>
> (Amina, SEAC worker)

However, although the workers acknowledged the importance of the parents' groups and parents being enabled to act independently, they appeared to prefer being involved with case work rather than spend time on the development work required to support the parents' groups (an issue returned to below).

Despite this enumeration of the 'sins' of professionalism, I wish to argue that the stance taken by the SEAC advice workers cannot easily be read off as oppressively paternalistic. For one thing, as I suggested earlier, the workers were subject to considerable constraints themselves, deriving from the Centre's position within a professionally orientated, public sector institution. I outline all three constraints here.

The first derives from the gendered workings of bureaucracies. The workers at the Centre, mainly women and doing 'feminine' work, attended to the emotions of their clients, listening to them (parents often commented that the SEAC worker was the first professional to listen to them), calming them, sympathizing with them, and working with them to help them present a calm, objective face to the education professionals as this is the only register deemed valid:

> [The worker has been] telling me what to do and how to go about it: calm down, now go and have a cup of tea, calm down, don't ring anybody up yet, calm yourself down and ring them up later.
>
> (White mother)

In this reading, the Centre operated as a safety valve for the bureaucracy, allowing the messy, personal, disruptive emotions of parents to be diffused safely and without threat to the system. This analysis highlights the extent to which SEAC is positioned as serving the needs of the *local authority*. The workers' sense of their own professionalism is also deployed to this end, and this presents them with inflexible scripts and modes of interaction from which it was difficult to depart.

The second point of constraint for the workers derives from working in a public sector organization which has been refashioned by managerial and performative priorities. As Stephen Ball argues, '[Another] aspect of [public sector] restructuring is the formation of new "professional" subjectivities. It is not simply what we do that is changed; who we are, the possibilities for who we might become are also changed' (Ball 1997).[8] Performativity also encourages the workers to emphasize solving individual cases. The manager of the Centre, Jane, described how individual case work had taken priority for the workers over development work. She suggests two main reasons for this: first, the workers' awareness of the demands of their case load, and second, that they found doing case work more comfortable and familiar:

> It's the combination of pressure, the demand from parents individually but also rather that you feel comfortable because it's familiar. And you could say it's possibly my fault for not giving more support and pushing them into doing more development work. But it's something that I've picked up, you know, that they have felt under a lot of pressure time-wise . . . Development work, spending a lot of time talking to parents, going to meetings, being with parent groups, it's very open-ended. You often don't see an immediate outcome . . . It comes back to this thing of just knowing that, you know they just see the files, they just see the number of phone calls, they see the number of letters, and they're aware of wanting to provide a good individual service.

Here the influence and constraints of both social democratic professionalism and performativity can be seen. The workers are under pressure to operate in a way that gives clear quantifiable results, and this is also the way of working with which they feel most comfortable. During most instances of casework, the professional–client boundary is clearly in place. Working with parents' groups, encouraging their sense of voice and agency, is to enter much more diffuse, uncharted territory, without any firm likelihood of success.

The third point of constraint derived from the workers' location as LEA employees. While the workers were clear that their role was to ensure that parents understood the often inaccessible educational, psychological and medical language around special education, and had space in which to ask questions, the notion of supporting parents in challenging the school or local authority was much more problematic. If a parent wanted to go to appeal, for instance, s/he would be referred to an independent organization which could provide support. This was a clear policy position. An area which attracted more uncertainty, however, was challenges to statements.[9] Given the general constraints on budgets which most local authorities experienced during the 1990s, many responded by trying to place limits on the rising demands for statements. Demand had been rising during the late 1980s and 1990s, because many parents lacked faith in both LEAs and schools to supply the provision they felt their children needed without the safeguard of a statement. Schools also saw LEAs' statement budgets as a potential resource. Some local authorities were trying to reduce the number of statements so that they could channel money from the statement budget to schools, thereby encouraging schools to take on responsibility for all their pupils and to intervene early before problems became severe. This approach is, of course, in line with the recommendations of both the 1994 Code of Practice and the 1997 Green Paper on special education. However, whatever the influences upon the local authority, the end result is that provision detailed on the statement is often written in more general terms than in the past. The amount of hours of extra help may not be specified, or may be limited.

> What's happened in [Tate] as well as many other areas is that even five or six years ago when we worked with statements for children with the more serious disabilities, it would say, 'Child needs speech therapy on a weekly basis', 'The child needs physiotherapy on this sort of roll' . . . Now we get something which says, 'May need appropriate paramedic support'. In terms of giving parents something useful and something to fight on, it's rubbish.
>
> (Worker from another agency)

Many of the parent-clients, being unfamiliar with the language and content of statements, were reliant on the SEAC workers for guidance in this area. However, encouraging parents to challenge a statement where the recommended provision was expressed vaguely with few specific references to times or qualified staff was seen by the workers as stepping beyond the boundaries of their role as LEA employees. The LEA, after all, saw SEAC as an agency that helped to ensure its target of zero statutory appeals. Additionally, the workers were unhappy with the idea of offering such direct guidance and intervention.[10]

Having now delineated a number of dimensions that serve to place limits and constraints upon the operation of the Centre, I now offer a more optimistic reading.

Possibilities

The work of SEAC can also be read in a way which highlights not only the limitations which operate within and upon the workers, but also the spaces which they identify and exploit. In an earlier article Simon Warren and I (Vincent and Warren 1997) argued that, at a local level, professional workers in our PCOs have a degree of 'space' in which to develop conceptions of their relationships with clients which may differ significantly from either social democratic or neo-liberal understandings of their role, so that they can, to some extent, approach parents as neither 'expert' nor producer. This may seem unlikely, given our earlier description of performativity, as a performative culture demands that its workers, as well as its clients, 'adapt your aspirations to our ends – or else' (Lyotard 1984: 64), but we suggested that there are occasions and situations in which professionals can avoid, or begin to subvert, the performative demands of their roles, in ways which foster their own priorities and agendas (see also Bowe *et al.* 1992). How professionals understand and use this space is influenced by particular aspects of their identities as well as the specificities of the contexts in which they work (see Vincent and Warren 1997). For instance, Simon and I have previously argued that Jalal, one of the advice centre workers, positioned himself as an advocate, on the side of parents to a degree that other professionals, non-frontline professionals, could not share. This understanding of themselves as a 'different kind of professional' applied to the other SEAC workers. As Jalal explains,

> Some parents they're very sort of unhappy when they go to a meeting and hear a lot of jargon words, and they've been promised that a lot of things will be done for them, [but] year after year, nothing changes . . . Being the professional here [at the Centre], we have a working relationship with the parents, they can rely, they can tell their problems. But these other kind of professional, high management professionals, they don't see them, they see only a three piece suit, maybe giving another speech, and, 'Oh, it's another speech,' they say.

He distanced himself from seemingly remote bureaucrats, particularly on the grounds of his ethnicity, feeling that he had access to the 'structures of feeling' of his Bangladeshi clients; they had in common if not the same 'language' in its entirety, at least access to the same social 'dialect' (Holub 1992). In Jalal's case he literally shared a language (Sylheti) with his Bangladeshi clients:

> I have had some teachers approach me, saying, 'I'm working with this family, but I'm not getting any response from them' . . . So we got involved . . . when I was speaking [the family's] language, I didn't take

the white professional with me. You know, they couldn't stop telling their problems, you know . . . The family thought, 'I don't want to tell my problem to an outsider.'

Similarly one of the other workers commented:

I kind of feel more like a semi-professional really, a go-between for professionals and families . . . Parents wouldn't class us in the same category as they would all these different professionals that they're involved with, you know . . . It helps to have another level that they see as more on a par with them.

(Sue, worker)

Sue's grounds for her partial identification with (some of) her clients differs from Jalal's; in her case it is their shared positionality as parents with children with special needs, and their shared social location as white parents with a developing, if embattled, sense of agency.

Some of the parents I've worked with are just as able as I am really, and I think maybe it's just experience. I think if I was in their position I would feel just as incapable in certain areas, I would need someone else to give me support, just to be sure that you know, you're always doing the right thing, because you get so many knock backs . . . I personally find it a nightmare every time I get a set of booklets, forms to fill out for my own children, and yet, I could sit alongside someone quite happily and do theirs . . . A lot of the time it's helping parents do it for themselves, but just giving them the extra support, you know. It might be completely different from [the bilingual workers' clients] but I find that the families I'm working with are able to do it, but just need the extra support and encouragement.

The other two advice workers also commented on the way in which their ethnic origin (Bangladeshi and Somali respectively) gave them access to particular clients' 'structures of feeling'. Such access provided benefits for the workers in terms of grounding them, and securing their sense of their own utility, and brought benefits to many of their clients who did feel that the worker spoke the same language (both literally and metaphorically) and shared their concerns (see below).

The workers rarely referred to possible grounds for *dislocation* between themselves and their clients, although it was clear that distinctions on the basis of race were made by both themselves and some parents. The division of the workload was implicitly racialized. Parents were mostly allocated the appropriately 'raced' worker to their case, the Bangladeshi workers dealing mainly with Asian and African/Caribbean families, Asha, the Somali worker, with Somali families, and Sue with the white families. This issue was briefly discussed at a staff focus group meeting:

Jalal: Very few, not many parents do 'phone and once they hear our voice, they want to know if there is any other English speaking worker

here. Very few, but you do get it. Is it because I'm Asian, and
they do not want to tell their story to me, or what is the reason?
[....]

Sue: I tend to think it's more just accent. It's difficult talking to
people on the 'phone with different accents, because it happens
to me in reverse doesn't it? Very often. Someone at the end of
the phone – and that's really very, very often – I can understand
what they're saying very clearly, but they still insist on talking
to Amina or Jalal, and I'm just out of the equation completely.

Amina: If any monolingual parents ring, I take the message first and I do
tell them we have a white worker, and you can choose . . . Sometimes they say yes, but most of the time they say 'no, no problem'.

There is a lot going on in the above extract, and it raises interesting questions about the individuals' approach to issues of race and racism, as well as
their interrelationships. Thus race appears as a crucial dimension in many
of the professional–client relationships, influencing the workers' access to
parents' structures of feeling. The importance of race in defining identity is
highlighted and strengthened by Tate's history of racism and racial harassment and the powerful discourse of exclusion directed by many among the
white majority at the Bangladeshi inhabitants. The reaction of the advice
workers to these racialized definitions of inclusion and exclusion is one of
accommodation and avoidance rather than resistance.

However, the black–white division made by the workers is overly simplistic,
and does not for example account for tensions within particular communities.
Jalal's sense of close identification with the local Sylheti-speaking community is clearly apparent in his long and passionate response to the issue of
discrimination against Sylhetis, particularly from other Bangladeshis:

One of my colleagues one day told me, 'I went to a family and she was
so well-dressed and I couldn't believe she was Sylheti.' I said, 'Come on,
what are you saying? I don't understand what you are saying. Are you
saying that Sylheti people are not well-dressed? How many Sylheti families have you visited? How many rich educated Sylheti families have you
visited? You are going to houses because they are in a mess, basically
because they are immigrants, they've got housing problems, they've got
job problems . . . You have an attitude problem. Don't say it again because
it annoys me. Because we must respect our clients.'

Jalal's understanding of his own identity and allegiances lead him to challenge this discriminatory portrayal of Sylheti parents. Some of the other
workers also drew on their experiences, values and beliefs to champion more
egalitarian professional–client relationships. Sue, for instance, felt her own
identity as the mother of two children with special needs informed the
egalitarian approaches she took at work and her promotion of a 'parent's
perspective':

I think I'm more confident at dealing with particular professionals [as a
result of her involvement with voluntary groups]. And able to always

have a parent's perspective in mind, because I've very often since I've been [here] been in meetings where I think if I hadn't had that experience of being a parent of children with special needs I would have maybe taken a different view. I feel like in a way it's a bonus that I've often been able to say, 'Oh just a minute, you're just viewing this from a completely wrong angle, and that's really not right.' So I think my experience has helped enormously.

While the other workers felt that they had a particular link with certain of their clients arising from shared social locations which contributed to similar perspectives, the Centre Manager, Jane, focused on the representation of parents as a distinct group. As noted earlier, she had worked in other local education authority projects aiming to increase parental participation in education. Her past career history, her experience of working in the special education services in Tate, her contact with parents over the years, and her professional contacts with other practitioners working to develop home–school liaison all led her to emphasize the need for fundamental change in the way in which local education services related to parents:

I've always felt that if you're going to have a long-term impact, you've got to make structural changes and part of that is to do with parents acting collectively. I don't think, although we've tried really hard, that the Parents' Forum has got off the ground. We're not going to give up on it. It seems to me that parents are still very isolated, that there are individual parents we can help to fight for what they want for their children, but we will actually achieve much more if we can get some collective representation of parents' views across to service providers. I think that's a long-term goal, but otherwise all you're doing is sticking plaster work.

Recurring in both staff and parent interviews was the view that although the advice and support given by the Centre was appreciated and produced benefits for individual parents, the ability of the workers to generate long-term or structural change was limited. The perceived limitations were partly practical (e.g. time, resources), but largely to do with the Centre being part of the authority. The establishment of parents' groups, however, offers a possible solution. Such groups have the potential to give parents a greater voice in relation to both schools and the LEA.

Parents' groups

There was, as several respondents noted, a lack of parent-organized support groups in Tate:

The model we've tried to develop, because we've been very conscious of being inside the LEA, and not independent, is this notion that as paid advice workers you're working directly with parents, but empowerment comes through enabling parents, giving the back-up to set things up for themselves and provide support for each other. I feel that's worked well with the groups we've set up so far. The focused groups, the dyslexia support group, the deaf children's society is pretty remarkable. In a very short space of time, where there were no voluntary groups, without paid workers, we've now got that.

(Jane, Centre Manager)

There's very limited practical services [in Tate], and there is no history of a campaigning agency, there is no history really of parental power within the borough. Parents have enormously low expectations of services and a very cynical view of service development, and that's fairly difficult to work with . . . I think the Parents' Centre has actually done very well in involving parents. I think sometimes it's quite difficult to involve parents because of the[ir] economic background, because of the day-to-day struggles of life, and so I think people [the workers] have done quite well. I think they identified small groups of parents who may not be representative actually of Tate's population, but they are still parents who live here and want to do something about life here and to get the best for their children . . . I've seen them at the Forum, I've seen them at parent groups, I've seen them in and around, they seem very comfortable at the Centre, the relationship with the staff appears to be very good, they obviously feel valued in the Centre. I think there are probably not that many parents involved [but] I think setting that against the background in Tate, it's a major achievement.

(Worker in another agency)

The groups themselves were special interest groups, bringing together, for example, parents with hearing-impaired children or parents with children deemed to have dyslexia. Although fathers were involved, the groups attracted mainly mothers. The groups were relatively successful in attracting and retaining parent members. There was also a generalist group known as the Forum, which was originally conceived as a mechanism for bringing parents of children with special educational needs together, in order for them to formulate an agenda of shared concerns and engage in a dialogue with the authority's policy makers.[11] However the Forum had trouble maintaining the numbers of those attending, and the group struggled to create an agenda and an identity. Several respondents suggested that the wide range of concerns which the Forum was willing to address (and which included transport, housing, the closure of a special school) made it too amorphous and diffuse a phenomenon to attract people consistently, and for those individuals to establish a common language. The specialist groups however catered to a particular audience and acted as sources of information and support for individuals. Cynicism on the part of parents regarding consultation procedures and participative mechanisms may also have contributed to the apparent apathy over the Forum. As a worker from another agency commented, the wheel had been invented several times over in Tate, but had not yet started to roll:

Tate's history of parental consultation is that we do something spectacular every now and again and we never follow it up. We've got a new Principal Officer in Social Services, and he says, 'I think we ought to ask parents what they need.' I have been strenuously saying to him, 'Don't do it.' We know exactly what parents need, what they need now, what they needed three years ago, five years ago, and we've gone and asked them and then we have never followed it through.

By 1999, two years after the end of the research period, the parents' groups appeared to have embedded themselves. The groups for parents of dyslexic and hearing-impaired children were well established, and two new groups existed. The Parents' Forum is now recognized as one of the LEA's user groups. There are also two groups specifically for Bangladeshi parents which are independent of the Centre but which have a working relationship with it.

Professional–parent relationships

Of particular interest throughout the research was the question of how the definitions of 'appropriate' parental behaviour disseminated by professionals working in parent groups, or the core parent members who organized groups themselves, were responded to by other parents.

In their case work, the workers generally felt parents should be 'active partners', and to this end they all encouraged their clients to be active on their own behalf and to act independently:

I will help them to do it, I'm not going to do it for them. I will show them the way so that next time they can do it for themelves . . . like some of the parents if the school gives them something to sign, they will sign it, nothing wrong, but I tell them you should know what's in there, you should know the contents before you sign. So I say to them, you tell them I'm not signing this until you find someone, or they can call me and ask me to help.

(Amina, advice worker)

However, this was sometimes done in a manner which, rather than negotiating, appeared to direct the parent to particular tasks:

We don't want them to rely on us only. So what we do is share the work, I'll tell you, you go and get a piece of paper, or ask that person to supply this information, and I'll do this work. We'll have a sort of agreement, you do this and I'll do this, otherwise we'll be writing letters year after year and they'll never, they'll learn to rely on us. For example, this particular case I remember, I could have phoned for him to be helpful to him to his doctor who is Bengali speaking. I said no, you're going to phone and you're going to tell him that you need this letter, because you can't say, I can't speak to him because my English is bad, because he has got a Bengali secretary and the doctor is Bengali as well. You should be able to do that. You bring that letter to me and I'll write a supporting letter . . . So it was partnership, I could have asked his doctor, but because I want him to be active in his problem, I said we'll divide the work, you take half and I'll take half . . . [Sometimes] I have to decide, am I asking too much? If this person can do that then why does he need to come to me? So I am not going to give him a job that he can't do.

(Jalal)

In this section, I consider how parents reacted in their relationships with workers and the extent to which these could be understood as 'active partnerships'. In conversation with parent respondents, Simon Warren and I heard again and again of negative impressions of the professionals whom they met and the procedures they went through. This held true for all the respondents. Regardless of ethnicity or social class, everyone had stories of professional arrogance, insensitivity or incompetence, bewildering procedures and frustrating periods of inaction. Parents commonly used a language of struggle; they spoke of having to 'fight' and 'battle' and of 'luck' if they came into contact with a helpful professional ready to listen to them.[12] These data were forthcoming despite the fact that the interview schedule was not designed to elicit information on problems and difficulties, but instead focused on the parent's relationship with SEAC (which was generally seen as a source of support). A few voices:

Father: I think it's very hard relying on other people with a child's education . . . You have no choice in life do you? You know, this guy says this, this and that. He's going to look at your case, and he can say yes or no . . . You've got to be, you're the only one who's going to fight for the child's rights and everything.

Mother: But we were *lucky* in respect with [the headteacher], because what we didn't know, he explained to us. He told us who the SENCo [special educational needs co-ordinator] was and what their job involved . . .

Father: The psychologist, we'd got really good friends there . . . so that we were *lucky* in that we had a really good teacher all the way through. We was *lucky*, I'd say. I must admit there are a lot of people who are not so lucky.

(White parents, my emphasis)

I've got to stand up for myself because no damn bugger else is going to do it, so it's only me, and I am the one. I'm frightened for [child], you know. One day I'm not going to be here, who's going to do it then? So if I don't do it now, what's he going to have for a future? It's a constant fight, constant battle with the authorities . . . Evidently, one of my files has got: Watch this mother, she's a bit of a bitch, and I went, 'Really, oh that's good.' They go, 'Don't you feel put down by that?' I go, 'No, because it is telling me I've made an impact.'

(White mother)

I found it [the statement process] quite confusing, very difficult to understand, and I don't think it was fully explained exactly what was going
on . . . even when they did explain I still felt totally clueless, and I didn't
know what stage he was on at any time.

(White mother)

Many parents described situations where they were completely alienated
from decision-making procedures:

There's not been enough help, there is no help apart from going to see
them [SEAC workers]. He thinks that he needs more practical help or
whatever, rather than maybe just advice . . . there's a lot of talking, it
will not get them anywhere . . . He's been like this for the last 15 years,
trying to be rehoused and seeing all different people, and people come
and visit and promise, 'I will do this and do that', but nothing's ever
happened, so at the moment you know, he feels not well enough to
chase all this up now, and he's just left it as it is.

(Interpreter translating words of Bangladeshi father)

She was present, and it was explained to her that the psychologist would
look at [child], and do whatever they do.

(Interpreter translating words of Bangladeshi mother)

[The mother] says that she's had help from individuals and groups over
the years [concerning her son], and she's not sure who is who. Over the
six years they have been in the flat, there have been a lot of different
workers . . . They have had no contact with anyone [apart from the school]
for over a year.

(Field notes recording translated response from Bangladeshi mother)

In response to what were frequently experienced as situations of exclusion,
parents insisted on their own knowledge of their children:

What the mother is saying is even if the school says, no, that he does
not need help, as a parent she feels that he does need help because of all
the time he's had off school [with illness].

(Interpreter translating words of Bangladeshi mother)

A child, no-one knows them better than the mother or father or the
carers . . . They write reports on my boy, I don't get to see what it's about.
I'm the mother, I should know what's getting put down on paper.

(White mother)

I think I've changed . . . I've had to fight for him [son], nobody else is
going to do it, and it's made me realize now that if you don't do it
yourself . . . they're telling you what your children need, and you as
parents should be telling them what your children need, not the other
way round, because you know your children . . . Us as parents can say,
'Hold on a minute, who are you to tell us about our children?' I mean,
to put it bluntly, 'Who do you think you are, what qualifications have

Table 3.1 Family strategies: a typology

Strategy	Number of families (17 in total)	Ethnicity
The detached approach	6 families	All Bangladeshi
The band-aid approach	6 families	4 Bangladeshi families 2 white families
The toolbox approach	5 families	All white families

you got?' Right, 'You might be sitting up there [but] all you do is read bits of paper about the children, we know our children'.

(White mother)

A typology of parental strategies

In dealing with the problems they faced, parents' responses could be grouped into three strategies – the *detached* approach, the *band-aid* approach and the *toolbox* approach.[13]

The detached approach

This describes strategies adopted by parents which were characterized by detached or relatively passive relations with professionals. Such an approach could have many sources, including parents' feelings of resignation, frustration or even despair that their situation could be resolved:

He feels very sad when people come and say, you know, they'll help him this way and that way and whatever, and then later on things are still the same. He feels he's very sad about this, but you know, what can be done? Because nothing seems to be happening, so he's just sort of like . . . leaving it for the time being.

(Interpreter translating words of a Bangladeshi father)

Quite often a detached approach was due to parents feeling confused and bewildered by the workings of the statutory assessment process and the range of educational and non-educational professionals with whom they had to deal:

We're getting parents who are coming in and their child is sort of on Stage 3 of the statementing process, and they're not aware they're on Stage 3, and they don't even know what the statementing process is . . . So there is an awful lot of parents that are going through all this, but without the support they're in a bit of a muddle.

(Sue, worker)

This absence of knowledge could prevent parents from acting on their own behalf even when they wished to do so; a situation similar to that found in the Tomlinson and Hutchison (1991) study of Bangladeshi parents' perceptions of the school system. The researchers on that project found that 'parental levels of knowledge about education and about their children's schooling is inadequate despite high levels of parental interest' (1991: 45). Even once the parents have contacted or been referred to the SEAC, they may feel constrained from taking up an active role. Several of the parents we spoke to faced multiple demands on their time and energies, and complained of illness and stress. Survival issues – housing, work, benefits – were of such major concern to some that they simply did not have the resources to cope with additional educational problems:

> The first thing would be to be rehoused, because there are nine people living in a three-bedroom flat, and the house is pretty damp.
>   (Bangladeshi father speaking through an interpreter)

> Ms—is very concerned over their housing. There are two other families beside hers living in the flat, 16 people in a four-bedroom flat. She has been on the waiting list for five years. She has two children and has just given birth to twins. The second child is the one she has had contact with SEAC about. He is quite jealous of the twins. She has problems with feeding him. Also her husband is away during the week, working. She is worried about how she will cope during the forthcoming summer holidays.
>
>   (Field notes recording a translated
>   response from a Bangladeshi mother)

In these circumstances parents wanted to leave the responsibility of dealing with yet another problem to the SEAC professionals. Such 'detachedness' does not mean that these parents were apathetic in their approach to their child's education. Rather this strategy can be seen as a realistic reading of the resources which they have available, and their apparent passivity is therefore a deliberate strategy, rather than a result of parental 'inadequacy' (see also Armstrong 1995 for a similar analysis).

The band-aid approach

These parents sometimes initiated their contact with the SEAC, though they were also referred by other agencies. They used the SEAC and other agencies to resolve particular problems – assessment of need, transfers, medicals, etc. As soon as the particular problem was resolved, these parents broke their association with the agency dealing with it. As far as the SEAC workers were concerned, these parents were similar to those using the detached approach, in that they tended to be rather passive in relation to the professionals. However, what marked them out was the fact that they would return again as new problems arose, using the SEAC to 'fix' things for them.

> Some of the contact is so minimal . . . they [parents] would just keep coming back for these very short actions that they want, you know . . . and that's their right, you can't insist that someone has more involvement . . . we must respect, if parents want to come with a specific problem, and that's it until the next specific thing.
>
>   (Amina)

He'll go for a certain problem, and then just come back home.
(Bangladeshi father speaking through an interpreter)

This again can be seen as a rational strategy. Parents perceived that there was a problem and felt ill-equipped to deal with it. They therefore sought out sources of help and support, and either approached the Centre directly or were referred by other agencies. If they found the advice workers to be helpful and effective, they returned again when another problem arose.

The toolbox approach

These parents tended to choose from a range of possible options open to them. Not all options were necessarily available at all times, and parents might not have had all the information required to make fully informed choices. They were constrained by who or what they knew, but attempted to use the resources they had available to them to their best advantage.

One SEAC worker described this approach in the following way:

I would probably do it, you know, if I've got a query about something, I would think, right now, where can I go about this? Um, maybe I'll give ACE [the Advisory Centre for Education] a ring. You're not doing it because you want someone to take over, but simply because it's a short cut. You feel that you can get the information quickly, you hope that if there is a centre that is established, it can tell you exactly who to contact.

(Sue)

These parents often had resources of social (e.g. personal contacts) and cultural (e.g. confidence, knowledge) capital available to them. This capital was in the same 'currency' as that of education professionals (largely from the same class background), whereas the knowledge and skills of other parents from different class backgrounds may have been of less use in such interactions (Gewirtz *et al.* 1995). These parents were more likely to work in an easily identifiable 'partnership' with SEAC workers, requiring from them initial guidance, moral support, and reassurance that they were doing the 'right' thing. One mother who adopted this approach described her contact with SEAC in the following way:

They listened to me and that was important because no-one was listening to me, and all I kept saying was, 'Look, keep putting up a brick wall and I'll go to your boss, because you've all got bosses at the end of the day, and I will climb the system if I have to . . .' [The SEAC workers] worked hard, they listened, and they helped . . . They then took over for me, and they dealt with all the authorities and sorted it all out, got to the bottom of what was going on. They believed me.

(White mother)

However, this mother's version of the workers 'taking over' is different, both qualitatively and quantitatively, from the detached or band-aid versions. She became very knowledgeable about many of the medical, legal and educational issues pertaining to her child's disability. She took with her to her son's annual review a copy of the Code of Practice and a SEAC worker. What she mostly required (and received) from SEAC was moral support.

> I knew there was a few people [who would be at the annual review], they thought in certain ways, they were going to do things, and I knew it wasn't going to take place that way. I thought for once I don't, because of my previous experience with them, I don't have to do this on my own any more . . . Sometimes when you've got children, especially with special needs, you do feel extremely lonely out there. You know, there's not much back-up for us.
>
> (White mother)

It was primarily parents from this group who were involved in the parent groups run at the Centre.

Social class and ethnicity

I suggest that the strategies adopted by parents are influenced by social class, and other connected factors such as familiarity with and knowledge of the education system, fluency in English, occupation and the material circumstances in which people live. However, this does not mean that parents adopting the toolbox approach are all middle class. That would be too simplistic. Several parent respondents who would be described as working class by the criteria of their housing, levels of education and employment nonetheless successfully adopted a toolbox approach. At the point at which a concern regarding a child is first identified, most parents, unless they happen to have a background in one of the relevant professions, start from a position of bewilderment, feeling they lack the knowledge and understanding to act on behalf of their children. Most parents, that is, start from a detached or band-aid approach. Certainly, parents with the social, cultural and financial resources commonly associated with the professional middle classes may be able to make the leap to assertiveness and agency more quickly than those without similar resources. However, other parents in our sample had undergone similar transitions. Quoted here are the words of parents from middle and working class backgrounds. One middle class mother described her first brush with the statement procedure as follows:

> I didn't know what questions to ask [the advice worker]. I didn't know anything about the statementing process, it was totally new to me. I didn't have a clue. I just wanted [the worker] to check [my contribution] . . . Even when [the Educational Psychologist] did explain, I still felt totally clueless, and I didn't know what stage he was on at any time.
>
> (White mother)

By the time the fieldwork was conducted, this mother was giving advice to other parents, running a support group, and was confident in her ability to find sources of help and support should she, or other parents, need them. Another mother who can also be classified as adopting a toolbxox approach was working class. She described herself as 'not educated' and having 'learnt the hard way'. A third mother said: 'You've got to learn, you've just got to learn, you know and that's what I've done. I've also made the big decision of getting myself back to school to learning' (white mother). These parents have all made the transition from passivity and dependence to activity and agency.

The authors of an evaluation of the SEAC conducted during our fieldwork commented on an earlier version of the typology described here, and stated that they felt there was an ethnic dimension determining differential responses:

> [Our] data suggests that Bengali and monolingual parents do tend to approach the SEAC in different ways. Monolingual parents may be more likely to come to the Centre to equip themselves with information and support they needed to help their child (the toolbox approach). Bengali parents are more likely to come expecting to hand much of this respons- ibility over to SEAC workers to deal with on their behalf (detached approach).
>
> (Evaluation report)

In our final report to the Centre, Simon Warren and I argued against drawing this conclusion from our typology, suggesting that the complexities influ- encing differential responses cannot be explained by a distinction drawn on ethnic grounds alone. Moreover, a binary division based on race may further perpetuate stereotypes and assumptions about the passivity of people of Asian origin. If professionals assume tendencies to particular types of behaviour, this can also act as a self-fulfilling prophecy, a scenario which can be described at best as unhelpful.

Most of the Bangladeshi parent respondents in the sample *did appear* to Simon and me to find the various procedures involved in special educational needs provision confusing and frustrating. However, there are many other considerations to be taken into account here before conclusions can be drawn. Factors ranging from the nature of the child's difficulty (problems with reading and writing which several of the Bangladeshi respondents cited may seem particularly amorphous and difficult to pin down) and the circumstances in which parents are living (i.e. to what extent survival issues dominate their lives) to their familiarity with the education system may all be relev- ant. Another issue is the difficulty white, professional researchers have, even when accompanied by a Sylheti-speaking interpreter, of accessing the thoughts and feelings of respondents of a different ethnic, cultural and, in many cases, class background (see Vincent and Warren forthcoming for details). It is therefore highly problematic to categorize parent respondents and their likely responses solely on the basis of ethnicity. The combination of occupation, material circumstances, cultural capital and familiarity with the education system are more important indicators than ethnicity alone.

Conclusion

My argument here is that, in order to avoid an inadequate account of the contradictions (and changes) inherent in the workings of professional bureaucracies, an understanding of the role of the professional needs to be firmly located within 'the historical specificity of real-world relations between professionals and clients' (Armstrong 1995: 125). Thus the concept of professional as a unitary category has to be disrupted or problematized. Analysis that rests on binary divides (i.e. whether professionals play an essentially emancipatory or oppressive role) is unhelpful as it overlooks the range of elements that contribute to the formation of a professional identity in different individuals working in different settings (see also Vincent and Warren 1997).

The advice centre workers therefore can be understood as 'active accommodators', working within and occasionally around the boundaries of their role. These boundaries had two sources: the traditional social democratic culture of professionalism which views the workers and their colleagues as having expertise, while positioning clients as the recipients of that expertise, and the performative regime now current in many public sector bureaucracies which encourages the workers to focus on quantifiable targets.

The gaps and spaces between and beyond these constraints were undoubtedly limited, fragile and partial. The opportunities – Jalal's challenge to deficit views of Sylheti-speaking parents, Sue's determination to introduce a parent perspective into professional discussions, the lengths the workers often went to ensure that parents understood the information given to them, to support them in meetings with professionals (in the case of some parents whose English was limited, quite literally to give them a voice in decisions on their children's care and education), and to listen to their perspectives – may indeed sound commonplace, limited and limiting. However, that the workers were engaged in so much basic work (delivering and explaining proposals to statutorily assess children, accompanying parents to medicals, mediating between parents and teachers, etc.) shows the depths of the cracks they were trying to smooth over, the degree to which many parents were alienated, bemused and angered by special education processes and procedures.[14] But as the quote from Michelle Fine at the beginning of this chapter suggests, smoothing over the cracks is a qualitatively different task, a different approach, underpinned by different goals and objectives to that of pursuing systemic change. Jane, the Centre Manager, had a wider brief than advice giving alone, one which she pursued in the cracks and fissures of running an advice centre: to encourage parent mobilization, so that parents could have an independent voice within local authority decision making, a voice that operated unmediated by professionals. Slowly fragile collectives, albeit organized around very specific interest groups, had started to emerge. The groups may seem an unconvincing exemplar of radical development, given that, as I stated earlier, a performative state needs to be involved in consultative processes for its own ends, and therefore would encourage some degree of involvement in service provision from user groups. However, the groups offered an arena for collective debate between parents (mostly mothers), 'a protected enclave' (see Chapter 1) through which and from which they could extend their own knowledge and begin to dissect and challenge professional understandings of appropriate parental roles and of deficit models of children with special needs. The data show that the personal support and information sharing the groups provide is important to their members. There are also traces and hints of the beginnings of collective questioning of existing procedures and assessments:

> If I didn't go to the advice centre I would have been lost . . . I wasn't even 100 per cent sure he was dyslexic. It [an ad in the local paper] said, Is your child dyslexic? Have they got problems with reading and writing, coordination? And it was going there and reading up, and they give you all the books and information. They talk about their children you know and they could be talking about yours . . . it's not very organized at the moment, . . . it's like a mother's meeting sort of thing, people getting it off their chest.
>
> (White mother)

> A lot of times, you know, if you can go and talk to people you go home feeling a bit better. We can't take problems away, we can't solve problems you know . . . but when you're there together you do find that although the child, all the children are individuals, and they've all got different needs, you always come up against the same barriers one way or another.
>
> (White mother)

> This is what comes out of the meetings as well: some of the parents are so disillusioned with the teachers; not all of them, don't get me wrong, there's some very good teachers . . . but they're [parents] not sure whether it's dyslexia or whether it's just the poor standard of teaching.
>
> (White mother)

These embryonic enclaves, with the exception of the group for families with hearing-impaired children, involved only a few, mainly white, parents. The group for families with hearing-impaired children, chaired by Jalal, had mainly Bangladeshi members. One of the workers commented on the difficulty of encouraging 'mixed groups'. There were, within Tate, some alternative and vocal sources of support within Bangladeshi communities for Bangladeshi families, and a well-organized Bangladeshi political lobby within the authority. However, as most of the active parents at SEAC were white, this may have contributed to an assumption among workers that Bangladeshi parents were more likely to be passive in their approach to their situation and dependent on the workers. As a result, one of the most marginalized groupings received the most professional tutelage.

The fragility of the parents' groups indicates the problems inherent in realizing the potential such collectivities theoretically have. The difficulties such groups face in forming a coherent identity and relatively stable membership cannot be underestimated, particularly in Tate where survival issues and racism, and the subsequent social and economic marginalization, mark the lives of many families. However, these groups do offer an alternative model, one which identifies not the needs and vulnerabilities of individual children and families, but rather those of the special education system itself, as the focus for critique and reform.

Notes

1 As it received national and local state funding, strictly speaking SEAC was not a civil society institution. As discussed in Chapter 1, civil society institutions are understood to be non-governmental institutions although, as also noted, there is a considerable degree of interpenetration between state and civil society institutions. Its location as part of the local state is identified in this chapter as a major influence upon the work of the centre, and the implications of this are discussed. As is also made clear, SEAC hosts a number of parent groups which can be understood as forming associational networks within civil society, micro-political public spheres in Keane's (1998) sense (see Chapter 1).
2 The fairly equal male–female balance in those parents who had interaction with PAC is explained for the most part by the involvement of Bangladeshi fathers, who in some cases were more at ease in English than mothers were. However the sample group also included a white lone father.
3 GEST funding is now replaced with the Standards Fund.
4 For example, Larson quotes Tawney as saying 'professionals may grow rich; but the meaning of their profession, both for themselves and for the public, is not that they make money, but that they make health and safety, or knowledge, or good government' (Larson 1977: 58).
5 As a result of an Audit Commission report criticizing the length of time Tate LEA took to produce statements, the workers are no longer allowed to hand-deliver assessment documents and they are all posted direct from the LEA offices, thereby allowing the LEA to comply with the Audit Commission's requirements to record assessment times with accuracy. This means that the SEAC workers are not always able to discuss possible options with parents before the parents formally respond.
6 The Centre Manager however had become 'bilingual' (see Chapter 6), and employed a managerialist language, talking of 'customer care', 'an accountable service' as well as 'empowering' parents to bring about 'structural change' within the system. Commenting on a draft of this chapter, she also suggested that by 1999, the growing case load dealing with exclusions and lack of provision by schools at the early stages of the Code of Practice has meant the workers placing an increased emphasis on consumer rights.
7 In the six month period from April to October 1997, the SEAC received 1017 phone calls and 529 referrals.
8 Performativity also requires the schools and the LEA to legitimate themselves through increasing efficiencies and cutting costs. The Centre is actually situated in a building that also houses other special needs services, such as speech therapy, hearing impaired services, and support teachers. While this one-stop centre is useful in aiding communication between the different services, it is the result of scaling down special education services in order to cut costs. The professional role of rationing scarce resources therefore persists, whether under a social democratic or a performative state. Similarly, the Centre officially contributed to the fulfilment of the LEA's targets (which included an Ofsted recommendation to reduce expenditure on 'high-cost' services), although, unlike other LEA services, SEAC is a service to parents rather than schools.
9 A statement of special educational needs is a written document detailing the child's needs and the provision required to meet them.
10 By 1999, the Centre Manager felt that the situation had changed and workers were much more involved in helping parents to argue the case for more support.
11 A performative state finds consultation with users helpful of course.

12 Generally, parents did not distinguish between professionals from different services (i.e. health, social services or education).

13 I am grateful to Simon Warren for suggesting these names.

14 In one instance a family was referred to SEAC because the parents were concerned over their son's progress. The advice worker discovered that the child had been issued with a statement three years previously. The school and the LEA had not adequately explained their actions to parents.

Education for motherhood?
With Simon Warren

Introduction

The focus of this chapter is the operation of a parent education group, and the experiences and understandings of both the course leader and the students. It seeks to illustrate the way in which hegemonic discourses concerning mothering (in this case, what has been called 'sensitive mothering') are disseminated, and gives the example of the ways in which one group of mothers responded.

Parent education and parenting classes are a growing phenomenon. They seek to offer parents support as they address aspects of their relationships with and their management of their children. Most courses are purely voluntary of course, but from April 2000, compulsory parenting orders for the parents of young offenders require parents, usually mothers, to attend parenting skills courses. Questions have been raised over the efficacy and ethicality of such courses and their enforcement. They can be understood as attempts to 'train' parents to interact with their children in particular ways, while ignoring the context for that interaction and the material basis underpinning many families' circumstances (for a mostly positive review of one pilot course, see Freely 1999). One of the questions raised by this chapter is whether similar criticisms can be levelled at voluntary parenting courses.

The course considered here was quite particular in its orientation. Unlike some parenting education classes, its focus was the development of practical skills. It offered parents (the students were all female)[1] an accredited practical skills course, which involved them in making educational materials for use with young children. In order to receive the accreditation, students had to fulfil a number of critieria such as 'personal effectiveness – assess own performance', 'problem solving – identify and use appropriate techniques'. They did this by completing the activities (e.g. making story books, maths games, doing science experiments, etc.) and also compiling a folder of writing which contained their descriptions and evaluations of undertaking the activities as well as longer pieces of work in which the students often chose to reflect on their own childhood. In tutor-led discussions and informal conversation, the students' feelings about motherhood, its difficulties and rewards, often surfaced (for example, the group did an exercise where they ordered in their own degree of priority what could be called 'family rules', such as 'apologize when you're in the wrong').

This chapter considers a number of areas. The first is the nature and scope of the course as it appeared to the researchers. The second is the discourse of 'sensitive mothering' (Walkerdine and Lucey 1989) and a consideration of the extent to which the course promotes adherence to such an approach. This raises issues about the relationship between the professional tutor and the student clients, similar to those discussed in the previous chapter. The third theme revolves around understanding and incorporating the accounts of the women students involved in the course. Their experiences appear to contradict the way in which the analysis has been shaped up to this point. As a result the concluding section of the chapter seeks to understand and partially resolve this conflict. We also discuss ways in which the focus of the course could be, potentially, redirected towards increasing the students' sense of agency within the public sphere, particularly in relation to state-sponsored institutions (in this case, schools).

In and out of the field: researching Elliott's parent education group

The parent education group met in 'Elliott', an inner-city primary school within 'Tate' LEA. The group as a whole comprised two subgroupings of women, with a total of approximately 18–20 members. During the study, most members of the two groups were or had been involved in taking the accredited practical skills course. The first group had completed the course the previous year, but several of its members still met weekly at the school. On the same morning, the second group of approximately 12 women had a two- or three-hour session where they undertook various activities designed to fulfil course requirements. It is this second group with which one of us (CV) spent most time during the research. The course was managed and organized by Christine, an adult education tutor with considerable experience of conducting parent education work. She was helped by Peggy, one of her former students. Their work in Elliott was funded by a local charitable trust, while Christine and Peggy were employed by a further education institute.

The women who attended the course were working class women from the surrounding area. The second group included both white women and those of Bangladeshi origin. The original group was mostly white apart from two African/Caribbean women and one Bangladeshi woman.[2] They mostly ranged in age from mid-20s to mid-30s. Christine was older, and therefore able to be, as she suggested, 'a mother figure'. Data were collected primarily through semi-structured interviews with Christine and Peggy, and 11 of the women students, 10 from the group currently undertaking the course, and one from the first group. Carol also participated in six course sessions, and occasionally stayed to the communal lunch, which a group of the women cooked for themselves and their children. Relationships between the researchers and the students are considered in a separate article (Vincent and Warren forthcoming). Here, we briefly recount the events surrounding dissemination of the research, and consider what this incident revealed about the power relationships shaping researcher–respondent relations.

A crisis of representation

Most qualitative social science researchers today are familiar with the arguments around the crisis of representation and accept that their work is an interpretation of the social setting in which they are working; certainly an interpretation grounded in data, carefully argued and illustrated and giving readers enough information about the parameters and conduct of the study for them to be able to make their own judgements upon the acceptability of the researcher's interpretation. So, as researchers, we accept intellectually that the process we are involved in is not a simple one of description and presentation, but rather one of recreating and re-presenting the lives of respondents as a result of our critical engagement with the data. However, despite this, researchers (including ourselves) routinely write in a fashion which privileges their accounts, sends out implicit messages of authority, correctness and 'truth' (Coffey 1999). 'Conventional ethnographic discourse can render the "observed" as mute, deprived of a culturally legitimised means of expression; visible and audible only through the eyes, voices and consequent text of a dominant group (the observers)' (Coffey 1999: 144). This was brought home to us when we sent a first draft of the analysis of the group's work to the tutor, Christine. This draft, like this later version, juxtaposed an initial reading of the parent education course with the more positive interpretation of the students, and asked questions about the meaning of this apparent contradiction. As a research team, we had arrived at this position because we felt that this tentativeness, this attempt to 'deal in paradoxes and resist theoretical closure' (Ball 1997: 268) was a strength. However, we had overlooked the power which accrued to us, as authors, through the process of fashioning an account. This was strongly brought home to us by Christine's reaction. The tentativeness, the openness to other readings, the nuances of academic writing was, to her, a chimera. Instead she read our account as sweeping and insensitive, the theorizing as alienating and abstract. Her anger and feelings of betrayal were evident. We spent a long time talking to Christine, to each other, and to other colleagues to try and understand how this situation had arisen. We found a tale of similar dissonance between researcher and respondent in the writing of Colleen Larson. Talking about life history research, she highlights the problems inherent in understanding the stories people tell through distanced lens . . . The lives of both researchers and research subjects are defined within systems of gender, race and class and are lived out in particular temporal, social and cultural moments. The social and personal experiences that people have had make some narratives possible for some and impossible for others.

(Larson 1997: 459)

She recommends engaging in 'deliberative dialogue' that would allow the negotiation of meanings between the researcher and the respondent. Indeed we accept that we should have spent more time discussing the developing analysis and its theoretical underpinnings with the group *as a whole* (for the students' reactions and responses are still missing). This form of dissemination and negotiation is an ethical practice much praised but – despite some notable exceptions especially among feminist researchers (e.g. Lather 1996) – more infrequently practised by social science researchers. Christine made some important comments which have contributed to this chapter. Carrie Paechter (1996), writing about apparently 'confessional' research, argues that the author is still in control, the arbiter of what is revealed and what is not. Similarly, despite this attempt at collaboration, we acknowledge that the power of this account, the way in which the written word generates implications of authority and 'correctness', still rests with ourselves as authors.

The parent education course

In this section of the chapter, we outline our perceptions of the course gained through participant observation. However, as explained above, our understanding should not be read as discounting alternative interpretations.

Having been primary school teachers, we were immediately struck by the extent to which the content and presentation of the course resembled a primary school classroom. There were three main manifestations of this. First, activities were planned and announced by Christine and their execution generally revolved around her.

I think like, she [Christine] does have a plan [of work], but she just takes us step by step. I don't think she wants to put too much onto us in one go, sort of thing.

(Deborah)

Second, 'classroom' talk tended to be directed by Christine. Occasionally the women students took it in turns to teach an activity to others, but it was Christine who regulated this event (e.g. its timing, the direction the discussion took, etc.) and remained clearly in control. She also revealed a certain amount of displeasure if the women were late arriving, talked when someone else or she herself was talking, or had not done activities they had promised to prepare at home. Third, in line with child-centred practices, discussions and activities might flow from one particular, spur-of-the-moment event. For example, on one occasion, Mary (a student) brought in an exquisitely embroidered/painted picture of a dragon which she had done with her daughter as part of the school topic. A discussion then took place about dragons and other mythical creatures including those that feature in Bangladeshi culture.

The following example, extracted from field notes and describing a science experiment morning, gives a flavour of the course content and ethos:

> After tea, Christine does the 'magic water experiment' which is again discussed enthusiastically – Shajna puts up her hand at one point [to answer a question, although this was clearly not expected practice]. Deborah then demonstrates the bizarre properties of cornflour mixed with water . . . We all think of words to describe the consistency of the cornflour: 'slimy', 'smooth', 'silky', etc. – 'lots of S words' as Christine says. She writes up the magic water experiment on a large piece of paper stuck to the board in order to demonstrate the form they should use for writing up their own experiment. She uses this to introduce some grammar and spelling rules ('You lot don't like using capital letters', the difference between 'piece' and 'peace' and 'brim' and 'rim'). It's not passive copying down, as people suggest what to write, but they are all very concerned (as am I) with writing down whatever version Christine writes down. We discuss what illustrations to put in the border [surrounding the writing].
>
> (CV's field notes 15/10/96)

In teacher training and related courses (e.g. nursery nurse qualifications), it has long been an article of faith that the trainee teachers should experience the learning process surrounding each activity. An enhanced empathy with the learner is seen as a useful way of helping them improve their teaching. However, we would argue that in the parent education group the women were not just temporary learners, being shown the techniques of various activities so that they could pass them on to children; they were often, as they were aware, the intended recipients of the learning. Indeed, Christine's pedagogic style can be understood as a way of guiding, directing and supporting students who have not, on the whole, had positive past experiences of education. The extract quoted above may be seen as a sensitive way of introducing basic literacy points in a supportive environment (no-one is put on the spot for instance). Similarly, the activities were not entirely directed by Christine. The students took it in turn to teach particular activities to each other. This involved them in what was, for many, a nerve-wracking task, as they planned and executed their teaching, and evaluated it alongside comments from their peers and the tutor. So how, then, can we understand the course's pedagogy?

A case could be made for some resemblance between the pedagogy of the parent education group and Bernstein's (1973) concept of 'invisible pedagogy'. The control of the teacher is implicit, rather than explicit, and the teacher arranges the broad context for learning from which the students select options, having autonomy over the structure and time-scale of the activities (Atkinson 1985: 157). However, the demands of the accredited course undertaken by the parent education group meant that there was an explicit emphasis on the transmission of particular skills (those involved in writing evaluations, for instance), and explicit, non-negotiable criteria for assessment (both features usually associated with 'visible' pedagogy). However, Bernstein makes another connection which is relevant to the preceding account of the course. He suggests that the significance of 'invisible pedagogy' lies at the ideological level, rather than that of practice. That is, invisible pedagogy realizes some of the cultural assumptions embedded in the ideology of the 'new middle classes'. It is not possible to do justice to the sophistication and complexity of the theory here, but the most important point for our purpose is that he identifies the importance, to the new middle classes, of women as agents of cultural reproduction. Atkinson summarizes this neatly:

> As women become crucial agents in cultural reproduction, mothering thus becomes 'professionalised' in the new middle class home. Commenting on the role of women in pedagogic innovations leading to 'invisible pedagogy', Bernstein writes 'women transformed maternal caring and preparing into a *scientific* activity' (1973, original emphasis).
>
> (Atkinson 1985: 162)

Can the parent education course be understood in this way? Is it the case, for instance, that during the parent education course, the working class women students are introduced to, and try out, a particular aspect of child-centred culture, 'invisible' pedagogy, for use with their children at home (see also Beck and Beck-Gernsheim 1995)? A pedagogy, moreover, which resembles that of the school as well as the new middle class home? In the next section, we look more closely at the discourses informing mothers' pedagogic practices.

Sensitive mothering

Parental responsibility for improving their children's early learning and their psychological well-being is emphasized by the media (especially women's magazines), and through the work of health and education professionals (Beck and Beck-Gernsheim 1995). As noted in Chapter 2, such responsibilities are highly gendered, the target audience being specifically female. The absence of fathers in these scenarios is striking. Generally, however, their absence is surrounded by silence which suggests that women are the 'natural' recipients of this advice.[3] Such information teaches women what is expected of them as educators (Brown 1993: 198; David et al. 1993: 53).

One of the most thorough and recent attempts in the UK to explore the normalization of particular forms of child rearing is contained in Walkerdine and Lucey's (1989) concept of 'sensitive' mothering. They argue that while mothers have long been responsible for the development of their children's moral, emotional and social development, over the last 20 years or so it has become increasingly accepted that mothers are also responsible for their children's early educational development. Walkerdine and Lucey studied this phenomenon in relation to class, gender and the way in which the two intersect. They looked at transcripts, originally collected by Barbara Tizard and Martin Hughes (whose analysis is reported in *Young Children Learning*, 1984). The transcripts detail the interaction between a group of working class and middle class mothers and their preschool daughters. They describe tellingly the way in which 'sensitive mothering' – a combination of educational and psychological discourses – requires mothers to behave in particular ways in relation to their children. Household tasks, for instance, are presented as opportunities for endless pedagogical stimulation. Mothers are required to reason and debate with their children rather than overtly exercise their powers of control over them. Anger and frustration are seen as negative emotions which should be denied and ignored. Walkerdine and Lucey argue that the mothers in their sample who strived to follow this ideal – primarily middle class women – experienced considerable emotional and practical burdens, the former from the stress of trying not to misunderstand or misinterpret the child's behaviour (something for which mothers are routinely blamed, see for example, Everingham 1994), and the latter from the constraints imposed on their time and energy by having constantly to interact sensitively with a young child. Similarly Griffith and Smith argue that

> The discourse of mothering supports a standard family organisation: the complete nuclear family. No concessions are made to the variations in the practical and material contexts of mothering work . . . Exposure to guilt, invidious comparisons and anxiety: all are constant hazards for mothers participating in the discourse.
>
> (Griffith and Smith 1991: 91)

Carole Pateman (1992) suggests that this regulation of mothering, this standardization and the pathologizing of those mothers who do not act in a 'sensitive' manner, reflects the state's interest in the quality of the population, and that encouraging women to be 'good' mothers can be understood as an attempt to ensure that children receive the 'correct' moral, social and educational training, especially in the preschool years. Walkerdine and Lucy further argue that such training is integral to the maintenance of liberal democracy, and the production of a child who will prove to be 'a reasonable citizen [who] imagines herself to be empowered, autonomous and free' (1989: 101).

Of course adult education as a whole, and the parent education course specifically, does not exist in a vacuum, and the contextual importance of the political climate needs to be considered for its contribution to the broader social and political framework within which messages about, in this case, 'appropriate' parenting can be disseminated. The nuances and emphases given to this message may alter over time in response to the changing social, economic and political context. For example, Thatcherite neo-conservatism encouraged a narrowing of the disciplinary 'gaze' onto individuals and individual families. In broad terms, the manifestation of this ideology in policy took the form of restrictions upon welfare state spending, and the whole-scale restructuring of public sector services, to enhance the role of individual consumers. In the late 1990s, the focus for action changed. Policies and initiatives operated on a smaller canvas, more focused in their regulation (although in aggregate they form powerful policy ensembles). And many of these initiatives are being proposed by the New Labour government. We are thinking here of the political momentum behind parenting classes, the parenting orders mentioned in the introduction, and more punitive, overtly controlling home–school agreements (see Chapter 2). Ministerial and Prime Ministerial pronouncements since 1997 have concerned children's bedtimes, curfews for young people, homework and the prevention of teenage pregnancies. In 1999, the Prime Minister, Tony Blair, identified what he saw as the need for a new moral settlement with the well-regulated family at its heart:

> We need to find a new national moral purpose for this new generation. People want to live in a society that is without prejudice but is with rules, with a sense of order. Government can play its part, but parents have to play their part. There's got to be, if you like, a partnership between Government and the country to lay the foundations of that moral purpose.
>
> (Rawnsley 1999: 8–9)

Together, all these micro-policies, proposals and pronouncements structure a climate in which mothers – for the focus on the mothering role is quite explicit – are expected to prepare their children for school, then support the school once their child is a pupil there, while being primarily responsible for behavioral and moral standards in their offspring.

'Sensitive mothering' is, therefore, an obvious example of the type of discourse the research project was designed to analyse. It is implicitly sanctioned by governments, perpetuated by health, welfare and educational professionals, and directed towards women, particularly working class and minority ethnic women (see, e.g., Nazroo 1997).[4] As such we were particularly concerned to see whether sensitive mothering was Christine's view of 'appropriate' mothering, and how strongly she disseminated her views to her students. The second part of the equation was the way in which the women reacted: did they accept, challenge or ignore her messages?

Access to what?

Christine saw the course as having two main sets of objectives. One was that it was an access course, both in the technical sense of gaining a certificate which the women could use to further their education or employment prospects, and in the sense that the course had a role building, or rebuilding, the students' confidence. The second objective was more subtle and intangible. Talking about her earlier experiences of parent education, Christine said:

> We started off with a Mother and Toddler group and that's almost always how we begin. Then people get fed up with just sitting there and gossiping, drinking coffee, smoking their heads off and yelling at their children. So you begin to, then, infiltrate if you like, all other sorts of ideas . . . You have to begin to sort of open it up to get people thinking about other things that they would like for them[selves]. So it's very much treats for parents as a kind of beginning, if you like . . .

Indeed this is how the group at Elliott started off, as Chrissy, a student, explained:

> I don't know how it happened but Christine got involved by coming into our parents [and toddlers] group and she said about starting to make things, so we started like making things for Easter . . . then she said would we like to go to a parents' conference . . . To us really it was just a laugh, you know, but when we went there it was just amazing what we seen . . . There were people from Liverpool, there was about 16 of them, and they'd all done this course, what Christine's doing . . . and they did their presentation and got their certificates, and all that. Really, really good. So when we come back we couldn't stop talking about it . . . And so she [Christine] said, 'Would any of yous like to do something like this?' and we went, 'Yeah, we do, it would be really interesting', and that's how it started.
>
> (Chrissy)

Talking specifically about the group at Elliott, Christine continued,

> I think people feel that they, they love doing those story props. It may be quite a struggle, but then they have this lovely thing to take home and really do with their children. Now that *improves* their relationship with children, probably more than them sitting down, and listening to me spouting on about, you know, you ought always to be positive to your child. Or you shouldn't scream and yell at your child, and I think these are subtle vehicles, if you like for *improving* the way that families behave with each other.
>
> (Christine, our emphasis)

'The problem of . . . middle class niceness' (Christine)

Although parenting (or more accurately, mothering) advice is not exclusively directed at working class parents, it is these families that are and have been the target for the most intensive scrutiny (see Finch 1984a; David 1985, 1993; also Chapter 2). Christine was very wary of giving the impression that there was a 'correct' way to bring up children. She was also aware that social class and racial differences between herself and the students meant that the women were living within social, cultural and economic contexts which contrasted to her own background. She had two main responses to this issue. One was to recognize the difficulties and deprivations experienced by some of the women in the group, and the differences between her lifestyle and theirs:

> I just have huge admiration for the parents, I really have huge admiration for them, because I can't imagine how I would cope in the circumstances that they have to live in, and I know I would be a heap on the floor if I had to live in such crowded conditions, if I had come from Bangladesh and didn't understand the flipping language, or what on earth was going on and it was freezing cold. Oh I just don't know how they survive, I

think they're just wonderful, and I know that I can get myself on that tube and go back to my middle class home, with my middle class values, etc. and I think there but for the grace of God you know, go I.

Peggy, the assistant tutor, also felt sympathy and understanding for the predicament of many of the students. Her understanding was particular, however, based on her past experiences of living in similar circumstances to many of the white women students. Thus she felt that she and the white (but not the Bangladeshi) women shared a common 'structure of feeling', their 'mental map of feelings, assumptions and experiences', to which Christine, the course tutor, had only limited access (see Chapter 2):

> Sometimes I think Chris understands everybody. I think she's very good at what she does, but I think she understands it because she's learnt it. I actually understand it because I've been there . . . I mean I'm not saying Christine's had it all a bed of roses, she hasn't, but she's had a slightly more middle class background to what I've had, and a lot of these parents have had . . . I feel I've been where they've been, and I'm not saying I understand them more, I'm really not saying that, but I think I've been where they are and I try to take that on board.

Christine was aware of this social distance between herself and the women,[5] and in response favoured an approach whereby both she and Peggy worked with a group of women:

> I think that is good because I think that then puts the middle class and the working class person on the same level, working with the group, so I think Peggy and I learn a lot from each other. I learn a lot from working with her, and she learns from working with me, and I think that's a really good mixture . . . That in a way can get round a lot of the problems if you like of trying to overlay the whole course with middle class niceness.

This meant that while both Christine and Peggy had very positive relationships with the students, they were qualitatively different. Their social class positions also determined their differential responsibilities vis-à-vis the course. The performative demands of piloting the students through to successful completion of the course meant that Christine often felt she needed to be 'bossy' with them, while Peggy could and did take a more relaxed approach.

Christine's other main approach to the issue of class in the parent education course was to appeal to the common bond of mothering:

> It is the hardest job in the world, yet we're all thrown in the deep end with practically no experience, or help, or support, or anything . . . and I think we all need help and support, but it's not from an expert, it's more from group experience, and I see myself, although I can be very bossy because I'm trying to get them through the course, I do see myself more as a facilitator, than as somebody who thinks I've got it all right, 'cos having three children of my own, I know I didn't get it all right.
>
> (Christine)

As a result, the 'messages' which Christine disseminated retained a 'soft' focus, out of kilter, for example, with the 'harder' tones politicians were using during this period to discuss the enforcement of particular types of parenting (see above, and also Vincent and Tomlinson 1997). Indeed, she, on several occasions, went to meetings organized by policy makers to speak against the introduction of more authoritarian policies. She was also unhappy with the idea of including overt 'parenting skills' in the course:

> I think there is a tendency . . . there can be, to be very patronising and to feel that a middle class way of bringing children up is the only way. We had a very good discussion this morning about a programme on television . . . and about the grandmother character in that. I mean she's a hard swearing, hard drinking, old battle axe . . . from a middle class point of view, she's always got her flask . . . she swears like a trooper, she's got a fag hanging out of her mouth . . . yet she's there for every single one of them [the children], and it's wonderful. I think there's a huge danger of thinking that parenting is only done properly if it's done in a middle class way.

The students all confirmed that Christine's precepts were generally phrased.

> She is always saying about spending time with them, making time for them and making things with them.
>
> (Sarah)

> *Sue*: Not strong [ideas about child-rearing]. She wouldn't force it on you, you know what I mean, she's got her opinions and we've got our opinions
> *CV*: What sort of things does she suggest?
> *Sue*: Spend more time with them.

> She'll probably give advice to parents that ask her for advice, but not generally speak out on how things should be done . . . What she hasn't given to parents is, 'Oh you should do this or do that or whatever' . . . Nothing, like, you know, nothing like to a personal level . . . I think she does it professionally or is professional enough to leave it at that and not extend it.
>
> (Ruckshana)

> It's really good to get involved, and it's really good fun to do things and they grow up . . . [She says] here's some ways that could, not necessarily improve your relationship, but it's sort of an added sort of, making parenting a bit more fun.
>
> (Mary)

Christine's own focus, therefore, is upon improving parent–child relationships and encouraging the women to create 'family time' (Brown 1993):

> I suppose what I hoped they would go away with is that children need encouragement and praise, that would be my number one thing. The whole business of how you have to tell a child that maybe some days,

you don't like it, but you love it, yes? But that is the message I think is very important, and that children who get praised and children who are encouraged, whose parents listen to them are going to be happier, more fulfilled human beings.

(Christine)

As a principle, spending time with your children and carrying out 'educational' activities with them could be said to transcend social class. 'Good' parenting can be, and often is, presented as a class-neutral as well as gender-neutral philosophy. Yet just as the burden falls on women rather than men, the weight of good parenting advice, as I noted earlier, is heaviest upon working class rather than middle class women. Andrew Brown's critique of the IMPACT project (a home maths project) presents a useful parallel here. In the following quotation, Brown presents a textual analysis of the IMPACT booklet for parents:

> The text [makes] a number of statements about what good parents do or should do. They are good listeners, discuss activities with their children, work with their children at home, and enjoy doing so. They are members of a distinguishable family unit that has identifiable family time together, that share activities, that has fun together. They are involved in their children's schooling and work with teachers . . . Even such a simple communication contributes to the setting up of a normalising discourse.
>
> (Brown 1993: 207)

Thus the focus of this 'soft' discourse is on the private, interior sphere: interaction between family members, and, implicitly, how such interaction can be improved. There is little space in the course for considering the effect the 'outside' world can have in constraining, directing, or moulding family relationships. In her reading of an earlier draft, Christine took issue with us on this point. She argued that, although the accredited course (about which she had reservations) did not formally deal with these issues, they were taken up by the women in more informal contexts when they met together as a group. This activity does not feature greatly in our data, which in themselves raise interesting points about the partial nature of attempts to represent the totality of a social experience for the group under study.

Adult education: '"The practice of freedom" or an exercise in producing conformity' (Finch 1984a: 92)?

The emphasis on self-improvement which pervades the parent education course places it neatly within the traditional social democratic understanding of the purposes of adult education. Personal enrichment, but of a type that also benefits 'society', is the classic aim of adult education for women (Finch 1984a). The women on the course were benefiting personally from learning new skills, gaining a certificate, and enjoying themselves, while at the same time learning new activities and techniques that they could share with their children and others. Mary Hughes (1993) argues that women involved in adult education often feel guilty about being away from their children and their domestic responsibilities. The parent education group offered a way out of this dilemma as the women were embarked on a course that had bene- fits for their children as well as themselves. However, as we have shown, the benefits for the child are clearly understood as emanating from changes in the mother's behaviour in relation to her child. The course therefore appeared to focus on women within the private sphere. Mary Hughes sums this up well:

> Adult education for women has been primarily concerned with the home- based life of women as mothers . . . The process has helped define women into home-based roles, whose boundary stops at the front door or maybe at the school gate.
>
> (1993: 152)

However, Hughes continues by acknowledging the way in which the unthreatening, supportive ethos of many adult education classes has helped women back into education, improved their confidence about their abilities, and opened up further opportunities for them. This is one of Christine's hopes for the course, and one it seemed to fulfil. Over the course of 1996, members of the group got jobs as lunchtime supervisors at Elliott, and under- took courses to become special needs classroom assistants, and preparatory courses for nursery nurse and other childcare qualifications. Former students had also gone on to a range of other jobs and courses. This form of support is recognized by Christine Everingham, who comments with reference to family support programmes in Australia:

> Social institutions such as family support programmes . . . are guided by the ideal of helping women achieve autonomy, while recognising the fact that their everyday lives remain embedded in kinship . . . Workers explicitly state their goals in terms of 'empowering' women through a personal supportive orientation that takes the particularities of each woman's situation into account.
>
> (Everingham 1994: 135)

However, there is another discourse surrounding adult education that dis- tinguishes itself quite sharply from the social democratic view propounded by Everingham. As Janet Finch (1984a) argues, adult education has long been seen as a vehicle to promote the advancement of working class groups as a collectivity, and in this context she cites the Workers' Educational Associ- ation, and Richard Johnson's (1979) concept of 'really useful knowledge'. Such a tradition highlights the importance of education in developing coun- ter-hegemonic ideas and knowledge. In more recent times, this tradition has taken on the form of 'critical pedagogy' (Middleton 1993). Such an emphasis appeared to be absent from the parent education course. Whereas 'empower- ing' women in Everingham's context means focusing on individuals, and enabling and supporting a (necessarily slight) expansion of individual oppor- tunities, radical adult education seeks to focus attention on broader structural conditions which constrain lives. The idea of opening up these issues for discussion and learning in the context of adult education is analogous to the thinking behind 'protected enclaves' (see Chapter 1) where groups can discuss their own situations, and work out their own agendas before going into the public arena. The women students at Elliott leave the school, and return to, in many cases, their overcrowded housing, their families' financial struggles, and, for some, the racism and sexism of the wider community. Yet the parent education course has its roots in the social democratic tradition of community and adult education, and is therefore ill-equipped to engage with structural issues. Nor should it be forgotten that the parent education course itself exists on the margins in several ways. Its funding is continually precarious and it is one of the last survivors of several similar initiatives run in inner London by education authorities over the last 20 years. To talk, then, of the ability of social democratic adult education to 'empower' seems to overstate the case. The course seeks to alter the margins of the women's lives, to affect a slight redrawing of the boundaries. What it cannot do in its present form – and nor does it seek to do – is address the nature of those existing constraints, and how they can be challenged. Christine disagreed strongly with us on this point. She maintained that the social network opened up by her collaboration with mothers at Elliott over a number of years (the accredited course being the latest manifestation of this work), has allowed a space to emerge in which such issues can be, and are, discussed and strategies for coping with them formulated.

However, the analysis up to this point suggests that, given the discursive framework in which the parent education group at Elliott operates, it could easily be seen as another manifestation of what Foucault referred to as 'the swarming of disciplinary mechanisms' (1977: 211). It is easy, in fact, to draw conclusions along these lines – except when one considers the reactions of the women students on the course (see Ribbens 1994 on the need to include the voices of mothers in any analysis of child rearing).

Speaking for themselves

The women were, of course, a self-selected group. They did not have to attend the sessions, or complete the work. However, most of the second group had attended sessions regularly for about 14 months, a considerable commitment. There was only a small number of drop-outs during this time, and the constant attendees were quite unanimous in their enjoyment of the sessions. They gave three main reasons for this: the achievement of gaining a certificate at the end; their enjoyment of doing the course itself and carrying out the activities with their children; and the injection of confidence and independence to which many attested as a result of the course.

All the women felt that attaining a certificate was an important motivator. It was tangible proof of their achievement and was something they could show to future employers or colleges. For those Bangladeshi women who were not yet completely fluent in English, the certificate proved that they could complete a course run in English, as this extract from interview notes illustrates:

> They are both sure that they will finish the course. They want to get the certificates. For Rehana, this will be proof of her ability to speak English and will help her get a job in a clinic or a school or go to college. Jaya's NVQ course [in child care] finishes in July. With that and her certificate [from the parent education course] she may go and do a nursery nurse diploma.
>
> (Interview notes, 23/4/96)[6]

The women's weekly experience of the course was generally positive. They had a chance to talk to each other while carrying out particular activities either individually or in groups. The completion of these activities was in itself a source of achievement, worthy of note. For example, Amina, after her 'micro-teaching' activity (teaching the whole group to make knitted flowers), produced the camera she had brought in, and took pictures of everyone with their completed flowers. The students also enjoyed learning aspects of child development and being able to undertake activities with their children, which would be beneficial for them. In addition to the educational input, this was, as many of the women made clear, a real source of pleasure. Overall, what they described is a move towards ways of behaving that can be categorized as 'sensitive mothering'. However, their words illustrate that such experiences are not necessarily perceived as oppressive. This is a useful addition to Walkerdine and Lucey's (1989) polemic against the discourse. They state, for example, that 'mothering is clearly both painful and intensely pleasurable' (1989: 157) but their analysis seems to emphasize the former rather than the latter. The Elliott students presented a different perspective:

> Doing this course has made me realize that sometimes I was too busy cleaning, I was too busy getting the dinner, too busy doing washing and ironing to spend time just sitting with them . . . I do find a lot more time now. I have got this extra energy from somewhere I don't know where. But I have a lot of time now. It's this course has made me realize that life's too short and you have got to do things, and I take them out a lot more, and I take them to the park. When we are in the park, I am saying, 'Oh look, how many ducks are there?' and I am getting them to do things. I might have done that before naturally, I don't know, but now . . .
>
> (Sarah)

> I've got young children and it sort of gives you a bit of an insight into how to, I know you do know how to play games, and play with the children, but it just sort of pushes you that bit more to put more effort into it you know, where the classrooms are full now, they need that bit of one-to-one . . . I just feel, it's a little bit more, they enjoy me making things with them at home, and they help me, whereas before you tended to get on with other things, you sort of make time now.
>
> (Deborah)

Although the women enjoyed undertaking the various activities, these extracts reveal some ambiguities. How do they manage to make more time? Deborah for instance has five children; Chrissy, quoted below, has four, and Sarah has four and a job as a childminder. There is absolutely no suggestion that their partners provide extra help with either the domestic responsibilities or the childcare. So shopping still has to be bought, cooking and washing to be done. Where is this extra time, effort and energy they refer to coming from?

> CV: Is it difficult though, making time? You've got five kids, how do you find the time?
>
> Deborah: Just being a kid like they are. I'd rather make things than make the dinner. That's my excuse.
>
> CV: And do you find it all right managing things at home, because you've got four kids haven't you?
>
> Chrissy: I let them get involved with things ... Three or four years ago, there's no way I would have done that. I'd have been sort of putting them to bed and sitting watching the telly ... The other day, I got a lolly stick and started making puppets with them. I mean I've got a 2-year-old to a 12-year-old and all ages, they were all in there, all interested in doing it ... Then they made a puppet show, really good, and I was getting so much out of it just watching them. Fantastic. But as I said, if I hadn't started this course, you don't think, you'd play with your children, but you don't think about doing creative play with your children, and what do they get out of it. I mean, I've got two little 'uns who are so confident, they're totally different to the two older ones.

Sarah offered similar explanations; she was able to find the extra energy because she was enjoying what she was doing *and* felt it was benefiting her children. By comparison, as Deborah and Rita pointed out, housework was tedious, and very isolating:

> Deborah: I think it's [the course] given me more confidence, talking to other people; when you're indoors you sort of shut the street door.
>
> Rita: It's mostly housework and shopping that you do, but [here] you know, you can sit and chat. I mean after lunch we sort of sit together in the room, we're all having a chat. You get in a rut when you're at home, don't you?
>
> Deborah: It fetches you out. You sort of tend to get set in your ways, you know. Take the kids to school, tidy up, go and pick the kids up, dinner's in the oven. Like you're just mum. This way you tend to get out ... you start taking more pride in yourself, you don't just muck around in T-shirts ... You tend to sort of make the effort.

Mary and Sue focused particularly on the beneficial effects the course has had on them as individuals.

> It's nice getting out of the house, talking to adults. I don't know really, it's sort of, I suppose it's my one morning a week or one day a week if I stay for the afternoon where it's sort of my time . . . Even though a lot of it does involve doing things that [my daughter] would like, it's me doing them because I want to rather than you know, having to do them.
>
> (Mary)

> *Sue*: It's given me a bit more confidence, whereas before if I knew there was something wrong I'd just sit there and not open my mouth, but now I don't care, if I think someone's out of order, I'll tell them, but it has, I'm a lot more, how can I explain it? I go places by myself now, whereas before I wouldn't dream of doing it . . .
>
> *CV*: And you work as well now [as a lunchtime supervisor]?
>
> *Sue*: Yes, it's just picking me up again. This may sound stupid I know, but I was married at sixteen and a half, and now it's like from that time to now I've brought up the kids and they're getting off out, and now I'm getting my independence back . . . This is for me, nobody else can sort of like invade that. I'm doing this for me, nobody else, for me. So I'm getting my independence back and at the same time I'm enjoying what I'm doing . . . Sort of like my own little world where I can shut myself off.

Only one woman, Ruckshana, who got very behind with her course work (although she eventually completed it), talked of the pressures that it added to her already full life. She had a full-time job in a health centre, close family ties and three children. She was also a parent governor at Elliott School:

> I'm never actually completing anything . . . Sometimes I actually wonder, even though I'm teaching myself these skills or whatever, you know, am I actually going to sit down and do all these things that I've learned . . . ? You know, are my children actually benefiting? Because I just don't have the time for them to learn anything or for me to teach whatever it is that I am learning.

It may be that Ruckshana's paid work, which she found fairly stressful but also very absorbing, provided her with a source of stimulation, independence and adult interaction that the other women found, to some extent, in the course itself.

To conclude this section I refer to Neckel's (1996) argument that social, political and cultural changes disrupting the traditional class hierarchy have resulted in the causes of social inequality appearing individualized. Thus feelings of inferiority have become a symbolic construction of deficient individuality. He argues that self-restriction is an inevitable outcome as 'limiting one's own interests and ambitions serves to reduce the feeling of inferiority' (1996: 25). The words of the women at Elliott seem to suggest that the parent education course had begun to alleviate such feelings, and to allow the women to recognize and exercise the talents they possessed.

Impasse

So how do we as researchers analyse the social relationships, understandings and experiences which constitute this course? Do we conclude that the 'oppressed' women students are unfortunately deluded and that our status as researchers, our access to knowledge they do not have, places us high above them, able to see and understand what they cannot? In *Getting Smart*, Patti Lather (1991) talks of the difficulties and discontinuities thrown up by hearing the voices of her students on her introductory women's studies courses. It would be easy for her to position herself as a 'transformative intellectual', a 'critical pedagogue' bringing light and understanding to those gripped by false consciousness. However, it is her students themselves who disrupt and problematize such a reading, just as it is the women on the course at Elliott School who disrupt and problematize our original reading of the course as constraining – inducting them into a particular set of practices. 'To what extent', Lather asks 'is the pedagogy we construct in the name of liberation intrusive, invasive, pressurised? . . . Many [students] speak of the 'shoulds' that add another coercive discourse to their lives, a discourse designed to shake up their world, but which often loses touch with what that shaken-up experience feels like' (1991: 143). The question we are left with is who is adding another 'should' to the lives of the women at Elliott? Is it researchers like ourselves and Walkerdine and Lucey, insisting upon the oppressiveness for women of discourses such as sensitive mothering, arguing that such courses are designed to make working class mothers, especially, function in ways that the state deems more acceptable? Or is the parent education course itself adding another 'should' to the women's lives, by defining, however implicitly and with whatever qualifications, a model for 'good' motherhood?

Conclusion

It is tempting to conclude that both readings possess equal validity. That, following Foucault, the discourses disseminated by the parent education course 'both liberate and enslave . . . empower and subject' (Ball 1994: 56). Of course, as Gramsci argued, it is precisely the multidimensionality of hegemonic discourses that gives them such power. In this regard, Gramsci talked of the significance of 'common sense', a constantly fluctuating discursive mix, that accommodates apparent contradictions, allowing one social group to hold views and opinions that do not appear to serve their particular interests' (Kenway 1990: 179).

Thus for the women students at Elliott the practice of particular activities and ways of interacting with their children takes on the status of 'common sense' understandings and knowledge. The activities are presented, and largely accepted, as being good for the children and enjoyable and beneficial for the women themselves. Any resulting burdens which call on their time and resources are seen by most of the women as worthwhile, because of the extra dimension added to their relationships with their children (see also Urwin 1985). Additionally, attendance at the sessions offers them the chance to meet other adults, and experience success in a learning situation. The course, therefore, *does* appear to be inducting the women into 'sensitive mothering' – but it is a discourse which cannot be understood in terms of a binary. It is not wholly 'oppressive' nor 'liberating'. It is only by recognizing and holding these opposing readings of the course in tension that an analysis can be formed which appreciates both its strengths and weaknesses.

The course in its current form centres on the students themselves as the focus for change, and in particular (though not exclusively) how they operate within the private sphere of the home. It would be possible, in theory, if the students were agreeable, to conceive a similar course which would engage with 'public' issues; to use the group more overtly as a 'protected enclave', but seeing that protection, that closeting within the private sphere, as a starting point, to take the women's concerns and demands as working class women and mothers out into the public sphere. To some extent this did happen. Christine acted as an emissary, taking the women's experiences, and sometimes the women themselves, to talk to various policy forums and professional groups. The women also contributed to a conference for social welfare professionals and parents in Tate local authority on home–school relations, where they performed a play about their experiences of the course.

The women's experiences were therefore beginning to reach a more public arena but not their demands, their questions or their challenges. We suggest that the arena of the school would be an obvious starting point (see also Moss 1999 for a similar argument with reference to early childhood institutions). Elliott School had a good reputation for parental involvement. Parents had been consulted on school policies and involved in curriculum events, and students from the course worked in the classes with small groups of children. The students also had children at other primary and secondary schools, and two specifically contrasted the welcoming atmosphere at Elliott with the more impersonal and intimidating surroundings of other institutions. Problems and concerns to do with school and their children's progress were often brought up by individual women and were discussed informally. This could easily be incorporated into the main body of a course. What sort of information do parents get from their children's schools? Are they informed about the progress their children are making in ways that are meaningful to them? Is it easy to visit the teachers and ask questions? How does the school respond to parents' concerns? What is the school's approach to literacy, numeracy, special educational needs, behaviour, supporting bilingual children in English, and so on? Tackling such issues would not only involve informing the women about the education system, but also encouraging them to critically assess the current provision and ethos of their children's schools. Such an emphasis would also serve to shift the focus for change away from the women's behaviour towards that of schools and teachers.

Acknowledgement

Chapter 4 is a revised version of a 1998 paper which originally appeared in the *British Journal of Sociology of Education*, 19 (2). We are grateful to the editor and publishers for letting us include it here.

Notes

1 The course tutor was in favour of opening the course to men in the future, in order to encourage men to take a more active role in relation to their children. Both she and the students had doubts about how well a mixed group would work and whether men would accept the activities as valuable. The women students were generally in favour of keeping their space women-only.
2 Although an exploration of the impact of race and ethnicity on the views and opinions of the students would be valuable, the limitations of space mean that this issue cannot be properly explored here. This issue is addressed in relation to the parent education group, although again not in exhaustive depth, in Vincent and Warren 1997.
3 There has been in recent years an intensification of concern over 'feckless fathers'. However the specific responsibilities of a father's role – apart from financial support – are not as clearly defined as those of the mother.
4 This report shows that Black Caribbean women have a disproportionately high rate of interaction with health visitors and social workers. It is unclear whether this is because of the increased demand from this group or professional perceptions of their disproportionate need.
5 A similar distance separated Carol and the women students; see Vincent and Warren forthcoming.
6 If the women did not wish to be tape-recorded, as was the case here, I took full notes.

CHAPTER FIVE

Parents, collective action and education

Introduction

As noted in Chapter 1, the democratic process in many Western countries is widely understood to allocate citizens a largely passive role, their activity centring on voting in elections. In search of remedies for the limitations of representative politics as it is currently constituted (Stewart 1997), theorists of democracy emphasize the importance of a dynamic civil society composed of a network of local, associative groups, wherein citizens can actively participate in decisions which affect their everyday lives (see for example Young 1990; Yeatman 1994; Benhabib 1996b; Fraser 1997a).

In this chapter, I focus on two of the four case study PCOs, the two which most clearly present examples of parental collective action. These are the campaigning group, which was composed from a network of local protest groups mobilizing to demand increased funding for education, especially schools, and the self-help group, a small group of African/Caribbean women who provide a network of mutual support and information concerning educational issues.

It is difficult to ascertain the degree and extent of collective lay mobilization on educational issues. There is some evidence that there are instances of local activity around special education.[1] There are also thriving networks of supplementary schools in most urban centres serving minority ethnic populations, although these do not necessarily see campaigning or influencing policy as a major part of their role (see for example Reay and Mirza 1997; Mirza and Reay 1999). Therefore it appears that sustained collective action on the part of parents, qua parents, is relatively uncommon in the UK. As a result of this lacuna there is a tendency in some areas, including my own earlier work, to celebrate uncritically the appearance of collective action, or to recommend its development without subjecting such claims to close empirical consideration. What are the aims of such groups? Who are their members? What are the consequences of their activity for the policy-making process in education, and for the role of parents as a collective in relation to policy making? What can such groups tell us about citizenship and civil society at the turn of the century?

In this chapter, I consider these questions in relation to the two parent groups mentioned above, the campaigning group, referred to here as PIE (Participating in Education), and the self-help group, which I have called ACES (African/Caribbean Education Support). The two groups were very different on a number of indices – their organization, their aims, their understandings of their purpose. Yet on closer examination there are also some interesting similarities. First, I give a brief introduction to each group, their aims, organization and membership. Second, the body of literature concerned with the analysis of new social movements is invoked in order to consider the very different social and political location of the two case study groups, their possibilities and constraints. I conclude that the operation of both groups was heavily influenced by their professional, middle class membership, and briefly consider the likelihood of wider recruitment to such collectivities.

PIE (Participating in Education)

The PIE campaign was particularly active throughout the UK between 1994 and early 1997 (an assumption of a Labour victory meant that action ran down in the immediate run-up to the 1997 general election). Its primary stated aims were to contest the cuts in funding for state education; to campaign for sufficient funding for a fair, equitable and accessible state education system which meets the needs of all children; and to attain the statutory definition and implementation of national standards through state education.

The campaigning group was initiated in 1994 by two headteachers whose schools were located within a shire county authority. They organized a public meeting in response to reports about expected cuts in the county's education budget. The turnout was much greater than expected with hundreds of people attending that first meeting. A local group was formed from participants, and the campaign grew from there. It developed a relatively sophisticated two-layered structure very quickly after its establishment. It had an overarching national committee and a range of local and regional groups, bringing together parents based in particular schools. These local groups could be established in any area where there was sufficient interest and support to sustain the process. It is important to note, however, that the original and strongest of the local groupings were situated outside major urban centres, clustered instead around the shire counties and towns of the Midlands. Thus its primary constituency was often referred to by activists themselves as 'middle England', a broad and rather imprecise term which generally refers to the conservative political and cultural tendencies of large numbers of white-collar workers, especially service-class professionals in small towns and semi-rural settings (Urry 1995).[2] During its first two years of life PIE organized two national demonstrations, and a concerted series of events designed to

highlight education funding and provision. Between national events, different regional groups organized local events and protests in response to the
situation in their areas. In line with the quiet conservative middle England
image, most PIE members in our sample had not previously been involved in
campaigning, and were, in many cases, unused to collective public protests,
demonstrations, and the type of media-oriented publicity stunts which PIE
practised.

The research was based on two neighbouring local groups. One was a
branch of PIE which covered a county, 'Midshire', the other a smaller group
drawing its members from a particular suburb ('East River') of Midshire's
main city. Members attending the group meetings often acted as representatives of their children's particular schools. Data are drawn from observations
of PIE meetings nationally, as well as local meetings at East River and Midshire,
and from 16 semi-structured interviews conducted in late 1996 and early
1997 with individual activists. Five respondents from the Midshire group,
seven from East River and four from the coordinating national committee
participated in the research. Respondents had various levels of involvement
with the campaign which are categorized here as *key* (centrally involved at a
national and/or regional campaign level), *core* (closely involved with a local
group) and *peripheral* (involved at the level of the individual school).

ACES (African Caribbean Education Support)

The self-help group was a small group of black parents, all of whom were
women[3], who 'offer[ed] support and guidance to parents of children at school
. . . and network[ed] with agencies and departments within the [City] Education department' (promotional literature). The city in question, 'Midcity', is
a large urban centre, with considerable suburban settlement, and a well-
established African/Caribbean population.

Members felt that ACES had two main functions. First, providing information and a forum for debate, as well as offering skills and support to individual parents who were experiencing difficulties with their children at school,
and second, improving parent–teacher relationships and expanding parents'
views of their appropriate role in relation to schools. The group had been in
operation since 1992. During that time membership fluctuated considerably.
At one point it had nearly 100 members on its mailing list. In 1997, during
the period of study, that number was down to just over 50. Meetings were
held every four to six weeks in a community centre. Turnout varied, but
regular attendees numbered about 10 to 15 women in their 30s and 40s.
Responsibilities tended to fall on a core group of three to four. The group
organized talks, often with outside speakers. Issues of behaviour and discipline in school, school choice and forms of parental participation were
recurring themes for the group as these were the ones that parents regularly
'stumble over' (mother). Approximately once a year the group organized a
day conference on a variety of issues to do with education and black children.
The group's coordinator was employed by a voluntary sector educational

organization which provided the group with some funding. Through her work for this organization, the coordinator, Annie, was involved in school governor training, and placed particular emphasis on encouraging black parents to become governors. Seven women members of ACES, the regular attendees and among the more consistently active members of the self-help group, participated in the research, and were interviewed during late 1996/ early 1997.

Who participates?

The social profile of collectivities clearly plays a key role in determining their priorities, their choice of tactics and strategies, the relationships between participants and between the group and the outside world. As I noted at the beginning, the two groups appeared to be very different. PIE operated in the public domain with a straightforward protest agenda, seeking to persuade the government, with a factual and largely quantitative argument, to increase the resources given to state education. ACES had an apparently more inward-looking focus, offering advice, support and information to individuals within a particular community. However, as illustrated below, ACES was also concerned to challenge dominant understandings of black children in the education system, understandings which located those children as problematic.

Race is the most obvious dimension of comparison between the two groups. Midshire City has a small but significant minority of black and Asian residents among its population, but despite this the respondents and those members who attended the PIE meetings we observed were all white. The ACES group members were either African/Caribbean or mixed race. Race and ethnicity were not seen as salient by PIE members. In comparison, ACES members spoke at length of the importance of having an all-black group which provided like-minded people to talk to, and reinforced their sense of both 'self' and 'community' (see below and Vincent and Warren 1999 for details).

At a cursory glance gender appears to be another difference between the two groups, as a considerable number of men were involved with PIE. A closer examination however reveals an interesting, if unsurprising, similarity. Within PIE, the activists organizing at school level were overwhelmingly female. Men became more involved at regional and national levels, coordinating local groups and sitting on the national committee. Similarly, although no men regularly attended ACES meetings, they were better represented on the course for potential black governors. Asked about this, one respondent replied, 'Power':

I mean it's a management post isn't it, and I think men would probably see themselves more as, I mean going to a parents' group probably sounds a bit wishy-washy to men, whereas if you say I'm going to be a school governor it's a different light.

(Black mother, education manager/administrator)

Table 5.1   PIE respondents

Level of involvement	Occupation	Gender breakdown	Previous campaign involvement?
5 key players	3 teachers 1 health professional 1 solicitor	2 women 3 men	2 men and 1 woman had campaigning experience
6 core activists	1 social worker 2 self-employed 1 teacher 1 retired teacher 1 full-time carer (ex-civil servant)	5 women 1 man	1 had been active in a trade union
5 peripheral activists	3 full-time carers 1 civil servant 1 full-time student	5 women	2 had campaigning experience

This illustrates men and women's differential involvement in their children's education (see Chapters 1, 2 and 4 for further comment). As Lisa Dominelli (1995) argues, this gender imbalance is common in other areas of community activism as well as education. Women's organizing in the community often revolves around 'family lives . . . and a host of issues linked to women's caring roles' (1995: 134). Further, she argues that such issues have often been labelled as 'soft' and therefore accorded secondary status by male community activists. Heidi Mirza (1997), writing about black women's agency in relation to education, also argues that the nature of collective action is heavily mediated by gender. Moreover, she maintains that the dominant forms of analysis of black collective action recognize only particular, masculine forms:

> Urban social movements, we are told, mobilise in protest, riots, local politics and community organisations. We are told that it is their action, and not the subversive, covert action of women that gives rise to so-called 'neo-populist, liberatory, authentic politics' (Gilroy 1987: 245). This is the masculinist version of radical social change; visible, radical, confrontational, collective action, powerfully expressed in the politics of the inner city, where class consciousness evolves in response to urban struggle.
>
> (Mirza 1997: 272)

In this quotation, Mirza suggests that not only gender, but also social class (and relatedly place and space) affect the type of collective action practised. It is to social class that I now turn. The social class profile of the two groups suggests that most activists were in professional middle class public sector occupations. The occupations of the respondents are shown in Tables 5.1 and 5.2. This profile reveals a dominant professional middle class grouping. With particular regard to black employment, local government has been

Table 5.2 ACES respondents

Occupation
2 education managers / administrators
1 school ancillary staff
1 teaching supervisor
1 community worker, currently unemployed
1 education social worker
1 social worker

Note: All the respondents were women and all had some other involvement in community activities in addition to ACES.

noted as an important sector for employing black people in professional and managerial as well as administrative roles (Daye 1994; Modood *et al.* 1997). There also appears to be a general correlation between public sector employment and activity within a social movement. Rootes (1995) has argued that participants in social movements are disproportionately drawn from middle class groups who have two characteristics: they have experienced higher education with its presumed liberalizing effects, and they work in public sector occupations, particularly within the 'caring' professions (education, welfare and health) (see also Bagguley 1995, 1997). Eder (1993) argues that there is a direct bridge between social class and action and that occupational culture is clearly a key dimension in determining people's involvement in social movements. Having sketched out a profile of the two groups and their participants, I turn now to explore the phenomenon of collective action.

Understanding collective action

Education as a site of collective lay activity has received little critical attention, except in the area of race and education (Troyna and Williams 1986; Gibson 1987; Formisano 1991; Mirza 1997). This seems unusual given that as several commentators have noted the scope and form of public sector welfare provision is a key post-industrial issue (Bagguley 1995). As I suggested above, much activity is small-scale, local and episodic and therefore does not lend itself to analytical attention, either from sociologists looking at social movements or political scientists concerned with interest group activity. The literature that does exist on collective action is a sprawling, multifaceted one. Only a small fragment of it can be deployed here, with particular attention being paid to the insights garnered by new social movement theorists.

The development and direction of social movements has been and continues to be the focus for considerable analysis among both European and North American social scientists.[4] To give some sense of the field, themes for investigation have included the social class composition of social movements (e.g. Eder 1993, 1995; Maheu 1995), their cultural characteristics (Melucci 1985, 1988, 1995; Eyerman and Jamison 1991), their interaction with the state

(Pickvance 1995; I. Taylor 1996) and their potential and limitations in terms of inciting social change (Touraine 1985; Plotke 1995). There has been a plurality of approaches to social movement analysis. Della Porta and Diani (1999) identify four, for example, although they acknowledge the artificiality of imposing too neat a typology on such a vast and interconnecting field. The dynamic area of new social movement theorizing, just one of their categories, provides, as they note, some valuable insights for those seeking to understand collective action, whatever its form.

'New social movements' (NSMs) are usually defined as large-scale collectivities, albeit usually composed of smaller groups: the peace, ecology and women's movements, for instance. Such groupings are broadly characterized by their progressive nature. The reference to 'new' refers to collectivities which cannot be adequately understood with reference to orthodox Marxist binaries of working class groups versus capitalist bosses (Melucci 1989; Plotke 1995). Analysis of NSMs has often focused on the way in which they challenge established meanings in a particular area and attempt to construct new understandings and identities. Women's groups, for example, have challenged dominant discourses concerning the role of women within the home and the workforce, and the acceptability of various forms of institutional and individual male behaviour towards women.

'Old' social movements, such as trade union groups, are deemed to be large-scale, formal organizations; their focus for intervention being conventional political structures, and their method, interest group politics. Their main concerns are with economic growth and redistribution. New social movements, however, are defined as more informal and spontaneous groupings involved in protest politics. Their main concerns are with 'quality-of-life issues and with the definition and valorisation of personal and collective identities' (Plotke 1995: 117; also Melucci 1989; Johnston and Klandermans 1995). However, several theorists claim that this binary divide is inaccurate and unhelpful (Calhoun 1995; Melucci 1995; Plotke 1995). Plotke for example points to the US civil rights movement as just one very eminent social movement which clearly combined legal, distributive and cultural elements. It viewed institutional and social frameworks *and* dominant cultural understandings as legitimate targets for attention and intervention.

As I noted above, much social movement analysis has concentrated on the potential of groups to initiate social transformation. Castells's work (1983), for example, focusing on 'the urban', described sites for struggle around collective consumption issues. But Castells also extended his analysis to argue that such contestations can also be understood as promoting for participants a redefinition, challenge or change in the meaning of the urban setting (also Lowe 1986). Again, there is an emphasis on creating and recreating meanings as a crucial part of current analyses of new social movements. Mueller refers to the capacity of social movements to 'generate oppositional meanings' (cited in Mirza and Reay 1999: 8). Similarly, Melucci emphasizes their ability to create a 'symbolic challenge'; that is a symbolic contestation and resistance of dominant hegemonies. He argues that what is valuable is the daily production of alternative frameworks of sense . . . Concrete concepts such as efficacy or success could be considered unimportant. This is because conflict takes place principally on symbolic ground, by the challenging and upsetting of dominant codes upon which social relationships are founded in high density informational systems. The mere existence of a symbolic challenge is in itself a method of unmasking the dominant codes, a different way of perceiving and naming the world

(Melucci 1988: 248)

Eyerman and Jamison (1991) contend that such a challenge to existing power relations is particularly important in that it also entails the construction of new knowledge. They refer to this process as 'cognitive praxis', whereby a social movement defines and (re)formulates its own knowledge, concepts and values (also Johnston and Klandermans 1995: 10).

A note of caution has to be introduced here as the transformatory power of social movements is highly likely to be limited by the influence of existing social hierarchies which structure and inform the organization and operation of social movements. The example given earlier of the women's movement is relevant here too. Commentators have argued that in the early phases of the women's movement, testimonies reflecting the experience of only a small minority of women (primarily white, middle class women) were given universal status. Internal challenges by women of colour have asserted the heterogeneity of the category 'women', and the different needs and desires which particular women prioritize (Mirza 1997). As a result of the way in which social movements reflect existing power relationships, Plotke asserts that their transformatory power can easily be overstated. Revolutionary potential was, he claims, granted by sympathetic analysts and participants in social movements, particularly those of the 1960s, but this was, in many cases, too heavy a label to attach to transitory and often fragile movements (Plotke 1995: 115).

A reading of social movements as progressive, even radical, in their concerns excludes some active groups (Roche 1995; Apple 1996; I. Taylor 1996). A sense of time is important here. Social movements may organize against dominant discourses of their time but they are also, and inevitably, in and of their time. A useful example here is the work of Kari Dehli (Dehli and Januario 1994; Dehli 1996) who maps the changing nature of parents' groups in Toronto, Canada, throughout the 1970s and 1980s. Parental voices arguing for their inclusion in educational governance on democratic grounds were replaced by those arguing for their inclusion as consumers. Support for multiculturalism and bilingual education became support for 'standards' and teacher accountability.

Ian Taylor (1996) points to the importance of movements organizing around the defence of privileges, such as NIMBY (Not In My Backyard) protests in the UK, tax-cutting movements in the USA, and various nationalist groups in Europe. The focus of Taylor's analysis is on what he terms 'suburban social movements': small, locally based groups of a conservative nature.[5] He defines them as a subgrouping of social movements concerned with institutional provision and quality of life. Using the example of concern with the prevention of crime and the variety of measures taken by local collectivities in suburban Greater Manchester to try and ensure their own safety and that of their property, he argues that suburban social movements are

> a very different animal from those which have been the focus of the classical analysis of social movements in sociology: above all they are movements directed not at social change and reform in a classically 'progressive' sense, but rather at the defence of privileges to which the socially and economically successful believe they are entitled.
>
> (I. Taylor 1996: 316)

In a contentious claim, Taylor argues that what he calls the 'blinkered empirical gaze' of some new social movement theorists, including the influential work of Alain Touraine, appears to recognize only the strong, progressive movements, dismissing smaller, more conservative action as 'evidence of bourgeois self-interest . . . or intolerance' (1996: 319).[6] Taylor argues that the motivation to form suburban social groups is characterized by a *mix of fear, anxiety and aspiration*. The groups arise as part of a 'middle class and suburbanite search for personal economic safety and neighbourhood security . . . [with respect to] the private home . . . [and] in the sphere of private consumption (iconically represented by the quality and variety of local shops) and public provision (the provenance and safety of the local park)' (p.321). Taylor doesn't mention education, but perceptions of the quality and safety of local schools would clearly fit into his analysis.

> These new 'social movements' must be understood as emanating, more or less spontaneously from individual suburban households or out of groups of neighbours coming together . . . These groups of what in North America are called 'concerned citizens' are the vanguard of a very contemporary form of local social movement, which whilst it does not generate the mass membership or collectivism of the movements described by Touraine, is nonetheless an archetypal and 'popular' movement of the mid to late-1990s, not least in the anxious private households of the English suburbs.
>
> (I. Taylor 1996: 327)

Taylor's suburban social movements have some similarity in form and motivation to Eder's middle class *moral crusades*:

> The moral crusades of the NSMs are collective reactions to the cultural modernisation which has increasingly widened the gap between morality and the life world . . . Fear and the overcoming of it in forms of collective protest are a reaction to this cultural modernisation.
>
> (Eder 1993: 155)

Therefore, suburban social movements are posited as insular and conservative groups, concerned with the defence of existing privilege. I want to consider whether this is an appropriate analysis of PIE and ACES. Given the middle class professional profile of most of the activists in the two groups concerned, this could be a possible explanation for their activity, namely that in the face of what they perceive to be problems besetting the delivery of quality educational provision, they have come together in collectivities the better to further their individual ends, and as a result to secure their relative class advantage in the education marketplace. Their concern then would be not with creating and recreating meaning, not with symbolic challenge or 'unmasking dominant codes', but rather with preserving and defending the status quo and rejecting change.

Locating the case study groups: PIE

I suggest here that there are three relevant factors to consider in relation to PIE in order to locate and explain the activities of the group. The first is its use of a universal rhetoric, positioning itself as an organic grassroots group. At a national level PIE used an inclusive language to describe its campaign – 'we speak for parents and children' (key player, teacher). Activists, especially key players, stressed that the campaign had broad-based support from 'ordinary people who were pushing prams, grannies and pensioners as well, who have been on our marches' (key player, teacher). This was the case because the campaign was 'fighting for something that every single parent in the country wants' (core activist, retired teacher). However, as explained earlier, PIE members were drawn primarily from specific social groupings. The National Committee for instance was composed of

> two solicitors, well the Chairperson, as I say, is this woman who works in the National Health Service, the vice-chair is somebody who runs his own business . . . the Finance Officer, he's a teacher, and the others are things like solicitors, solicitors' clerks. They are just . . . people.
>
> (Key player, solicitor)

The dominance of the professional middle classes at a national level is reflected locally, as this activist's description of her local group, East River, makes clear:

> Typical East River busy-bodies . . . Maybe people of professional backgrounds, often working, often busy, but you know, who still feel very strongly that they have to do something about matters like this, and they're concerned about their children's education, but that's typical of people in East River.
>
> (Core activist, carer)[7]

The homogeneous nature of campaign activists (in social class terms) can lead to universal claims being made for the opinions and experiences of what is actually a specific social group. One of the respondents made this point:

> Most of us assume other parents are just like us; this is not deliberate. We are not thinking about all parents. We are thinking about white middle class parents like ourselves.
>
> (Peripheral activist, carer)

The second factor is PIE's concern to present itself as a grassroots campaign in the sense that non-educational professionals played a leading role. A parent-led campaign has a powerful symbolic significance, conjuring up as it does the image of an outpouring of frustration from 'ordinary people'. However, activists also described considerable teacher involvement in the campaign, and a certain amount of privileging of teachers' knowledge and experience.

> [The involvement of teachers] only strengthens it [PIE] because I think there are a number of issues in education that are more fully understood by teaching professionals.
>
> (Key player and trainee teacher)

> I think parent groups, without being a sort of dominant figure in it . . . I think maybe need a little background information of what it's like from the school's point of view, you know, what it's like at the chalk face.
>
> (Core activist and retired teacher)

Thus teachers were presented as having specialist knowledge which could inform the campaign's activities. By contrast, parental experiences of the education system tended to be overlooked as a source of information or a potential guide for future activities.

A third area for consideration in trying to locate and explain PIE's actions is the focus of the group's campaign. The overt focus was resource allocation. In a phrase which reoccurred in the data, PIE wanted to see 'adequate and equitable funding' for education. Key players (those centrally involved in the campaign) were particularly concerned with compiling and quantifying the resources which the campaign felt should be directed towards education. They emphasized a direct relationship between plentiful funding for education and the creation of learning environments able to encourage educational success. The persistent linkages made by activists between outcomes, opportunities and resources successfully formed a counter-argument to the rhetoric of John Major's Conservative government which, of course, assumed a relationship between positive learning outcomes and leaner, apparently more efficient educational units.

PIE's aims were characterized by a concern with distributive justice; that is, the argument was that large class sizes, or poor school buildings, or cuts to local special education budgets interfered with children's access to the social good that is education (Young 1990; Troyna and Vincent 1995). As an organization, PIE was not concerned with the content of the education that children receive. There were hints and suggestions in the data of an implicit conception of an improved system of state education (a few activists strongly voiced their opposition to selection for instance), but they remained muted and marginal to the overriding concern with funding. In any case the stances taken by those members who did position themselves in opposition to selection were reactions to government policy and pronouncements, rather than proactive constructions of an alternative agenda. Official PIE policy made no comment upon the National Curriculum, or upon the pedagogies used to implement the curriculum. It did not, therefore, challenge the state's view of 'official' knowledge in the way in which, for example, the groups of conservative parents described by Michael Apple (1996) managed to. In this sense, PIE does not fulfil the requirements of some theorists for NSMs, namely that they challenge existing understandings and values, in this case what education is or what its function is. Indeed, among activists, the predominant discourse concerning the function of education was inscribed by human capital theory – investment in Britain's economic future. This illuminated a chain of correspondence to which nearly all the activists subscribed. Increased funding → higher standards for 'all' → greater economic competitiveness. The group's emphasis upon the funding rather than the content of education or the organization of the education system limited its understanding of social justice and education to issues of distribution.

By this reading, the primary motivation for mobilizing and participating in PIE, and for members joining, does appear to connect with Ian Taylor's understanding of suburban social movements; members were concerned to 'defend privileges to which the socially and economically successful believe they are entitled' (I. Taylor 1996: 316). This analysis is reflected in the reasons PIE activists gave to explain their motivation. Unsurprisingly, personal motivation was frequently cited:

> I went into it for very personal reasons because I could see that what I thought *I'd secured for my children as a good education* was just going to be swiped away from under their feet, basically through cuts to education, and basically that was the point I started at.
>
> (Key player, trainee teacher, my emphasis)

> I fear for them [the children] . . . if I could afford it I would have both my kids at private school, purely for the class size issue
>
> (Peripheral activist, civil servant)

> East River is in a rather cosy position in that the schools are all quite, you know, reasonably good, and we don't want them to get worse.
>
> (Core activist, carer)

> I think that if you are an articulate, and to use the jargon, a middle class parent, whose child is likely to do quite well out of education, you know, if somebody comes along and says, 'I'm sorry, the chances of that are going to be reduced', they might need to actually react against it because yes, they do relatively well out of the system.
>
> (Key player, health professional)

There are clear similarities here with Eder's portrayal of middle class pressure groups, which he describes in the following terms. Political pressure groups are 'fighting against the euphemistic treatment of or complete disregard for social problems, thus against [their] own decline in the status system' (1993: 155). This form of activity is 'a response to the problems connected with the crisis of the welfare state, frustration and disillusionment with the party system and with bureaucratisation' (1993: 150). Protest is articulated through an 'alternative public opinion' which is set apart from 'mass public opinion' and competes with 'the elitist public of ruling political culture'. The cultural capital of such groups allows them to marshal and present their arguments effectively, to use expert opinion and professional public relations.

However, motivation was not always described in personal terms alone and several activists generalized from the particular to the universal. It is possible that involvement in the campaign increased a sense of identification with the broader issues raised and therefore a more communal outlook (for similar argument see for example the work of theorists on deliberative democracy, e.g. Barber 1984, also Chapter 7). I would argue that PIE cannot be neatly analysed as simply an entrenched, insular and conservative social movement, concerned with the defence of existing educational privileges for the children of an elite but anxious class fraction. The group reflected many elements of this characterization, but to employ it as an entire explanation is to overlook important features of PIE's identity and organization. It did, for instance, operate upon the national stage and employ a universal rhetoric in defence of all children's education. Undoubtedly it provided a focus for a range of parents to protest about cuts in education, even if simply through being present on a march. In addition, the group's very existence and rhetoric legitimated the increased democratization of education governance. In other words, PIE was itself an *implicit* argument for the right of any and all parents to become directly involved in, and try to influence, the distribution of resources to and within a key public sector service. It should be remembered, however, that parental involvement remained mediated and guided by education professionals. Additionally, it remains the case that PIE members were seeking a tightly defined change: the adequate resourcing of welfare state institutions. The group clearly did not have an agenda for more fundamental change, which would require challenging dominant discourses concerning the nature of state education, its content, pedagogy and organization. Indeed, given the loose coalition of teachers and parents which PIE represented, any more detailed campaign about the content of education would find it hard to create and sustain agreement among members, and the resulting fractures would risk dissipating the sense of belonging and shared vision (see della Porta and Diani 1999).

ACES

It is in relation to this dimension, namely articulating a challenge to dominant discourses shaping the operation of the education system and the relationships formed therein, that ACES differed from PIE. At first glance this may seem an unlikely conclusion; ACES shared with PIE characteristics which suggest it too was fuelled by liberal individualism, a concern to secure educational advantage within the existing system. In writing about the group elsewhere (Vincent and Warren 1999) Simon Warren and I identified a gently reformist and generally positive approach to the education system which was held and disseminated by core members. We suggested that this was shaped and influenced by these members' professional identities within education and related professions. Thus their emphasis was on working within the system's limits to resolve particular individual problems:

> If people feel that education is what schools do, and it's something that happens nine 'til three thirty, then they are not going to get involved until their child is ill, hurt or in trouble. If parents only respond when there is a problem, then the group will not be able to attract people when there isn't an immediate problem to be resolved. So it's about *selling the support for education.*
>
> (Mother, social worker, my emphasis)

> Rather than saying, 'Oh the school is wrong, or you are wrong', because I don't think that helps anybody, because what we're trying to do is build the relationship, not destroy it.
>
> (Mother, education manager/administrator)

> So a lot of parents, a lot of the parents who are parents now, are letting all that come out, their anger and frustration at the system, and their children you know . . . I guess if you're not within the system and can actually see how it works, you tend to feel that there is definitely them and us, but it isn't.
>
> (Mother, education social worker)

Simon Warren and I suggested that the group promoted a role of 'critical friend' as an appropriate mode for parent–school relationships.[8] This role placed a high premium on parental voice, on questioning, on being at school and on being involved. It is much easier for someone to adopt if they have high levels of confidence and knowledge about the education system (ACES was, of course, trying to support other black parents while they acquired these attributes). The approaches and attitudes of core members may not necessarily be accepted by those parents whose experience of educational institutions has led them to conclude that, contrary to the words quoted above, there is indeed a 'them' and 'us' situation and that power is firmly accrued by 'them'. The professional members of ACES explained the non-involvement in school of other black parents in terms of their lack of confidence and knowledge and of schools not being welcoming. They did not however foreground the degree of alienation and distance which it has been suggested characterizes the relationships of some parents, including both black and white working class parents, to educational institutions (Vincent 1996; Reay 1998).

However, ACES' adoption of a largely reformist approach did not interfere with the women's clear and consistent portrayal of their concerns and complaints around the education provision available to their children, and the nexus of discrimination therein (see Vincent and Warren 1999). Indeed, the self-help group provided a space for these professionals to act without the constraints imposed by the boundaries of their particular occupations. This is illustrated by the comments of the coordinator, Annie, on the genesis of the group:

Many issues came out, and there were a lot of, I suppose, professionals on the [governors' training] course, who were in education and they were quite aware of some of the issues, but weren't in a position to do anything about it in their particular roles, their professional roles, and I guess myself as well felt that we could do something more concrete, if you like, in a voluntary capacity, a self-help capacity. So we thought that if we met regularly and tried to discuss the particular issues, contact various people as [a group], rather than as a teacher or an education officer or something, that we might get more done . . . If we met regularly as a proper group, got some funding, maybe we could start having conferences, having seminars, and, you know, bring the debate to the public and carry on from there.

However, despite their criticisms, group members did not dismiss the current education system in its entirety. Their concern was to help as many parents as possible support their children as they navigated a path through educational institutions, hopefully to emerge, successful, at the end. This understanding articulates with the work of Heidi Mirza who argues that success for black children traversing a white-dominated education system can be seen as an oppositional strategy, reworking and challenging dominant educational discourses which see black children (especially boys) as disruptive and underachieving:

> For black women strategies for everyday survival consist of trying to create spheres of influence that are separate from, but engaged with existing structures of oppression . . . Their desire for inclusion is strategic, subversive and ultimately far more transformative than subcultural reproduction theory suggests . . . In certain circumstances, *doing well can become a radical strategy*. An act of social transformation.
> (Mirza 1997: 276, 270, 274, original emphasis)

Furthermore, Mirza and Reay (1999) argue that a reading of supplementary schools – apparently conformist organizations with an agenda of promoting educational success, often through traditional pedagogies – is incomplete if it defines them simply as examples of individualized agency. For these teachers and pupils, narratives of success within the school system are intertwined with concerns about recovering black history, and establishing a space for 'a blackness which is neither vulnerable nor under threat; rather a blackness comfortable with itself' (Mirza and Reay 1999: 23). As I hinted earlier, ACES played a similar role. For some members, belonging to a black group helped reinforce a sense of 'self' and 'community':

> I often felt that being brought up in [part of city] we were actually losing out in a sense in mixing with the black community because, you know, being the only black girl in the class, and looking around at other black families and I've always wanted to be more involved in the community.
> (Mother, social worker)

Another said,

> You can't be too black [if you're to succeed] . . . I don't know how you
> define 'too black', there's got to be some conformity . . . the higher we
> move up . . . a little bit more of yourself you have to give up in order to
> fit in, because you've got to be able to fit in.
>
> (Mother, education social worker)

To the members of the group who were themselves education professionals
the idea of 'giving something back' to support the education of the next
generation of black children was an important motivator, a responsibility
and a personal obligation (see also Reay and Mirza 1997). To this end, core
members took their 'insider' knowledge of the education system to the group
which operated as a reciprocal network, with the emphasis on mutual support.
The boundaries of the space which encompassed only African/Caribbean
women allowed them to develop a sense of community to which they could
contribute and from which they could receive:

> I think the idea of a network is that it's a self-support group and that
> there are people within the group who are sort of supporting each other
> from their own personal experience. Sometimes I think the danger of
> having an organization that says, 'We will solve your problems', well,
> some of the problems can't be solved . . . We all face the same problems,
> whether we're professionals or not, whatever we classify ourselves as . . .
> we've all got children, and I'm no expert in bringing children up, and
> nor are they, but we can always support each other.
>
> (Mother, education manager/administrator)

In effect the group provided an enclave, a space for 'making sense of what
they saw' (Mansbridge 1996: 57). As I argued in Chapter 1, ACES can be
described in Melucci's terms as an 'invisible network'.

> These 'submerged' networks, noted for their stress on individual needs,
> collective identity and part-time membership constitute the laboratories
> in which new experiences are invented. Within those invisible laborator-
> ies [social] movements question and challenge the dominant codes of
> everyday life.
>
> (Melucci 1989: 6)

Several theorists (e.g. Scott 1990; Young 1990; Fraser 1992; Mansbridge
1996; see Chapter 1) argue that such spaces are crucial for the development
of a more participatory democracy. They allow groups, especially marginalized
groups, to identify and explore their own interests in an atmosphere of
mutual support, thus creating the potential for the formulation and expression of counterdiscourses, 'a shared critique of domination' (Scott 1990,
quoted in Mansbridge 1996: 58), which can then be disseminated outwards.
    The form ACES' counter-discourse took was a response to, a challenge to,
what the women perceived as the dominant understanding of black children. It is expressed succinctly here by one member:

I think the concern is that we can see that the research shows that a lot of our youngsters are being expelled from school, we can see that we're sort of at the bottom of the league tables, whatever table comes out we seem to be at the bottom, except for unemployment and crime, we're top of those.

(Mother, education manager/administrator)

Particular social groups construct their own understandings, challenge dominant understandings of who they are, and how they should behave and make space for themselves in different ways. An account of the experiences of young, black women involved in the 1980s raregroove scene (Bakare-Yusuf 1997) provides an interesting development of this point.[9] For aspirational young black women, participating in a multiracial, socially diverse milieu, and one that was not seen as traditionally 'black', allowed them to express their particular identities as black, non-traditional, upwardly mobile young women. ACES provides its members with a different way of making space for themselves and their children. Despite the differing nature of the examples, the comparison illuminates the way in which both groups create and use that space, to reinscribe a new cultural identity, and challenge dominant understandings, whether those concern what music black women should listen to, or how well black children should perform in schools.

Conclusion

This chapter has examined two small parent-centred groups, examples of parental collective action in relation to education. I have argued that the campaigning group, PIE, worked effectively within a narrow agenda focusing on the popular rallying cry of an increase in funds to education. The group's work remained therefore almost entirely within the category of conventional pressure group lobbying, and it did not fulfil the grandiose claims made for NSMs and their ability to affect cultural transformation. But neither was the group as insular or conservative as the suburban social movements described by Ian Taylor. In its rhetoric and public activities PIE sought to co-opt all parents to its campaign in defence of state education.

Liberal individualism is also – and to a greater extent – an incomplete explanation for locating the work of ACES. Following the analysis of Heidi Mirza, I have argued that this group of African/Caribbean women have created a space for themselves and others in which they can share concerns, pool their resources and gain support and strength in engaging with a white-dominated education system. The women are attempting, with few resources and limited time, to articulate publicly a different set of assumptions and expectations about black children from those they feel currently hold sway within the education system, and to create the conditions in which their children and those of others can succeed.

Both groups propagate a notion of active citizenship. Bryan Turner's (1990) typology of four political contexts for the institutionalization or creation of citizenship rights draws on combinations of a public/private division and a passive/active distinction. He locates the development of English citizenship within the passive/public cell. 'Passive democracy recognises the legitimate function of representative institutions, the courts and the welfare system, but there is no established tradition of struggles for citizenship rights' (p.200). This characterization broadly reflects the generally passive nature of the turn-of-the century polity in England. By this reading, groups such as PIE and ACES are valuable for challenging the inevitability of public passivity.

However, both PIE and ACES activists are drawn mainly from professional middle class groupings, particularly those involved in the 'caring professions'. This professional middle class orientation affects the way in which the groups operate: the mechanisms they set up (e.g. PIE's relatively formal structures), their orientation (e.g. PIE's privileging of the knowledge of professional educators), and the strategies they choose to promote (e.g. ACES' dissemination of the appropriate parental role as that of 'critical friend'). The 'subject positions' (Apple 1996) which the groups made available for parents were limited in their appeal to those who have the knowledge and confidence, the existing cultural capital, to allow them to consider such an engagement with the education system. The challenge therefore is to identify ways in which currently disenfranchised groups can share the sense of capacity, of capability for agency that the PIE and ACES parents for the most part possessed; to identify participative strategies that are rooted in people's immediate experience and realities that will allow more parents to feel that collective action is a useful and available strategy. Both groups help, in a modest way, to create an animated and dynamic civil society. But without a focus on those people they do not reach, it will remain a civil society which is only open to and enjoyed by a few.

Notes

1 In some collaborative work which I undertook with the Advisory Centre for Education (a parental advice centre and information point) in 1996, we identified a range of local groups organizing around special educational issues.
2 Urry also notes the diverse lifestyle and politics of the service-class group taken as a whole.
3 Men were not excluded from the group, but none had ever consistently attended.
4 A collection edited by Lyman (1995) tries to plot some of the differences between the two contexts, and one by della Porta and Diani (1999) claims to synthesize the differences in orientation.
5 For an opposing view, see Eyerman and Jamison (1991), who reserve the designation 'social movement' for large-scale phenomena which 'touch basic tensions in society' (p. 56).
6 Taylor may rather overstate the case here; there is work looking at conservative social movements, e.g. Sommerville (1997), and other work referenced here earlier.
7 In the East River group particularly, existing relationships and friendships had been important to the formation of the group and contributed to its maintenance. This also had the effect of increasing the group's homogeneity.

8 The label is our own, although the group reacted favourably to the idea when it was fed back to them in a case study report.

9 'The raregroove scene developed in London in the early 1980s at warehouse parties and on pirate soul radio stations . . . Raregroove music, then, is an eclectic mix of black musical genres . . . funk and early rap which reflect urban experiences, issues and black consciousness' (Bakare-Yusuf 1997: 84).

CHAPTER SIX

An alienating system?
With Simon Warren

Introduction

The preceding chapters of this book focus on the field of education to consider ways in which formal citizenship rights can be transformed into new forms of citizenship engagement and interaction, through the development of opportunities to encourage lay participation and agency, and drawing on forms of parental activity and mobilization that exist outside any one school. In this chapter we shift the focus somewhat. The subject of this chapter is refugee and asylum-seeking families who cannot take for granted formal citizenship rights. The emphasis also moves back to the school system, and the study of parent–teacher relationships within schools. Many of the same themes persist however: the difficulties surrounding lay participation, professional notions of appropriate parental roles in relation to schooling, and the constraints under which professionals operate.

This chapter draws on data collected on a small-scale qualitative project which focused on links between refugee families and the primary schools their children attended.[1] It focused in particular on school responses to refugee populations. In this chapter we endeavour to contextualise the experiences of refugee children in relation to schools by briefly considering the impact of 'survival issues' (e.g. status, housing, benefits) on their families' lives. Second, we focus on home–school relations, and argue that the way in which a school (and we highlight in particular the role of the headteacher) defines a balance between its academic and pastoral priorities and responsibilities helps to shape the nature of home–school interaction. We conclude by suggesting that relationships between refugee parents and families reveal and reflect absences and distances which exist between many marginalized families and schools.

The research

There is relatively little information on the educational experiences of refugee children once they have arrived in the UK. Quantitative information collected by the Home Office relates solely to the asylum process, and while several local education authorities (LEAs) in London collect data concerning the distribution of refugee children among their schools, these are very much local, ad hoc initiatives. The nature of the available database is in itself revealing of the overriding concern to categorize and survey refugee movements with a view to control (an example of Foucault's analysis of the state's desire to categorize, group, segregate and control; Richmond 1994). Most of the existing literature on settlement is concerned, not with education, but with refugee families' access to and experience of health, welfare and housing services (e.g. Balloch 1993; Gammel *et al.* 1993; Bloch 1999). The nature of links between race, ethnicity and educational progress and achievement has been the subject of several recent government-sponsored reports in the UK (e.g. Gillborn and Gipps 1996; Blair *et al.* 1998; Ofsted 1999), although the experiences of refugee pupils and families are largely absent. We have tried in a small way to rectify this in the research reported here.

During 1997–8, we worked with four case study primary schools in two inner urban areas, which, between them, had a range of experience of having refugee pupils and addressing their specific circumstances. We conducted 71 semi-structured interviews (through interpreters where appropriate) with refugee parents, teachers in the schools, workers employed by local education authorities specifically to support refugee children, refugee community activists and local authority officials. Thirty-three refugee parents from Bosnia, Kosovo, Somalia, Iraq, Iran, Sudan, and the Congo participated in the study. They came from a variety of backgrounds and had different experiences of flight from their home countries to settle in the UK. They included parents who had been here for six or seven years and those who had been here a few months. Not all of the parents we talked with shared exactly the same views or confronted the same problems. However, despite the heterogeneity of this group of respondents, there was a great deal of similarity in their experiences of the education system, and in the aspects they identified as problematic. We were expecting more differences than we actually met. Differences of view may possibly have emerged if we had been able to interview larger numbers and also to conduct a higher number of repeat interviews with respondents (see, e.g., Bloch 1999).

We also observed parent–teacher meetings in school and analysed relevant school and local authority documents. The observations of parent–teacher interactions proved an effective method of gathering data on relationships and also triangulating data gathered through interviews (see Chapter 2 for more information on methodology, for the same broad approach was applied in both projects). For reasons of space, this chapter describes two of the four sample schools, referred to here as Freshfields and Greenford Schools (for details of the other two schools which we called St Peter's and Southcote Grange, see Vincent and Warren 1998). Freshfields and Greenford are in a

London local authority which we are calling Northway. Northway is a small, densely populated Labour-controlled London authority. During the 1990s it witnessed a tenfold increase in the number of refugee children in the schools, the total standing at 1700 in 1997 (report to Education Committee, September 1998). The demand on its resources, especially housing and hostel accommodation, is severe, and during 1998 the authority was forced to employ a former school building as a temporary emergency shelter. In the field of education Northway funded a refugee support team whose workers had been supporting both schools mentioned here. Statistics were kept concerning the distribution of refugee children throughout the borough, and there were plans to try and improve the collation of information concerning the achievement of refugee pupils as a group.

Migration to the UK

Before going on to discuss the research findings in more detail, we wish to draw attention to the wider issues of migration, displaced populations, reception procedures adopted by Western states, and the process of settlement. Western European nation states share with other affluent countries a so-called 'pragmatic' approach to immigration (Richmond 1994), which reflects the existing balance of political and economic power. Although attempts are made to mitigate the situations within countries from where refugees are or might soon be flowing, the emphasis is on 'state security . . . translating into a preoccupation with border control' (Richmond 1994: 221; also Marfleet 1996; D. Taylor 1996: 20). This approach in Europe is deeply inflected with a Eurocentric body of thought, drawing on images and ideas dating back to the time of European imperialism and the expansion of repertoires of racism (Gabriel 1994). The black 'other' becomes an 'absent presence' (Apple 1999) in policy.

Defining terms

In this chapter, the term 'refugee' is used to include both asylum seekers and those who have already been granted refugee status. A refugee is someone who has left his or her home country 'owing to a well-founded fear of being persecuted for reasons of race, religion, nationality, membership of a particular social group or particular political opinion' (Article 1 of the 1951 UN Geneva Convention).[2] With increasing levels of migration worldwide at the turn of the century, it is difficult to generalize about particular groups. However, the primary characteristic of a refugee is the involuntary nature of flight. It is possible to draw a rough distinction between migrants, who are *drawn to* a country, and refugees, who are *driven from* their own country: 'Immigrants are deemed to be propelled by hope to better their life whereas refugees are trying to rebuild some part of what they have lost' (Joly 1996: 144):

Refugees had to leave as a result of factors which in the last analysis were not primarily economic and they did not make a decision with primarily positive connotations. What all refugees have in common is that they left their country of origin because a dramatic change jeopardised the life they were leading, although this change need not always be sudden. If things had continued as before the change, they would have stayed. Their move also involves a collective character. In that, they differ from so-called economic migrants as the latter have an individual project to change their life circumstances, to improve them.

(Joly 1996: 149)

However, we would add to Joly's definition the observation that the term 'economic migrant' is one much used by UK government spokespersons to justify refusing entry to those not defined as 'genuine' refugees. Yet it is of course possible to be driven from a country by economic causes which can result in the disappearance of job and livelihood.[3]

Daniele Joly also goes on to argue that refugee attitudes towards settlement are influenced by their relationship to their country of origin and whether they wish or hope to return. Many of the parents we spoke to did indeed have what we termed a *project of return* (see also Marfleet 1996). This was an important factor, influencing their attitude towards their children's schooling, and injecting it with a sense of urgency. They saw it as crucial that their children be well-educated in order to help rebuild countries shattered by civil war or suffering oppressive regimes.

The context of settlement

Immigration legislation: fortress Europe

Immigration legislation has without doubt been getting more limited and punitive since the 1980s, leading to a 'culture of restrictionism'. This phenomenon is observable in many Western states; as borders within Europe slowly dissolve, the border around Europe hardens and solidifies (Richmond 1994; Joly 1996). In the UK, the 1993 Asylum and Immigration (Appeals) Act and the 1996 Asylum and Immigration Act have reduced the rights of asylum seekers to be housed in permanent local authority housing and reduced their rights to welfare benefits. *iNexile*, the magazine produced by the voluntary organization, the Refugee Council, comments that 'over the past two years the system of support for asylum seekers arriving in the UK has descended into chaos' (Refugee Council 1998a).

Refugees are generally drawn to settle in large cities with more heterogeneous populations, more chances of work and temporary accommodation. In the UK this translates into London and over 80 per cent of the refugee population in the UK have settled there. This means that most inner London schools and other welfare agencies have some experience of meeting the needs, if not specifically of refugees, of bilingual families.[4] For this reason, it is of particular concern that the newest piece of restrictive legislation, the 1999 Immigration and Asylum Act, emanating this time from a Labour government, institutes a system of 'no choice' housing which will disperse refugees outside London. The Act also removes asylum seekers from the mainstream benefit system, establishing a new agency (the National Asylum Support Service) to run a national 'safety net' programme of support in kind (i.e. cashless), worth about 70 per cent of Income Support.[5] Concerns have been voiced about the impracticality of vouchers and the way in which they mark out and stigmatize their recipients. The overarching ideology of the policy as a whole, running though proposals for support, detention and decision making, remains deterrence, or as *iNexile* put it, 'deterrence through destitution' (Refugee Council 1998b: 13). For those existing asylum seekers, the Labour government has put some measures in place to deal with the backlog of cases awaiting decisions, but this is proving a very slow process. For many, their future remains uncertain:

> The immediate problem a refugee faces is his status. Am I accepted here or am I not accepted here? That is the basis, everything will flow from that, because if you are thinking everyday, 'Will I be thrown out?', you won't do anything at all.
>   (Northway community group worker; see also Bloch 1999)

The 'bogus' refugee
The concern of affluent nations to protect and conserve their resources means that those seeking to make a claim on them have to be subjected to stringent procedures to assess their worthiness. This task is less problematic if all claimants are positioned as potentially unworthy. Indeed, individual moral unworthiness is not the only criterion used; refugees are also positioned as a danger to security (see also European Parliament 1990; Gabriel 1994; Richmond 1994). This can be personal security with stories of criminal asylum seekers (Refugee Council 1999a) as well as the security of the nation state or collection of nation states. Gabriel (1994) notes that the European Community (EC) group which deals with issues of immigration is known as the 'Trevi group, an acronym which stands for "terrorism, radicalism, extremism and violence"' (p.162).

The figure of the 'bogus' refugee, in the UK simply to exploit the benefit system, has become, to use Cohen's (1980) term, a powerful 'folk devil'. The debate on asylum and immigration is generally conducted in terms of numbers and cost, while references to the moral obligations of the host country are marginalized. During the research period (1997–8) there were a number of instances of hostile coverage of refugees in both London local and national press (see also Refugee Council 1998c, 1999c). Even in the supposedly liberal environment of local government in Northway, and moreover within a team charged with responsibility for policy making on issues involving refugees, the stereotypes appear to have infiltrated the collective consciousness:

> The discussions are frequently interspersed with jokes, you know, a sort of flippant approach, which kind of, what shall I say? . . . kind of reveals the degree of scepticism that's working around whether or not these are real refugees or real asylum seekers . . . It comes out as well with comments

like refugees seen to be using mobile phones, giving the impression that that's not appropriate, those sort of ... You get anecdotal evidence of stories about refugees being involved in business and trading, etc., attempting to claim benefits ... There isn't any kind of discussion about what, if that is happening, why it's happening, and there aren't any discussions about understanding behaviour.

(Northway employee and member of policy-making team)

Welfare provision – housing and local government

Recent legislation[6] has restricted refugee access to public *housing*, although local authorities still have a responsibility to house families with children. As a result many families find themselves in a series of temporary accommodations. Homeless families face difficulties finding school places, maintaining the children's regular attendance, and participating in the life of the school. Lack of space and facilities adds to the stress families are already under in trying to make a new life, and the academic progress of these children may suffer through frequent disruption. Schools also face considerable demands in terms of settling new children who may then move on quickly and without warning (Power *et al.* 1995, 1998). Yet statistics on pupil mobility are not widely gathered, so its effects are overlooked (Dobson 1998). One case study school, St Peter's, was close to a large bed and breakfast hostel and we spoke to five of the families living there who had children at the school. We include here a quotation from an interview with three of those families, all Kosovo Albanians who are speaking through an interpreter.

They think that one of the reasons why the children are not doing such good is because of the conditions they are living in. They are not very good, especially for the children. They see that even in their [rooms] they don't have any sort of desks where the children can do their work or read something or do any drawings so maybe that is one problem ... Then the problem is if they bring [homework] home, they haven't got good conditions.

(Interpreter)

Local government in the UK underwent a fundamental reorganization during the 1990s. Two common features of that reorganization have been a decline in funding from central government and constraints on ability to raise local taxes, and a concomitant emphasis on value for money. This clearly impacts on the money available for supporting nascent community groups, as one Northway employee describes:

Most of the [refugee] groups have come into the borough in the last six years I would say, and that has also coincided with the timing of major cuts to all the borough's services. That is a very difficult time to come in and try and put your roots down ... There was some indication that there might be more council money [for community groups] but it's not proved to be the case. I suppose I really did think that some of [the refugee communities], by this point, would have established themselves and located themselves in offices . . . have their own space and a working environment. It's almost not the case as I am sure you have seen. They really are struggling . . . in what feels like a very crisis-ridden environment in the borough.

(Northway refugee support worker)

It is an obvious point, but one worth restating here, that marginalized groups such as refugee groups clearly face extra difficulties in mobilizing themselves. The more recent the rate of community arrivals, the bigger the problems. New arrivals are likely to have little spare money or time, or the knowledge of a variety of systems – the assets which allowed ACES and PIE to establish themselves (see Chapter 5).

Another feature of local government in the 1990s was the introduction of values and practices imported from the private sector to accompany the wholescale restructuring of the sector. The aim has been to revolutionize what was commonly portrayed as local government's inefficiency, bureaucracy, wastefulness and partisanship. The introduction of market forces into service delivery, combined with reduced public sector funding in the late 1980s and early 1990s, was intended to foster efficiency, value for money, and direct accountability to customers (Cochrane 1993; Radnor *et al.* 1996). This ideology, combined with the general marginalization of the claims of refugees outlined earlier, has resulted in a situation where other priorities take precedence over a desire to respond to all those in need:

The agenda now is, runs right through the Council, is value for money and efficiency and high-quality services, and that's not a bad thing. I think we'd all support that and would not support waste anywhere, but there is also a cautiousness . . . [The social services department] would see their prime function as protecting the public purse and ensuring that claims that are made against it come from genuine need . . . There's a climate, the sort of climate which is driven by financial constraints, rather than personally you're looking at best meeting the needs first, and this council, I can see why they've got to be like that, in the sense that they have to control the limited funding they've got, but I get the impression that there's a greater acceptance of hype around bogus refugees . . . [The council policy group on refugees] are still individuals who are genuine, they're there, in that team, because they're interested in the work and want to do the best . . . but I can see that it hasn't got the drive to protect the interests of refugees as the first priority, you know, it's to protect the public purse.

(Northway employee)

This situation was not, of course, unique to Northway and the authority in comparison to other urban authorities was and remains active and supportive in this area.

The contextualization of education policy: the education market
The education system cannot be studied in isolation from the political, economic and social context. We have already mentioned the developments in

immigration, welfare and housing policy which have affected the reception and settlement of refugee families. It now remains to trace the effect of the competitive market place in education which has developed over the last decade, and in which schools now operate, on pupils, such as refugee pupils, deemed to have additional educational needs.

The competitive environment in which schools now exist does not reward them for attracting pupils newly arrived in the UK. Such students are often expensive in terms of additional provision, and may not provide an instant payback in terms of results. These children, who may speak little English, are unlikely to score highly on standardized tests, at least at first. Two of the four case study schools in particular realized that the dominant focus on output measures had a detrimental effect on their positions in the local 'league tables' (ranking schools via their national test results), and that the process did not reflect the progression and achievement of pupils during their time at school, which was often quite dramatic. Therefore there was strong support from the headteachers of the case study schools for 'value-added' measures which would show how pupils had improved while they had been at a particular school, rather than simply measuring their performance when they left. However, in this regard, the DfEE sounded a positive note when it announced in July 2000 that newly arrived children from overseas, for whom English is not a first language, will not have their test results included in school league table results for a two year period.

As funding is largely pupil-led, all schools are under pressure to attract as many pupils as possible. The need to increase school numbers, of course, conflicts with the ability of the school to serve a transient homeless population. If a school is full, it will not be able to take in pupils who arrive without warning mid-term. Thus refugee pupils tend to be clustered in less popular (and therefore poorer) inner city schools. Concern about the effects of a competitive, quasi-market structure on other groups within the pupil population have also been expressed (see for example, Gillborn and Youdell 1999 on achievement and ethnicity; Slee *et al.* 1998 and Corbett 1999 on special needs pupils and discourses of inclusion).

Home and school – worlds apart?

As was noted in Chapter 1, it has become commonplace to talk of parent–teacher 'partnership'. Yet despite the frequency with which this concept is employed, its manifestation in practice often differs from the rhetorical support for 'partnership'. Indeed, it has been claimed that relationships between parents, particularly working class and some minority ethnic parents, and education professionals are marked not by the equality which the term 'partnership' suggests, but rather by an imbalance of power in favour of the professionals (e.g. Lareau 1989; Vincent 1996; Vincent and Tomlinson 1997; Reay 1998). One of our respondents described home–school relations in the following way:

It's about power and who has the power and how much a parent is really going to be given an opportunity to really know about that, and is there space for change there, and could you think about teaching in a slightly different way at least initially . . ? How much can one shift, what is shiftable and what isn't. But of course, it's very difficult in schools at the minute because they are tied down with other things.

(Northway refugee support worker)

Most teachers of course do not see themselves as particularly powerful individuals,[7] although their professional knowledge and their location within an institution can give them a position which some parents find intimidating. This introduces the need for a view of power which sees it as having diverse sources and being heterogeneous in its manifestations. Iris Marion Young cites Foucault as suggesting that we should look beyond an understanding of power as dichotomous in being, a model of dominant and subordinate groups, and instead emphasize its dispersal through the action of many individuals who are 'simply doing their jobs or living their lives, and . . . do not understand themselves as agents of oppression' (Young 1990: 42, also Todd and Higgins 1998).

Social class has been posited as a key variable (often *the* key variable) in determining parents' relationships with teachers (e.g. Lareau 1989; Vincent 1996; Reay 1998). Working class parents are generally understood to have little effective voice in relation to a school and to be positioned by teachers as in need of tutelage concerning appropriate forms of parenting and interaction with the school (Martin and Vincent 1999). In contrast, there have been instances of middle class parents strongly influencing the organization of schools as well as teachers' pedagogic styles and curriculum content (see, e.g., Apple 1996; Reay 1998; Chapters 1 and 2). However, the home–school relationship will depend not only upon the range of social, cultural and material resources open to parents and their willingness to deploy them in seeking to make the school act in a particular way, but also the micro-political processes, interests and relationships which shape the school's responses. Indeed, refugee parents do not fit neatly into the working class/middle class dichotomy. Many come from middle class backgrounds in their countries of origin, but the easy fit between their family 'habitus' (dispositions, assumptions and expectations) and that of the school, usually assumed to exist between the homes of professional middle class groups and schools, is lacking. To quote Gewirtz *et al.* (1995), their cultural capital is in the 'wrong currency', something the parents we spoke to felt keenly. They all commented on the differences between the English education system and that pertaining in their countries of origin. The most commonly identified points of difference were the style of learning encouraged in primary schools (aimed at developing independence in the pupil and with less reliance on texts than some formal and more traditional systems) and the nature of adult–child relationships. Both were seen as more relaxed and less formal than parents were used to. While disapproval of these changes was by no means universal, their existence did mean that 'the English system' differed radically from, as one parent said, what was 'normal'. This required them to negotiate between systems, changing their ideas, assumptions and expectations quite dramatically.

Institutional cultures

Our data indicate marked differentiation between the case study schools in terms of their approach to home–school relations in general. Clearly the priorities identified by schools help to shape their ethos, what they stand for, their mission.[8] Our discussions with refugee parents and teachers led us to become particularly interested in the ways in which schools defined the boundaries between themselves and surrounding communities and, particularly, how teachers understood the balance between pastoral care and academic care. In Rutter and Jones (1998), Crispin Jones asks what we consider to be a key question:

> And one question remains uninvestigated: what is the effect of the balance that each school places on pastoral and academic issues, however crudely defined? Does the time . . . put into pastoral care detract from academic care and subsequent academic performance and vice versa?
>
> (Jones 1998: 179)

We can define pastoral care as a concern with the non-academic progress of children, which is likely to be heavily influenced by their family circumstances. Schools can see pastoral care and academic care as potentially in tension with one another or in support of one another. To put it another way, and to paraphrase one of our respondents, should knowledge about the child's background be seen as background knowledge, or is having and deploying such information central to the educational project? Schools' decisions on this issue will influence their approach to home–school relations, and in particular the nature of the boundaries they maintain between home and school. However, we do not wish to be understood as suggesting a simplistic dichotomy between 'achieving' schools and 'caring' schools (Power *et al.* 1995; see also McClure and Lindle 1997). Such a divide would be far too crude. Rather, as we noted earlier, it is a matter of how home–school relations are understood. What does the school see as the purpose of parental involvement, of community links? To what extent, if at all, would a school choose to get involved with other aspects of the child's life outside school? A school could focus on a child's educational progress, by abstracting the child as far as possible from other elements of his/her life. A school with more permeable home–school boundaries may want to learn as much as possible about a child's life, seeing that as affecting the child's education.

Role of the headteacher

Our point here is that schools find their own answers to these questions, their own settlements. The nature of that settlement, what it looks like, is greatly influenced by the values and priorities of headteachers. Research on the values and ethics of the market in education (Gewirtz *et al.* 1995; Grace 1995, 1997) suggests changing discourses and practices of leadership as heads seek new settlements which reflect the changing constraints and opportunities in managing a school at the turn of the century. Gewirtz *et al.* (1995) identify a number of overlapping characteristics which describe a move away from older forms and styles of leadership based on a public service ethos and traditional professional values (a state they refer to as 'bureau professionalism' or 'welfarism') to those based on the need to respond to and survive within a market-driven climate (which they refer to as 'managerialism'). Gerald Hanlon (1998) describes a similar division opening up in many different areas of professional work, between what he describes as 'social service' and 'commercialized' versions of professionalism. He suggests struggles to achieve validation for the two competing understandings of professionalism have split what were previously relatively homogeneous professions. We suggest below that some of the tensions he describes are played out in the differing headship styles of Freshfields and Greenford headteachers.

Hanlon, Gewirtz and her colleagues, Grace and other commentators (e.g. Clarke and Newman 1992; Yeatman 1993; Whitty *et al.* 1998) are describing a trend towards management practices associated with the private sector which are taking centre stage in education. This has led to the development of features such as a reliance on quantifiable output measures and performance targets; the devolution of management control; the development of new reporting, monitoring and accountability mechanisms (in the case of education, Ofsted, the national inspectorate and the national tests fulfil this function); the imitation of certain private sector management practices such as the use of short-term labour contracts;[9] and the development of corporate plans, performance agreements and mission statements (Boston 1991):

> The New Management discourse in education emphasises the instrumental purposes of schooling – raising standards and performance as measured by examination results, levels of attendance and school leaver destinations, and is frequently articulated within a lexicon of enterprise, excellence, quality and effectiveness.
>
> (Gewirtz and Ball in press: 10)

Similarly, Hanlon (1998) defines commercialized professionalism as stressing three factors: the technical ability to practise in the professions, managerial ability and financial skills, and entrepreneurial ability.

While there is some measure of agreement among commentators on the features of managerialism, it is harder to identify with the same degree of accuracy what may be being left behind, apparently sacrificed to the need to maintain competitive advantage. Hanlon suggests social service professionalism is centred around the principle of providing a service on the basis of need rather than ability to pay. However, a corollary of this is that professionals positioned themselves as experts providing solutions to a passive and largely ignorant population (Hanlon 1998: 50). In specific reference to education, Gewirtz and Ball (in press) argue that what they refer to as 'bureau-professionalism' or 'welfarism' embraces a range of values and practices. Some of these have attained central status within the profession, become 'condensation symbols' (Edelman 1964). That is, they are accepted as a 'good thing' even though they remain difficult to define, and may mean different things to different people. Examples of such concepts include 'valuing all children equally', a 'caring' ethos. Other values which can be associated with 'welfarism' but have not attained widespread acceptance and usage, even before the advent of managerialism,[10] include anti-racism and community and parental involvement in education. With regard to the latter, Stephen Ball (1997) argues that managerialism articulates with, and feeds off, existing bureaucratic values, the most salient feature of which in this case is its ambivalence towards the involvement of parents. Similarly Gerald Grace (1997) notes that the autonomous traditions of school leadership, and trends towards professional insularity, resulted in often defensive reactions to initiatives to widen decision-making powers to include parent and community involvement.

It has been suggested that, given these two competing 'languages', managerialism and welfarism, heads in the 1990s are *bilingual* – not a term of our own invention (Clarke and Newman 1992), but a particularly appropriate one for this project. Clarke and Newman use the term to refer to heads who learn to speak the new language of management while retaining some values and priorities characteristic of their role as educators. Headteachers therefore use (at least) two languages to address their several concerns. Indeed, Ball and Gewirtz (1997a) suggest that they are multilingual, moving between an 'older' language of public service and several 'newer' languages of school management: the language of the market (e.g. PR, marketing), financial management (e.g. the budget, plant management), organizational management (e.g. corporate culture, human resources) and the curriculum (e.g. programmes of study, achievement levels). The incursion of the newer language(s) inflects the old, giving rise to a different set of priorities and nuances. Movement between the different registers can offer heads some scope to become 'active accommodators' (see Chapter 3).

The balance, the accommodation, the degree of interpenetration between welfarist and managerial languages may be influenced by the headteacher's own values and beliefs, and the particular situation in which a school is in, its recent history, the head's relationships with and perceptions of the pupil and parent body, the teaching staff, the local authority and the governors. As Gerald Grace notes, 'the established cultural practices and the old leadership settlements are breaking up and new patterns are emerging' (1997: 314). Heads may also deploy different languages in different contexts and situations. The way they present their priorities, the spin and emphasis they put on their words, may vary depending on who the listener is. What we are suggesting therefore is that the particular nature and extent of the head's bilingualism will affect the way he/she defines 'appropriate' home–school relations. We now seek to illustrate our arguments with reference to Greenford and Freshfields schools, both in Northway LEA.

Greenford Primary School

Greenford School, with 430 pupils, serves a large housing estate in an area with a reputation for racial tension. The school expanded rapidly during the 1990s as Bangladeshi families moved into the area. Over half the school's pupils are of Bangladeshi origin and the school has worked hard to provide a secure environment for the pupils. The numbers of refugee children have grown rapidly, and the headteacher (a white man who had been in post eight years) attested to the school's struggle to switch its self-image from one of a school which had one dominant minority ethnic group to one with a more varied ethnic population. In 1998 the school had a high rate of pupil mobility (approximately 25 per cent).

To return to the relationship identified by Crispin Jones between the academic and the pastoral, the headteacher at Greenford suggested that the relationship was a tense one. He described how in the past, at his school, the academic had been sacrificed to the pastoral, and spoke of his strong reaction against what he saw as an old, outdated and ineffective notion of welfarism in education. In his view, teachers' interest in the lives of their pupils, their concern to encourage their personal and social development, had been in danger of exceeding their focus on raising achievement. As such it had been a complacent culture:

> Lots of teachers liked to come to Greenford because it was a multicultural school, and they felt they would like to be the guardians of multicultural education, yes? . . . One of the areas I had to shift – and it took me quite some time to shift it – was the issue that teachers aren't here to teach. You respect, you have knowledge of other cultures or children you are working with, but at the end of the day, achievement is what we're after. Quite a number of people left within the first few years . . . I took away a kind of power base [from those teachers who left]. How can I put it? It's very difficult to describe it in a way – but there was a culture in the school, held by some people, that was not very helpful to education basically. It was helpful in supporting families maybe, but it wasn't particularly helpful in terms of teaching children to read and write and to become academically successful. We have shifted that culture now by careful appointment of staff. You know, we are now looking at a team of people who, by and large, have that commitment to achievement . . . I think whatever the intake, our driving goal is achievement. You know, how we get there, we obviously then have to take into account the background of our pupils, and whatever, but that's the goal – to continue to raise achievement[11]. . . . I have to make it very clear to teachers that you are not social workers . . . by being clear of your role then you are of most benefit to all the children in your class . . . When I came here, there was a certain group of teachers, children had to learn to read by osmosis and things like this. Forget it; you want those children to have the tools to be able to learn as quickly as possible because that is going to help them. That ethos has changed and I think it's changed

nationally; anyway it's not just this school. But that was a big sea change; I felt that we really felt that teaching and learning is our job and Ofsted has put it into perspective in that sense.

(Headteacher, Greenford)

However, as the headteacher also pointed out, it is not feasible entirely to separate the academic development of a child from other factors influencing his/her total development. Talking about parents' evenings, Greenford's head described the incursion of personal, social, cultural and financial family matters into the school:

Parents get as long as they want really, but it's basically a 15/20 minute slot, and often, like in all parental consultations, what comes up is more than just so and so is getting on very well. You know, domestic issues come up, social issues come up, and during that fortnight, I get an awful lot of referrals from teachers about things that are happening . . . Almost all parents attend. Those who don't attend, we harass and telephone to get them into school because we think it's [contact with the family] very important.

Links with parents remained an important part of Greenford's concerns. Parent–teacher consultations were firmly focused on informing the parent of the child's strengths and weaknesses to date, and enlisting parental support in helping the child to progress. Thus parent–teacher contact was seen as part of the strategy to raise achievement, rather than an end in itself: 'Better communication helps achievement, you know; it's one of those things that does feed into achievement' (headteacher).

As we said earlier, heads can switch between the two 'languages' of welfarism and managerialism. The concern for the 'whole' child, a concern with the child's personal and social development, a concept more clearly associated with welfarism than managerialism, was retained by Greenford's headteacher. For example, he made a point of visiting the playground every day, saying,

It's my opportunity to look around the edges of the playground to see what's not happening, as opposed to what's happening in the middle of the playground . . . [To find a way] whereby those children [on the periphery] do become involved, with a little skulduggery, sort of setting up situations to some extent, to give those children support in the playground, because the playground can be a very, very lonely place if you speak no English, if you are worried, apprehensive, nervous or whatever.

Greenford's headteacher had defined the school's role with clarity. The school's task was to concentrate on success in the one major area of improving teaching and learning, and this strategy appeared to be working in terms of test scores. Greenford's 1997 scores for the achievement of 11-year-olds were above national and local averages in maths and science and showed a considerable improvement on previous years' results. Staff had a coherent remit and did not dissipate their energies trying to be all things to the pupils.

Constructing a consensus that excludes or minimizes other values is an identifiable aspect of what Willmott (1993) refers to as 'corporate culturism'. This has the effect of reducing ambivalence and correspondingly personal insecurity as to what teachers should be doing:

> One of the concerns is – and one we have got away from – is that, you know, we are not the housing benefit agency, we are not social services. Yes, we know where to send to, but we can't deal with it ourselves.
>
> (Headteacher, Greenford)

This last was an issue we asked heads about, the extent to which they felt able to get involved with the non-educational issues with which refugee families have to contend. Greenford's headteacher was often asked to write letters, particularly about housing, on behalf of families and would personally respond to requests, as well as referring parents on to other agencies.

The headteacher's bilingualism was strongly influenced by his perception of his school's recent past. He advocated an apparent narrowing of the school role to an almost exclusive focus on the task of raising achievement, as defined by test scores. Other concerns, and particularly the influence of often difficult family circumstances, were ruled out of court – something to be referred to, dealt with by, another agency. The child's happiness, the school creating and maintaining links with parents, were all means to the end of higher achievement. The headteacher at Greenford felt that this overriding emphasis on achievement would be welcomed by families with children at the school. The interviews we conducted with parents suggest that his assumption was correct. However, this symmetry in goals and aims was undermined by an asymmetry of view concerning how they should be achieved. It was difficult for parents from marginal and often pressurized situations to share in the school's educational project. The current arrangements for contact and communication were not, parents suggested, sufficient for them to access the school curriculum, teacher talk, and teaching and learning styles in a way that would allow them to become 'partners' with the school. This was expressed strongly by two groups of Somali parents:

> Every term the school needs to inform the Somali parents about the problems of their children, not waiting for parents' evening because there is this problem of language. It should be a more active way, of, how do you say, a policy, an active way of coming and meeting the needs of this community.
>
> (Interpreter)

> The breakdown is not because the Somali community lacks language but because the school is unwilling to contact, to come forward and to meet the needs of the community. [Another mother] is saying, 'I cannot communicate with the school, it should be the other way round, because the school has got the resources . . . We are not belonging to the mainstream, and the mainstream knows the system'.
>
> (Interpreter)

The school held two parents' meetings a year, which were arranged as a personal appointment with the class teacher. Those parents who did not attend were asked to come in at another time. However, interpreting arrangements were only made for the Bangladeshi population. It was assumed that other parents would bring someone with them who could speak English. In practice, as is common at many schools, this often meant that the children were used as interpreters.

The school had a worker from the local authority's refugee support team working at the school to develop closer home–school links. To this end she had organized coffee mornings for refugee parents. It was originally planned for teachers to attend these on a rotating basis. However, the responsibility slowly devolved to a relatively junior teacher who was the designated link with the authority worker. She explained the non-involvement of the other staff in the following terms:

> I think people at the school do think that parents are important and the relationships are very important, but at the end of the day you have got to do the National Curriculum and it's what you do in the classroom, that is your job.
>
> (Teacher, Greenford School)

We also gathered evidence that such discourses, seeing a school's pastoral role as in tension with its academic responsibilities, were being played out within the LEA. An administrator outlined this perception, describing it as being at odds with the approach taken by the authority's refugee support team:

> There's a perception that, how much of a myth it is and how much of a kind of element of truth might be in it, I'm not sure, but the [refugee support workers] ha[ve] tended to over-emphasize the welfare issues at the expense of the education issues. I think maybe within [the language support service], maybe within the [inspectorate and advisory body] there is a kind of automatic, or a tendency to resist consideration of welfare issues, because they see that that's welfare issues again, and [the refugee support teachers'] proper place is in schools, in classrooms, on achievement, not necessarily working with families . . . There have been complaints from headteachers about the balance not being right, and that there are teachers behaving like social workers . . . It's only in a few cases, and it's only because, it kind of mirrors the perceptions that exist in the department as well about the balance between work in schools and work outside schools.
>
> (Employee, Northway LEA)

A worker from the refugee support team described a similar attitude among teachers at another Northway school (not part of this project):

> [The staff were] slightly doubtful, a bit suspicious . . . just not really understanding why it would be so important to have a group of parents meet for coffee . . . 'How does that connect to the children? All this work

with parents is all very well, but we are interested in the children's education.'

This suggests that relationships with parents, any parents, are seen by some teachers as lying on the fringes of their rightful concerns, as having little immediate impact on a child's achievement. Under the pressure that ensues from frequent changes to schools' curriculum, pedagogy and procedures (the introduction of the literacy and numeracy hours and the special education Code of Practice for example), forging and maintaining relationships with parents are constantly downgraded in teachers' lists of priorities (although a historical consideration of home–school relationships suggests that this low priority is not entirely a result of the recent changes; Vincent 1996). Some parents have the will, confidence and capacity to forge relationships themselves, to maintain close home–school contact, and to oversee their children's academic and pastoral progress. Newly-arrived asylum-seeking parents have to overcome huge obstacles to demonstrate such agency, as they struggle with dislocation, foreign cultures and foreign systems, as well as pressing everyday survival needs.

Freshfields Primary School

Freshfields School, with 472 pupils, is housed in a Victorian three-storey building located in a generally affluent residential area. In 1998 the head-teacher, a woman of South Asian origin, had been in post two years. The school has undergone considerable demographic change over the past 20 years. In the late 1970s and early 1980s, the school's population was drawn from a more uniformly middle class population, which included bilingual children. That changed during the 1980s and the school now has a very mixed population in terms of social class as well as ethnicity. Many of the current pupils do not live in the immediate, prosperous locality.

Freshfields presented an example of a different balance between welfare and managerial values. The headteacher's language when describing the boundaries between home and school differed noticeably from her counter-part at Greenford. She presented a language of time, trust and building rela-tionships, and constructed her account of home–school relationships through the use of anecdotes about particular incidents and individuals:

> This Somali child that we had . . . he was constantly in trouble, constantly hitting out . . . What was useful was to call in mum and say to her, 'Look, I am not putting up with this behaviour. You need to do some-thing about it', but at a level for her to tell it as it is: 'Actually I can't begin to tell you what my life is like at the moment.' So although your expectation of the behaviour doesn't actually change, it has given you an in-road. I mean, I still see [the mother] regularly . . . That was the way into the family if you like. Now had that parent seen me as somebody who they came to and got told to take their child away, and I wasn't going to discuss it, etc., we would never have had that. . . . I think prob-

ably that is the thing I have learnt most is that you have to give people time, but you have also got to build up trust . . . I think that is the thing, it's that, time. I mean as far as I can see there are very few places that our parents, particularly our refugee parents, get time . . . other than school.

(Headteacher)

The headteacher's reasons for her approach were not linked to the school's history, as was the case at Greenford. One source of motivation was her own experiences, growing up as a child of Asian origin in a largely white environment, and like the refugee families in her school, having to negotiate an overt 'otherness':

[We wish to promote] things like that [in school] you know – that kind of pride in their culture, that kind of understanding, that kind of confidence will make a whole lot of difference. They won't go into school wearing pink tights because they want to be white, like I did . . . You know I do it partly because of my own experience.

Freshfields' headteacher also wrote letters to, and liaised with, various bodies (e.g. housing authorities). It was difficult to tell from their general accounts whether there was an appreciable difference between the involvement of the heads at Greenford and Freshfields in either the number of cases or the depth to which they took their involvement. However, Freshfields' headteacher saw such work as clearly within the remit of the school:

I don't think there is anyone else to do it, Simon, I don't, and actually as long as they are still getting their entitlement to education, as long as a child is still achieving, this is only an extra, [which], for peanuts, we can provide.

Like the head at Greenford, Freshfields' headteacher employed both managerialist and welfarist languages, although the balance was different. She was acutely aware of the competitive environment in which schools now exist, and the need for Freshfields to maintain its appeal and thereby its pupil population vis-à-vis other schools. To this end, she adopted an 'entrepreneurial', proactive approach to obtaining resources for the school and to promoting the school locally, activities which could take up a considerable amount of her time.

The school hosted community language classes, which were regarded highly by bilingual parents. The establishment of these classes, in Bengali, Albanian and Somali, provided another example of the head's bilingualism. She saw the main purpose of these as fostering the children's sense of identity and self-confidence, but was also ready to employ the argument that the classes would improve the children's learning of English too, feeling that this was the more 'acceptable' defence (an example of 'active accommodation', see Chapter 3). In her efforts to convince the governing body to fund the language classes, she marshalled the support of parents and teachers, aware that she needed to address the governing body's concern that the classes should prove value for money, but that it was hard to provide the governors with the argument they really wanted – the promise of quantifiable payback:

What [the governors] wanted, I suppose, was for me to able to say, 'This project will cost us £4000. What is that £4000 going to give us in terms of results?' and unfortunately that is what it's like, isn't it?

(Headteacher)

At Freshfields the pastoral elements of the school's relationship with individual parents were fairly well developed. Some parent-respondents spoke very warmly of the personal support the school had offered them, and they responded by supporting the school. However, the interface between school and refugee parents was the remit of just a few staff, the head and the two EAL (English as an Additional Language) teachers. The role of the EAL staff in particular was an example of the 'key person syndrome', where responsibility for a particular issue is devolved to just one or two individuals who are charged with developing and holding the school's store of knowledge on the particular topic. In addition, the headteacher's personalized approach had disadvantages in that it created close relationships with a few individuals, and did not necessarily reach the wider parent body. Thus there were instances when individual refugee parents closely involved with the school were seen by staff as representatives, standing for the community to which they belonged.

To some extent, therefore, refugee parents as a group still had difficulty in accessing the school. We observed some parent–teacher meetings at Freshfields where parents were often quite passive, not asking many questions. To give just one example:

The class teacher said the child had a general weakness, a 'deficiency' with fine motor skills, which meant his handwriting was poor. She suggested ways in which the parents could help at home, giving the child things to do with his hands, not just handwriting practice. [Somali mother] says nothing but nods occasionally. Teacher comments that the child is 'good at everything else though', but doesn't go into much detail. Asks the mother, 'Is there anything else you want to ask me?' before moving off. Mother shakes her head and thanks the teacher.

(Fieldnotes, Freshfields)

It is worth making the point that this feature of parent–teacher contact is not something confined to refugee parents or to Freshfields School, as earlier research suggests there is often a vagueness at the heart of parent–teacher interaction over children's progress (Vincent 1996; Reay 1998; Walker 1998; MacLure and Walker 1999). A Kosovo Albanian mother at Freshfields made the same point, saying, 'they say, "oh, he's great." That's it.' She continued by saying that she found it difficult to ask too many questions in case staff thought 'she asks too much for her son or daughter'. Such parental reticence and diffidence, while by no means limited to refugee parents, is arguably compounded by their awareness of their marginal status, their 'otherness', as they attempt to operate in an unfamiliar system with unknown assumptions and rules of behaviour. One father, explaining his support for Freshfields

School's language classes, clearly described this sense of 'otherness' which he felt would stay, not only with him, but also with his children:

> I know a person needs identity and I know they will never speak English as an English person, however they command it. I don't want them to lose their mother tongue . . . [They will be] British Somalis. Because they are black, English are white, right? Anyone who comes from anywhere else . . . if they have been here 100 years or 200 years, they are still where they come from.
>
> (Somali father)

Conclusion

We have argued that the broader social, political and economic context in which aslyum-seeking families exist is enormously disabling. They are 'denizens', not citizens, excluded from the formal citizenship rights most of the population take for granted. They then enter a school system which, by and large, caters for a stable, monolingual population (Power *et al.* 1995). In some institutions few concessions are made to their disorientation. Traditionally the 'real' work of schools has been seen as the teaching of the formal curriculum with minimal interaction with the pupils' homes. The current emphasis on school improvement means that schools are encouraged to co-opt parental support. However, this too allows parents little opportunity or autonomy to act as equal partners with the school. From a parental perspective, schools can seem impermeable and inaccessible (Vincent and Martin forthcoming). We suggest that the incursion of managerialist practices into education serves to emphasize the performance and achievement of disembodied pupils as measured by national tests. This directs schools to focus on the delivery of the curriculum and minimize other concerns, such as pastoral issues. Yet we believe that the relationship between the academic and the pastoral is worth overt and explicit consideration by schools. The balance between the two helps shape a school's ethos and practice and provides the context in which pupils achieve. The nature and scope of home–school interaction clearly reflects the relationship between the two. The two case studies, Greenford and Freshfields Schools, are two examples of the different balances struck. At Greenford, the headteacher took the view that the particular emphasis upon the pastoral which had previously been a feature of the school served to undermine the school's academic role. At Freshfields, the headteacher took a different position. She emphasized developing close links with families and finding out about their particular situations, although her more personalized, individualized approach did not reach all families. The refugee parents themselves wanted recognition of their circumstances and backgrounds. One example of this was the almost unanimous parental support for the inclusion of issues about migration and refugees into the mainstream curriculum. This would involve such issues as the forces compelling people into seeking asylum, as well as more general issues about loss, migration, change and belonging:

I think it's better if they have a chance to learn for everybody what is it brought him here or what brought her here and like why people have to come here because more I think, maybe I am wrong, but in most cases they think you are poor, and just came for the life here and that's what makes you angry . . . Most English people look at that problem [of the former Yugoslavia] and they don't know a thing about my culture, my country and what I was before and why I came here.

(Kosovo Albanian mother, spoken before the
outbreak of war in Kosovo)

She believes it's advantageous to make aware other children and even adults what 'refugee' means, because some of them believe that these people in all their lives have never supported their children, have never had homes, never worked for themselves . . . So it's advantageous to make them aware of what in the first place took them to become a refugee and that they had a life of their own before they came to Britain as a refugee.

(Somali mother speaking through an interpreter)

The telling them is good, and to explain not only by talk but by films. Yes I think it's good and I think this racism is less. To let the children know what the other children are suffering, you know that is very good . . . [The teachers] should tell them they moved from their country to this country to make themselves safe and sure for themselves, not for economy. Some countries about economy . . . but other countries they moved from the terrorism in their country, from the war, from the politics.

(Iraqi father)

The refugee parents participating in the study had questions and comments on both the way in which their children's schools currently operate, and the progress their own child was making. But many of those views and opinions remained hidden from the school, submerged in a web of conflicting concerns and competing priorities which may include, for example, housing, status, benefits and racism. Moreover, they may prioritize achievement, but most did so from a starting point of confusion and lack of knowledge about the UK education system; they spoke a different language and were met by an unfamiliar set of practices. An emphasis on the flexibility and accessibility of school systems and the permeability of home–school boundaries would, we suggest, help to address the concerns of refugee parents for the educational futures of their children.

Finally, we conclude that the findings from this project suggest that a study of the circumstances of refugee pupils in school is not simply a specialist exercise, of relevance to a relatively small group. On the contrary, it is suggested that the presence of refugee students 'reveal[s] problems that have always been there within the education system itself' (Jones and Rutter 1998: 2). We argue that the difficulties refugee families face in developing meaningful and positive contact and communication with schools may be obvious and tangible (not sharing a common language with the teachers for example), but in essence they also reflect the difficulties which many parents face, particularly those from black and minority ethnic groups. Currently other priorities are being piled on to primary schools in the UK and space and resources are limited. However we suggest that headteachers still retain a measure of autonomy and discretion, sufficient to enable them to encourage dialogue between the school and its different communities concerning the ways in which learning can be best facilitated.

Notes

1 This project was funded by the Nuffield Foundation and we are grateful to Dr Helen Quigley for her support.
2 Some refugees (programme refugees) are accepted as a group by the host country, others apply individually for asylum. While applying for refugee status, an individual is known as an asylum seeker. Asylum seekers in the UK can be granted refugee status and the right to permanent settlement, or Exceptional Leave to Remain (ELR, which gives them fewer rights), or have their case refused.
3 This process may be the product of a racialized division of labour which can force individuals and groups (e.g. Czech Romany) to seek migration as a solution to their marginalization.
4 Staff at one of the four case study schools, Southcote Grange School, located on the outskirts of a city in the Midlands, spoke of their recent uncertainty over how to respond to their first refugee pupils.
5 At the Third Reading of the Bill in June 1999, the government did introduce concessions to apply to asylum-seeking families which means that children in families will receive 100 per cent of Income Support (Refugee Council 1999b, 1999d). The new support system came into effect in April 2000 (Refugee Council 1999d)
6 Namely the Asylum and Immigration (Appeals) Act 1993, Asylum and Immigration Act 1996 and the Housing Act 1996.
7 Diane Reay gives an example of this when she refers to teachers in a predominantly working class school trying to reconcile mothers' demands 'for information, for extra resources and above all for educational outcomes that transformed their children's life chances' (1998: 124) with what they felt it was possible for them to achieve from within the classroom.
8 Of course, schools are far from autonomous in making these decisions and primary schools in the UK are currently experiencing a pronounced degree of regulation and central direction.
9 This is a particular feature of work for teachers with EAL (English as an Additional Language) responsibilities.
10 It is not being suggested that the postwar period in which welfarism was dominant was a 'golden age' of democracy and equality.
11 Gewirtz and Ball (in press) quote a new headteacher, hoping to turn around a 'failing school', adopting a similar position:

> In schools we care, but we need to express our deep caring through providing a learning environment and opportunities for work, so we need to take one step back from the indulgence of trying to solve all the students' problems. They have different backgrounds , but this is not a branch of the social services, and we are not social workers. Although we have to educate with a knowledge of students' backgrounds, we need to put work and education at the top of the agenda.
>
> (Gewirtz and Ball in press: 28)

CHAPTER SEVEN

Conclusion – including parents?

PCOs as counterpublics?

In this book I have explored the themes of citizenship, participation and collective action in relation to education. I have illustrated the way in which social class, gender and ethnicity affect differential rates and modes of participation and engagement. I have also emphasized attempts within the case study sites to engender agency, activity and confidence in those not normally heard in public discourse. However, such attempts are fragile, and it is this theme of fragility and partiality with which this concluding chapter engages.

In Chapter 1, I suggested that independent PCOs had the potential to act as 'counterpublics', 'protected enclaves' in the arena of education where different groups of parents could meet, discuss and determine their priorities, their agendas, their questioning of the 'way things are'. As a result some submerged lay voices could enter into a debate on education, contributing to a revitalized and expanded public sphere. Here I consider the evidence of the empirical chapters regarding this proposition.

Clearly not all the case study PCOs can be understood as 'counterpublics', although I would argue that they all made gestures towards that role. To varying degrees, they all provided a space for 'subordinate social groups to invent and circulate counterdiscourses, which in turn permit[ted] them to formulate oppositional interpretations of their identities, interests and needs' (Fraser 1997a: 81). 'Oppositional' is a rather blanket term to apply. Not all the parents' groups consistently and constantly gave voice to oppositional discourses; on the contrary, they were often conformist. The targets of their opposition, as the earlier chapters show, were varied – schools and teachers, the government, hegemonic discourses concerning mothering, a parent's role in relation to education, particular characterizations of black children and so on. It may be argued that in some of the examples given, such as the SEAC (Special Education Advice Centre) parents' groups (see Chapter 3) or the parent education group at Elliott School (see Chapter 4), the 'counterdiscourses' which emerge are too underdeveloped and incoherent to warrant the name. I accept this to some extent, but would point to the potential such groups carry within them (see Chapters 3 and 4). In other cases, such as that of ACES, the black self-help group, the case is more clearly made (see Chapter 5). It might also be argued that the members of the campaigning group, PIE, are not a subordinate social group, but almost entirely (in the local groups studied) members of the white, professional middle classes. Group members however *felt* subordinated in the sense that they believed themselves excluded by national government from consultation on funding policies for state education. It was lack of *recognition*, therefore, that led PIE members to feel themselves (along with other parents and teachers) to be a subordinate group. Yet clearly, on other indicators, PIE members formed a relatively privileged grouping.

Several theorists have been concerned of late with the relationship between issues of recognition and redistribution in a struggle for greater social justice (Fraser 1997a, 1997b; Young 1997b; Phillips 1999). Nancy Fraser (1997a), for example, insists upon an analytic distinction between cultural and economic inequality, in order to develop a more nuanced understanding of underlying causes and possible strategies for remedy. However, she recognizes that the two sources of oppression do not operate separately in practice.[1] PCOs, in the main, can only address the lack of *recognition* given to parents as a distinct grouping trying to ensure that parents as a whole and/or particular groups of parents are better heard and attended to. Here the blurring of the line between redistribution and recognition is already evident. The advice workers at SEAC spent some of their time ensuring parents received the benefits they were entitled to, and writing to the housing department on parents' behalf (distribution, if not quite *re*distribution), as well as championing parents' rights to comment on local special education procedure and policy (recognition). The campaigning group, PIE, had a universal, apparently redistributive goal deriving from its arguments for improved funding and smaller class sizes in all schools. But to a great extent, the PCOs were concerned with recognition, inserting parents' voices into the local and national debates about education.[2] The groups operated largely in a realm divorced from economic equality and this is a key explanation for the limitations of some of their activities. I shall return to this point in conclusion.

Disseminating discourses

In Chapters 1 and 2, I posed the question: did PCOs act as channels for the dissemination of hegemonic discourses concerning 'good' parenting? These earlier chapters suggested that there are a number of elements in play which can be read off from the current policy ensemble as defining 'good' and 'appropriate' parenting in terms of parent–school relationships. There are three such elements: the role parents should play, first as a *consumer* choosing a 'good' education for their child, second, once the child is in school, acting as a '*partner*' with education professionals, largely on the school's terms, and third, the *'responsible'* parent. The latter stresses familial self-reliance and independence, and the emotional, intellectual, social and physical work invested by the parents, usually the mother, in the development of a reasonable and reasoning child.

These dominant discourses were not accepted unproblematically by the case study groups. Instead the groups variously prioritized other conceptualizations, disregarded particular aspects, or sought directly to question hegemonic understandings. For example, ACES, the self-help group, sought to ensure all parents were able to act as informed *consumers*. Core members felt that one of the group's functions was to ensure parents had adequate information with which to make their choice. They themselves provided a particularly rich source as they acquired and disseminated both official, written information and also informal local opinion (see Chapter 5). However, the group's commitment to consumerism was heavily qualified by its members' emphasis on parental *voice* within school as well as parental *choice* of school. Similarly, SEAC sought to 'empower' parents, by legitimating and strengthening their voice within the special education system in addition to ensuring their consumer rights. Three of the groups, PIE, ACES and SEAC (the exception being the parent education group which was primarily concerned with parenting practices rather than parent–school relationships) implicitly challenged the discourse of 'partnership', by advocating a view of the parental role which had a far greater potential than that of junior *partner* with the teachers. By virtue of its campaign, PIE, for example, was asserting parents' right to be involved in decisions concerning the funding and organization of state education, in a far more immediate and significant way than the idea of 'partnership' generally allows. The notion of the *'responsible'* parent, emanating in its current form from a recent spate of authoritarian government policy prescriptions (see Chapter 2), was of particular relevance to the parent education group, concerned as it was with parenting practices. As described in Chapter 4, the tutor of the parent education group was critical of such policies, feeling that they placed an extra burden on mothers, like her students, who were struggling to bring up their children in impoverished circumstances. As a result the tutor's messages about 'good' parenting were muted. However, despite this, the focus for change remained the private sphere of interaction between family members and implicitly how such interaction could be improved. There was little space in the group for an explicit consideration of the effect the 'outside' world could have in constraining, directing or moulding family relationships.

As this example, and the earlier chapters, suggest, the PCOs did not adopt in their entirety 'official' discourses concerning parents' roles. But nor did they disseminate any radical counter-hegemonic understanding of parents' roles and relationships within the education system. The group that came closest to this was probably ACES, the self-help group. As discussed in Chapter 5, the professional background of the core members helped shape the particular orientation of the group and the boundaries of their activities. It is clear that the PCOs' conceptions of parents' roles varied and contained different nuances and priorities. However, they all disseminated one particular message about the role of the parent in relation to education: that parents had both a right and a *duty* to be involved. That involvement could be as *a critical friend* (ACES, see Chapter 5), maintaining close links with the school and supporting its work, but not unquestioningly; as alert actors involved in decisions concerning aspects of local and national policy (PIE and SEAC); and as informed individuals closely involved in monitoring their own child's education (ACES and SEAC) and supporting them at home (the parent education group). The exercise of the right to involvement and the fulfilment of that duty to be involved is clearly easier for some groups of parents than others, and the earlier empirical chapters have illustrated the difficulties and obstacles that some groups of parents experienced – those who were not fluent in English, those faced with survival issues (housing, employment, benefits) for example – leaving them with little of the energy, confidence or expectation of success which might motivate an intervention on educational issues.

Having considered the messages PCOs disseminate, the next part of the equation was to consider the reactions of individual parents. The case study chapters (3–5) considered whether parents accepted, resisted or reinterpreted the PCOs' understandings of 'good' parenting. It is clear that those individuals most closely involved with the groups perceived a close or at least a 'good enough' fit between their views and attitudes and those of the group (which is not to say that the groups themselves were not internally differentiated). The effects that membership had on particular core individuals were marked. Melucci (1989) comments that often belonging to social movements has a disruptive effect upon individuals as they come to question beliefs and attitudes they had previously accepted uncritically (also Lather 1991). However, the PCO groups did not have the all-consuming embrace of the new social movements about which Melucci mainly writes. Membership of women's groups, radical ecology and peace groups has a more obvious potential to challenge members' sense of identity, the way they lead their lives and how they understand the world around them. The PCOs by contrast offered help and support to people in roles and situations already constituted. The changes which resulted were more modest, more limited, but also more positively received, less disruptive to their sense of self. A number of participants spoke of their 'development'; they had learned new skills, and gained new resources, often of confidence and knowledge. In Chapter 3, the words of the small group of parents who worked with SEAC advisers and who adopted a 'toolbox' approach to change testify to their increase in confidence and sense of agency. Chapter 4 details similar changes, certainly in terms of an increase in confidence, in many of the women students who attended the parent education group. Another example is provided by one of the key players in PIE, Susanne. She spoke at length about how she had been changed by her personal involvement in the campaign. Her starting point was trying to safeguard her own children's education in the face of cuts to schools' budgets. Since then:

It has been a tremendous learning curve upwards . . . now I understand the intricacies and what's at stake and . . . what's going on . . . I get a tremendous amount of strength from that understanding, and then go out to schools and speak. I've never done any public speaking, but because I felt secure and happy with the knowledge I had it gave me the strength to go out and speak to parent groups and often I was speaking to two hundred-odd parents, just informally and I'd never done anything like that before . . . I hadn't worked since 1988 when my first child was born, so we're talking about quite a few years I had been a mum basically. I had lost an enormous amount of confidence over that time, not being in the workforce, not actually perhaps using my brain in that way to filter through ideas and arguments. So . . . it even took me quite a bit of strength just to go to that first meeting . . . I could possibly never have gone to that first meeting, because I was just so lacking in confidence, personal confidence . . . So the first meeting I went to I was incredibly nervous, incredibly nervous, thinking, 'What on earth have I got to say to any of these people?' I thought very carefully about what I was saying and tried to speak from a very personal point of view . . . And I have grown enormously since then, I mean I really have grown enormously.

She continued by talking more generally about the transformation that campaigning can have on women in particular:[3]

When the miners' strike was on, it was the women supporting the miners' strike [in this area] . . . and realizing the strengths and attributes that they never thought they had, and I think we're seeing the same thing also with the dockers' strike in Liverpool. Teams of women . . . who just say, 'We're only housewives' and suddenly they realize that they have got an ability to transmit knowledge and talk to people and let people know what's going on. And so a lot of people I'm talking about in this small group [East River] would perhaps be mums that have never been involved in a campaign before, like Julie Flannigan would be one, and she's subsequently gone on to be a governor at her school and she's also now a member of CASE [Campaign for the Advancement of State Education] . . . another one would be Jo Joyce who . . . has never done anything of this sort before, she's done a couple of public speaking engagements . . . and another one would be . . . the Acting Treasurer of Midshire PIE . . . She's got two little children, and even though . . . she's always worked so she hasn't lost that, perhaps that confidence side of her, I think she's also gained a lot from doing things with different groups of people as well. So it's touched an enormous amount of people, and I'm looking more at people who haven't perhaps been politically aware or campaigned or anything . . . I do think a lot of women are, I mean if I say trapped that sounds awful, because many women want to be the primary caretakers of the children, I'm not denying that, and I actually wanted to be the primary caretaker of my children, but I do think that is a lifestyle that is very insular.

Susanne's account and those of mothers from SEAC and the parent education group share one theme: the deleterious effect of motherhood upon their confidence and sense of efficacy in settings outside home. In addition, though, it is motherhood that has provided the catalyst for their activity, a point I return to below.

A brief summary of the argument might be useful at this point. The propositions of theorists of democracy and some commentators on social movements converge around the potential of groups to organize within the terrain of civil society, and as a result of their mobilization and activity to develop counter-hegemonic meanings – in Melucci's terms, new ways of naming the world. However, when this proposition is applied empirically to the PCOs, a convincing case is difficult to sustain. The case study initiatives are limited to local and fragile instances of participation and citizenship activity around education. They are also somewhat more conservative in tone than the scenarios envisaged for them by political theorists suggest (although, as Chapter 5 demonstrates, this conservatism can be read in a number of ways). As a result of these characteristics, PCOs affect individuals but not systems. As illustrated earlier, involvement with the case study groups changed the knowledge base, the perceptions of agency, and the social relations of many individuals from all four groups but especially those in PIE, in the parent education group at Elliot School and in the parents' groups at SEAC. The local education systems, specific regimes and procedures (such as special education policy and practice), the boundaries between educational institutions and parents were all less amenable to improvement and amelioration.

Particular parents

Another feature of PCO action and activity is that the groups operate around particular, not universal, concerns, namely safeguarding or improving circumstances for individual children and families. The difficulties of pursuing wider agendas, even if the group in question supports a more broadly based campaign for change, are clear in relation to all the PCOs. The lack of time, money and personnel loom large in the life of all these groups. Cutting across these practical factors is another order of constraint – professional boundary setting, parents' sense of powerlessness, a deference to professional knowledge and expertise, and a privileging of individual strategies over the possibilities of collective action. All these serve to deter involvement in collective action. The explanation for this orientation, this lack of faith in the possibility or utility of collective action, can be framed simply: we live in a passive polity. Excavating, in depth, the reasons for the predominance of a politics of 'domestication, containment and boundary drawing' (Benhabib 1996a: 7) would require a book in itself, but here I highlight three relevant points. These are lay persons' relationships with professional expertise; class-related strategies of risk management; and the particular and individual nature of many people's motivations to act.

The first point addresses lay individuals' approach to and relationship with apparent sources of expertise invested, in these examples, in professional educators and advice workers. The decline in deference to traditional sources of authority, the proliferation of forms of expertise and competing interpretations of 'reality' from experts within a particular field has ushered in a more complex relationship between individual and expert (see Chapter 3). As Giddens (1991: 7) notes, reactions from lay individuals to expert systems draw on a spectrum of possibilities ranging from trust, through pragmatic acceptance and scepticism to rejection and withdrawal. Nonetheless, the proliferation of forms of expertise is still capable of deskilling lay actors. The parent education group is one example here. As well as being given the opportunity to hone and develop their literacy and numeracy skills, the students were also encouraged to hone and develop their mothering skills. However, mothering has also been construed as 'natural' and not a necessary subject for instruction (although as Chapter 2 noted, historically, working class mothers have been more likely to be positioned as subjects for professional tutelage). SEAC could, in a pessimistic reading, also be an example of this process. Parents are encouraged to take their problems to local authority professionals who will identify a 'solution' (although of course the workers did attempt to encourage people to work *with* them, rather than have things done *for* or even *to* them and their children). However, Giddens also argues that 'the reflexive encounter with expert systems' (1991: 143) can empower individuals to develop their sense of agency and 'transform the conditions for their own actions' (p. 138). He gives the example of a woman with a back problem who becomes aware of the variety of orthodox and alternative treatments available and seeks to inform herself about her complaint and potential remedies in order to make a 'reasonably informed choice' (p. 141) about treatment. Giddens's description elaborates the type of 'toolbox' approach that I suggested was adopted by a small group of SEAC parents. The exclusivity of such 'reflexive encounters' is clear. The skills and capabilities of reflexivity are unevenly distributed across the population. They are far *easier* to adopt and practise if one has a range of resources – the money to pay for alternative treatments; the level of education needed to access even popular medical texts; the time to read and digest them; the confidence to question practitioners; and so on. All these factors operate to set boundaries on who challenges professionals, and makes their own choices and judgements, and who defers, regardless of the degree of scepticism and mistrust with which they might do so.

The second point also takes up class-related issues. Bill Jordan and his colleagues have argued that the strategies of risk management employed by middle class groups privilege the household unit over any other forms of collectivity (e.g. trade unions, community, collective political action). This prompts particular forms of activity (Jordan *et al.* 1994; Jordan 1996). Jordan argues that changes, emanating in the mid-1960s, to the structure of the national labour markets and the increasing interdependency of nations transformed the structures of opportunities and incentives for individuals within welfare states, and weakened institutional constraints that bound them to the particular collective action systems of such states – such as trade unions, local government services and social insurance systems. In consequence, middle class groups seek to handle risks to their household's position strategically and individually through, for example, making use of private welfare systems (Jordan 1996: 127). Those decisions in aggregate can affect a particular area of provision to the extent that not only are groups with fewer social resources excluded, but also the ambitions of the middle classes are vulnerable to frustration. This is partly due to the effects of congestion in particular markets, and the cycle this perpetuates – the continual raising of the stakes. Nevertheless, Jordan argues that with regard to education, the goal of higher education (in a respected institution) cannot be given up – although its attainment cannot be guaranteed – because higher education is seen as the gateway to a 'good' job and future security and fulfilment. Therefore middle class parents lay great importance upon the choice of a 'good' school and often utilize monitoring strategies within school, buying in extra provision (e.g. tutors, extra-curricular classes) as necessary (Vincent *et al.* 1999; Ball and Vincent 2000; Vincent and Martin 2000). Jordan (1996) argues that education is an example of a site within which the choices of the socially advantaged enable the formation of exclusive 'clubs' and mutualities as individuals attempt to develop assets and resources to best advantage and to manage risk. Collective action therefore is only necessary to preserve positional advantage (this argument is considered in Chapter 5 in relation to the campaigning group, PIE). Those who are in a less advantaged position are often too concerned with survival issues and working strategically within and around welfare (benefit) systems to have the energy and agency available for interactions with the education system.

Birenbaum-Carmeli (1999) picks up the importance of this division when she argues that policies that offer universal rights such as the right to be involved in one's child's education, or the right to choose a school for one's own child, can be exploited by resourceful citizens in pursuit of their particularistic interests:

> Extensive parent participation in the public school system represents therefore a certain indirect privatisation of the educational system, signifying a withdrawal from a more universal welfare policy. Whilst in principle, all parents are invited to participate in the educational process, in actuality only the more powerful ones can take advantage of this right. Moreover the realisation of democratic civil rights by privileged groups may turn into a silencing of other voices.
>
> (Birenbaum-Carmeli 1999: 86)

Birenbaum-Carmeli's paper is an example of the way in which parental participation is mediated by factors other than, or in addition to, a parent's access to and deployment of particular social, cultural and material resources. Particular national settings (she writes about Israel) as well as, on a more micro level, individual schools help shape the context in which participation occurs. The core of her account concerns parental influence on professional determination of curriculum content, an area on which parents in the UK have minimal influence. However, her point has a general relevance. Her protagonists are middle class parents, generally understood to be an influential grouping in terms of education (Reay 1998; Ball and Vincent 2000). Yet, as I have argued earlier, middle class parents as a group are internally differentiated and do not all find schools to be inevitably 'malleable' (see Chapters 1 and 2).

The third point addresses the nature and tone of what is deemed to be legitimate for discussion in the public arena. We have seen that the motivations of parents who become involved in the PCOs are informed by the desire to improve or safeguard the education and welfare of their own children. In some cases this concern became generalized to all other children, or to those of a particular group. In other cases the focus remained on an individual child. Such particularity is often deemed to be inappropriate as a spur for participation in public arenas. Birenbaum-Carmeli's (1999) account, for example, posits self-interest as inevitably selfish and detrimental to deliberation and debate. Similarly, liberal understandings of citizenship often position individuals as 'naturally' possessing the tendency to pursue their own self-interest and having to work to 'develop moral capacities to counter their basic selfish acquisitive inclinations' (Dietz 1992: 66). Nagel (1991) writes of the extreme difficulties of reconciling the 'duality of standpoints', the 'standpoint of the collectivity with the standpoint of the individual' (p. 3). He argues that finding a settlement between personal aims, interests and desires and the ability to abstract oneself from these and recognize that others have equally valid concerns is an unsolved (and largely unsolvable) problem. Yet such a solution is the basis of morally acceptable social and political arrangements.

Nagel was not, however, suggesting a binary; rather a complex intertwining of the personal and the impersonal. It is on this terrain that another reading of self-interest is possible: that self-interest is incomplete as an explanation for participation, or, to be more precise, self-interest which is narrowly conceived. As Jayne Mansbridge argues (1990), duty, love (or empathy) – two commonly recognized forms of altruism – and self-interest intermingle in our actions in ways that are difficult to sort out:

> When people think about what they want, they think about more than just their narrow self-interest. When they define their own interests and when they act to pursue those interests, they often give great weight both to their moral principles and to the interests of others.
>
> (Mansbridge 1990: ix)

Many writers within the (broadly conceived) deliberative democracy tradition have been concerned to acknowledge, even centre, the importance of the particular and the private in determining what is regarded as legitimate for discussion within the public domain (Young 1990; Mouffe 1993a; Fraser 1997a; Phillips 1999). Sara Ruddick, writing about maternal politics, political motherhood, accepts that this almost always begins with a commitment to a woman's own child and family, and that the movement from one's own to other's children is 'difficult and fragile' (1997: 374) but possible (see also Nagel 1991). Indeed, she concludes that such particularity is a strength because it acts as a strong source of motivation, as well as being valuable in itself for encouraging empathy:

> This passionate particularity is often seen as a limit of maternal politics. 'Real' politics should organise against all injustices; its causes are meant to be transpersonal and transcendent. I, however, see the partiality of maternal politics as part of its promise. People are passionate and local. What looks like the ability to transcend particular attachment is often defensive, self-deceived or the luxury of the strong and safe. Most political relationships have to be created in the midst of passionate particularity, not outside of it. Maternal politics, because it issues out of particular and familiar allegiances, can inspire a move from one's 'own' to 'other', from local to more general.
>
> (Ruddick 1997: 375)

Suppressing particularity will, as Mansbridge (1990) argues, detract from people's willingness to participate; Nagel's concept of 'duality' illustrates how intertwined the particular and the impersonal standpoints are. It is this exclusion of the particular as a valid set of concerns that makes certain traditions within civic republicanism appear so austere (Marquand 1994). Another reason for welcoming 'passionate particularity' is that the abstract equality of the universal privileges and reinforces the position of those already in power in particular social situations. On this point, Iris Young critiques Benjamin Barber's view that the conditions for a strong democracy require the 'transcending of individual needs and wants', arguing that to insist on a generalist point of view reinforces already existing privilege. She developed the ideal of communicative democracy to address this failing in some versions of deliberative democracy (Young 1989, 1996).

However, the preceding argument has suggested that it is those parents *already* in a position of social advantage who are using their particularity to consolidate that advantage, and moreover who may have the resources to mask that particularity with a language of universal concern (a criticism that could be directed at PIE; see Chapter 5). Another disadvantage is that particularity may be used to argue against specific provision on the grounds that 'my' child will not benefit from it. Therefore when the argument is weighed in relation to social justice concerns, it is clear that particularity can sometimes work against the interests of disadvantaged groups as well as sometimes in their favour (Nagel 1991; Phillips 1999: 109–10). However, it is far from clear that prohibiting the expression of particularity is a preferable strategy, as it is one which will lead to a confining, a narrowing of public participation as people direct their energies inwards towards the private household (Vincent 1992).

To summarize: three reasons are offered here for the existence of 'domestication, containment and boundary-drawing' (Benhabib 1996a: 7) which act to limit people's public involvement. First, that some sections of the population have few other realistic options but to defer to expert tutelage and guidance. Second, that middle class households have a tendency to prioritize the individual family over collective strategies. And, third, that particularity – most people's original source of motivation for participation – is often deemed inappropriate as a reason to enter the apparently objective public sphere. In particular, it is the class-related dimensions running through the first two points on which I want to dwell in the next section.

Inequalities in participation

In *Which Equalities Matter?*, Anne Phillips (1999) emphasizes the material conditions affecting participation and agency. She argues that the current focus on 'equality in the context of difference' (p. 9), on gender, racial and cultural hierarchies, has, productive and fundamental to the debate though it has proved, 'crowded out older questions of economic equality' (p. 14). She argues that people's sense of political competence, efficacy and even of interest in issues decided outside the home cannot be divorced from the economic conditions governing their own lives. There are two issues here – those of access and those of recognition:

> It is not just that the routinised nature of so many people's working lives deprives them of the opportunity to exercise their decision-making powers or that the daily confrontations with poverty leave them no time for political life [access issues]. The deeper problem is that the disparity between rich and poor blocks the recognition of equal worth . . . the profound lack of social recognition.
>
> (Phillips 1999: 80)

The lack of social recognition of all citizens is reflected starkly in how people's basic needs are met; the hegemonic positioning of people 'dependent' on state benefits, for example, as 'deficient', both in capabilities and morality. Phillips also refers to David Miller's argument that social segregation – the isolation of particular class groups in terms of housing, the services used, the schools attended – discourages the capacity to view others as equal (an argument that Jordan (1996) employs in his analogy of 'club formation', which was mentioned earlier) and is itself a process constructed around an exclusionary imperative.

Thus, Phillips emphasizes the economic factors underpinning problems of recognition. If we are to attain a more deliberative society, a more active and interactive polity, with a wider variety of associational groups at all levels, then greater political equality is necessary. A precondition for that more substantive political equality is substantive economic equality. This is a problem currently acknowledged by the Blair government, but one to which a very particular set of policy 'solutions' are posed. The concern is with attitudes and aspirations, personal responsibility and initiative. The political rhetoric describes 'promoting civic activism' and 'strong communities' (Blair 1998: 12), and strengthening the democratic impulse 'by finding new ways to enable citizens to share in decision-making that affects them' (Blair 1998: 15). Similarly David Blunkett, Secretary of State for Education and Employment, comments, 'Raising aspirations and building confidence within communities can lead to increased participation in the form of self-help groups, involvement in service-delivery and even in developing community enterprise' (1999: 14).

However, New Labour's proposals and policies operate at levels both too micro and too macro to address the issues raised by the research evidence presented here. Many of the policy proposals specifically focus on the micro level, on improving families, on isolating and remedying deficiencies in family organization, relationships, values and outlooks. The focus is on changing individuals, rectifying their home lives, not on challenging the exclusionary systems and procedures found in public sector institutions. Blunkett again:

Changing attitudes is of course very difficult. But it is vital that we do so. We need to be practical and realistic. In the past we have not got the balance right between the rights we accorded people under our benefit and other support systems and the responsibilities that they themselves needed to exercise. We are changing this. We are doing it by introducing systems which place a proper emphasis upon personal responsibility and so encourage personal initiative.

(1999: 20; see also quote from Blair 1998 in Chapter 2)

The macro proposals, the 'new democratic experiments', are far distant from the local groups and organizations in this book. The emphasis here is upon established, formal procedures: elected mayors, citizen's juries, public–private cooperation in the public sector. In all this economic inequality is recognized, but the solution is seen to lie not in its material underpinnings, but in the attitudes, the apparent indifference, apathy, and lack of ambition that deprivation engenders. The implication is that citizens rejuvenated through new opportunities will automatically go on to revitalize civil society. Yet the issues, questions and problems highlighted here remain. They concern professional–client relationships and the limited 'subject positions' open to lay individuals, the lack of tradition of citizen involvement in the public sphere, the exclusionary thrust of traditional approaches to citizenship premised on universalism, the complex ways in which gender, class and ethnicity interact to shape modes of participation, activity and inactivity. All these need to be addressed in practical terms if the resurgence and interest in generating greater political participation is to become anything more than rhetoric.

As things currently stand, there is little language, and few arenas for people coming together as citizens. Initiatives are often formal and somewhat bureaucratic, such as citizens' juries (Coote and Lenaghan 1997), rather than organic or grassroots developments, like social movements. In the education field, as elsewhere, lay associational groups, examples of collective action, are still relatively uncommon for the reasons outlined above. However, the PCOs, which have formed the subject of this book, have gone a little way towards the creation of a language and several arenas in which lay voices can be injected into what has been, hitherto, largely a professional preserve.

Notes

1 Instances of cultural inequality (e.g. the position of gays and lesbians) often have some economic element (rights to a partner's pension for example; Phillips 1999), and instances of economic inequality a cultural element (derision of aspects of culture, ways of speaking for instance traditionally associated with working class groups, Gewirtz 1997; Phillips 1999). Fraser (1997a) herself gives the position of women and black people as being paradigmatic examples of the way in which economic and cultural injustices interact.
2 Of course it is important to note that over the last 30 years other groups, notably the voices of LEAs, and in particular teachers, have been increasingly downgraded in terms of influence in the face of increasingly prescriptive central government policies.
3 Gender and not social class is seen as the differential here.

References

Adler, M., Petch, A. and Tweedie, J. (1989) *Parental Choice and Education Policy*. Edinburgh: Edinburgh University Press.

Alexander, T., Bastiani, J. and Beresford, E. (1995) *Home–School Policies: A Practical Guide*. Nottingham: JET Publications.

Anderson, P. (1994) Power, politics and the Enlightenment, in D. Miliband (ed.) *Reinventing the Left*. Cambridge: Polity Press.

Apple, M. (1996) *Cultural Politics and Education*. Buckingham: Open University Press.

Apple, M. (1999) The absent presence of race in educational reform, *Race, Ethnicity and Education*, 2(1): 9–16.

Armstrong, D. (1995) *Power and Partnership in Education*. London: Routledge.

Arnot, M., David, M. and Weiner, G. (1999) *Closing the Gender Gap*. Oxford: Polity Press.

Arnot, M. and Dillabough, J. (1999) Feminist politics and democratic values in education, *Curriculum Inquiry*, 29(2): 159–90.

Atkinson, P. (1985) *Language, Structure and Reproduction*. London: Methuen.

Bagguley, P. (1995) Middle class radicalism revisited, in T. Butler and M. Savage (eds) *Social Change and the Middle Classes*. London: UCL Press.

Bagguley, P. (1997) Review article: beyond political sociology? Developments in the sociology of social movements, *Sociological Review*, 45(1): 147–61.

Bakare-Yusuf, B. (1997) Raregrooves and raregroovers: a matter of taste, difference and identity, in H. Mirza (ed.) *Black British Feminism*. London: Routledge.

Baker, M. (1998) Decoding the Code: responsibility, dependency and restructuring. Inaugural address, Department of Sociology, University of Auckland, 24 September.

Ball, S. J. (1991) Power, conflict, micropolitics and all that!, in G. Walford (ed.) *Doing Educational Research*. London: Routledge.

Ball, S. J. (1994) *Education Reform: A Critical and Post-structural Approach*. Buckingham: Open University Press.

Ball, S. J. (1997) Good school/bad school, *British Journal of Sociology of Education*, 18(3): 317–36.

Ball, S. J. (1999) *Global Trends and Educational Reform: The Struggle for the Soul of the Teacher*, Education Policy Studies Series, no. 17. The Hong Kong Institute for Educational Research, Shatin, Chinese University of Hong Kong.

Ball, S. J. and Gewirtz, S. (1997a) *Schools, Cultures and Values: The Impact of the 1988 and 1993 Education Acts*, ESRC Final Report. London: Kings College London.

Ball, S. J. and Gewirtz, S. (1997b) Is research possible? A rejoinder to Tooley's 'On school choice and social class', *British Journal of Sociology of Education*, 18(4): 575–86.

Ball, S. J. and Vincent, C. (2000) New class relations in education: the strategies of the 'fearful' middle classes, in J. Demaine (ed.) *Education Sociology Today*. London: Macmillan.

Ball, S. J., Maguire, M. and Macrae, S. (2000) *Youth Identities and Structured Individualism*. London: Falmer Press.

Balloch, S. (1993) *Refugees in the Inner City: A Study of Refugees and Service Provision in the London Borough of Lewisham*. London: Goldsmiths College.

Barber, B. (1984) *Strong Democracy*. Berkeley, CA: University of California Press.

Beck, U. (1992) *Risk Society: Towards A New Modernity*. London: Sage.

Beck, U. and Beck-Gernsheim, E. (1995) *The Normal Chaos of Love*. Cambridge: Polity Press.

Benhabib, S. (1992) *Situating the Self*. London: Routledge.

Benhabib, S. (1996a) The democratic moment and the problem of difference, in S. Benhabib (ed.) *Democracy and Difference: Contesting the Boundaries of the Political*. Princeton, NJ: Princeton University Press.

Benhabib, S. (1996b) Towards a deliberative model of democratic legitimacy, in S. Benhabib (ed.) *Democracy and Difference: Contesting the Boundaries of the Political*. Princeton, NJ: Princeton University Press.

Bennington, J. (1977) The flaw in the pluralist heaven, in J. Raynor and E. Harris (eds.) *The City Experience*. London: Ward Lock.

Bentley, T. (1998) *Learning Beyond the Classroom*. London: Routledge.

Bernstein, B. (1973) *Class, Codes and Control, Vol. 3*. London: Routledge and Kegan Paul.

Bhatti, G. (1999) *Asian Children at Home and at School*. London: Routledge.

Birenbaum-Carmeli, D. (1999) Parents who get what they want: on the empowerment of the powerful, *Sociological Review*, 47(1): 62–90.

Blair, A. and Waddington, M. (1997) The home–school 'contract': regulating the role of parents, *Education and the Law*, 9(4): 291–305.

Blair, M. et al. (1998) *Making the Difference: Teaching and Learning Strategies in Successful Multi-ethnic Schools*, research report no.59. London: Department for Education and Employment.

Blair, T. (1998) *The Third Way: New Politics for the New Century*. London: Fabian Society.

Bloch, A. (1999) As if being a refugee isn't hard enough: the policy of exclusion, in P. Cohen (ed.) *New Ethnicities, Old Racism*. London: Zed Books.

Blunkett, D. (1999) *Social Exclusion and the Politics of Opportunity*. London: Department for Education and Employment.

Booth, T. and Potts, P. (1992) *Learning from Experience*, Course E242, unit 3/4. Milton Keynes: The Open University.

Boston, J. (1991) The theoretical underpinnings of public sector re-structuring in New Zealand, in J. Boston et al. *Reshaping the State*. Oxford: Oxford University Press.

Bowe, R., Ball, S. J. with Gold, A. (1992) *Reforming Education and Changing Schools: Case Studies in Policy Sociology*. London: Routledge.

Brannen, J. and Moss, P. (1991) *Managing Mothers: Dual Earner Households After Maternity Leave*. London: Unwin Hyman.

Brennan, D. (1998) *The Politics of Australian Child Care*. Cambridge: Cambridge University Press.

Brindle, D. (1999) Blair tells cynics: it's good to be a do-gooder, *The Guardian*, 22 January.

Brown, A. (1993) Participation, dialogue and the reproduction of social inequalities, in R. Merttens and J. Vass (eds) *Partnership in Maths*. London: Falmer Press.

Brown, A. (1999) Parental participation, positioning and pedagogy: a sociological study of the IMPACT primary school maths project. Unpublished PhD thesis, Institute of Education, University of London.

Butler, T. (1996) 'People like us': the gentrification of Hackney in the 1980s, in T. Butler and M. Rustin (eds) *Rising in the East?* London: Lawrence and Wishart.

Calhoun, C. (1995) New social movements of the early nineteenth century, in M. Traugott (ed.) *Repertoires and Cycles of Collective Action*. London: Duke University Press.

Castells, M. (1983) *The City and the Grassroots*. London: Edward Arnold.

Clarke, J. and Newman, J. (1992) Managing to survive: dilemmas of changing organisational forms in the public sector. Paper presented at Social Policy Association Conference, Nottingham University, July.

Cochrane, A. (1993) *Whatever Happened to Local Government?* Buckingham: Open University Press.

Coffey, A. (1999) *The Ethnographic Self*. London: Sage.

Cohen, J. (1997) Deliberation and deliberative democracy, in J. Bohman and W. Rehg (eds) *Deliberative Democracy*. Cambridge, MA: MIT Press.

Cohen, S. (1980) *Folk Devils and Moral Panics*. New York, NY: St Martin's Press.

Cole, I. and Furbey, R. (1994) *The Eclipse of Council Housing*. London: Routledge.

Coote, A. and Lenaghan, J. (1997) *Citizen's Juries: Theory into Practice*. London: Institute of Public Policy Research.

Corbett, J. (1999) Inclusive education and school culture, *International Journal of Inclusive Education*, 3(1): 53–61.

Crompton, R. (1987) Gender, status and professionalism, *Sociology*, 21(3): 413–28.

David, M. (1985) Motherhood and social policy: a matter of education? *Critical Social Policy*, 12: 28–44.

David, M. (1993) *Parents, Gender and Education Reform*. Cambridge: Polity Press.

David, M., Edwards, R., Hughes, M. and Ribbens, J. (1993) *Mothers and Education: Inside Out?* London: Macmillan.

Davies, C. (1996) The sociology of professions and the profession of gender, *Sociology*, 30(4): 661–78.

Daye, S. (1994) *Middle Class Blacks in Britain*. London: Macmillan.

Deem, R., Brehony, K. and Heath, S. (1995) *Active Citizenship and the Governing of Schools*. Buckingham: Open University Press.

Dehli, K. (1996) Travelling tales: thinking 'comparatively' about education reform and parental 'choice' in postmodern times, *Journal of Education Policy*, 11(1): 75–88.

Dehli, K. and Januario, I. (1994) *Parent Activism and School Reform in Toronto*. Toronto: Ontario Institute for Studies in Education.

Della Porta, D. and Diani, M. (1999) *Social Movements*. Oxford: Blackwell.

DfEE (Department for Education and Employment) (1998) *Home–School Agreements: What Every Parent should Know*. London: DfEE.

Dietz, M. (1992) Context is all: feminism and theories of citizenship, in C. Mouffe (ed.) *Dimensions of Radical Democracy*. London: Verso.

Dobson, J. (1998) Statistics are vital, *Times Educational Supplement*, 2 October.

Dominelli, L. (1995) Women in the community: feminist principles and organising in community work, *Community Development Journal*, 30(2): 133–43.

Donzelot, J. (1979) *The Policing of Families*. Baltimore, MD: Johns Hopkins University Press.

Dunleavy, P. (1991) *Democracy, Bureaucracy and Public Choice*. London: Harvester Wheatsheaf.

Edelman, M. (1964) *The Symbolic Uses of Politics*. Chicago, IL: University of Illinois Press.

Eder, K. (1993) *The New Politics of Class*. London: Sage.

Eder, K. (1995) Does social class matter in the study of social movements? A theory of middle class radicalism, in L. Maheu (ed.) *Social Movements and Social Classes: The Future of Collective Action*. London: Sage.

Eley, G. (1992) Nations, publics and political cultures: placing Habermas in the nineteenth century, in C. Calhoun (ed.) *Habermas and the Public Sphere*. Cambridge, MA: MIT Press.

Ellison, N. (1997) Towards a new social politics: citizenship and reflexivity in late modernity, *Sociology*, 31(4): 697–717.

European Parliament (1990) *Committee of Enquiry into the Rise of Racism and Xenophobia*. Series A. Document A3, 195/90. Brussels: European Parliament.

Everingham, C. (1994) *Motherhood and Modernity*. Buckingham: Open University Press.

Eyerman, R. and Jamison, A. (1991) *Social Movements: A Cognitive Approach*. Cambridge: Polity Press.

Femia, J. (1981) *Gramsci's Political Thought*. Oxford: Clarendon Press.

Field, J. (1999) Schooling, networks and the labour market: explaining participation in lifelong learning in Northern Ireland, *British Educational Research Journal*, 25(4): 501–16.

Finch, J. (1984a) *Education as Social Policy*. London: Longman.

Finch, J. (1984b) The deceit of self-help: preschool playgroups and working class mothers, *Journal of Social Policy*, 13(1): 1–20.

Fine, M. (1997) [Ap]parent involvement: reflections on parents, power, and urban public schools, in A. Halsey, H. Lauder, P. Brown and A. Stuart-Wells (eds) *Education, Culture, Economy and Society*. Oxford: Oxford University Press.

Fitz, J., Halpin, D. and Power, S. (1993) *Grant Maintained Schools: Education in the Market Place*. London: Kogan Page.

Formisano, R. (1991) *Boston against Busing*. Chapel Hill, NC: University of North Carolina Press.

Foster, P., Hammersley, M. and Gomm, R. (1996) *Constructing Educational Inequality*. London: Falmer Press.

Foucault, M. (1977) *Discipline and Punish*. London: Penguin.

Fraser, N. (1992) Rethinking the public sphere: a contribution to the critique of actually existing democracy, in C. Calhoun (ed.) *Habermas and the Public Sphere*. Cambridge, MA: MIT Press.

Fraser, N. (1997a) *Justice Interruptus*. London: Routledge.

Fraser, N. (1997b) A rejoinder to Iris Young, *New Left Review*, 223: 126–9.

Fraser, N. and Gordon, L. (1997) A genealogy of 'dependency': tracing a keyword of the US welfare state, in N. Fraser, *Justice Interruptus*. London: Routledge.

Frazer, E. and Lacey, N. (1993) *The Politics of Community: A Feminist Critique of the Liberal–Communitarian Debate*. Buffalo, Ontario: University of Toronto Press.

Freely, M. (1999) Teaching mothers a lesson, *The Guardian*, 29 September.

Funnell, R. (1995) Corporatism, self and identity within moral orders, in R. Smith and P. Wexler (eds) *After Postmodernism*. London: Falmer Press.

Gabriel, J. (1994) *Racism, Culture and Markets*. London: Routledge.

Gammel, H., Ndahiro, A., Nicholas, N. and Windsor, J. (1993) *Refugees: Service Provision and Access to the NHS*. London: College of Health.

Gewirtz, S. (1997) Post-welfarism and the reconstruction of teachers' work, *Journal of Education Policy*, 12(4): 217–31.

Gewirtz, S. and Ball, S. J. (in press) From 'welfarism' to 'new managerialism': shifting discourses of school leadership in the education marketplace, *Discourse*, 21(3).

Gewirtz, S., Ball, S. J. and Bowe, R. (1995) *Markets, Choice and Equity in Education*. Buckingham: Open University Press.

Gibson, D. (1987) Hearing and listening: a case study of the 'consultation' process undertaken by a local education department and black groups, in B. Troyna (ed.) *Racial Inequality in Education*. London: Tavistock Press.

Giddens, A. (1991) *Modernity and Self-identity: Self and Society in the Late Modern Age*. Cambridge: Polity Press.

Giddens, A. (1994) *Beyond Left and Right*. Cambridge: Polity Press.

Giddens, A. (1998) *The Third Way*. Cambridge: Polity Press.

Gillborn, D. (1998) Racism and the politics of qualitative research: learning from controversy and critique, in P. Connally and B. Troyna (eds) *Researching Racism in Education*. Buckingham: Open University Press.

Gillborn, D. and Gipps, C. (1996) *Recent Research on the Achievements of Ethnic Minority Pupils*. London: HMSO.

Gillborn, D. and Youdell, D. (1999) *Rationing Education*. Buckingham: Open University Press.

Gilroy, P. (1987) *There Ain't No Black in the Union Jack: The Cultural Politics of Race and Nation*: London: Hutchinson.

Giroux, H. (1994) *Disturbing Pleasures*. London: Routledge.

Goldring, E. (1997) Parental involvement and school choice: Israel and the United States, in Glatter *et al.* (eds) *Choice and Diversity in Schooling: Perspectives and Prospects*. London: Routledge.

Goodley, D. (1997) Locating self-advocacy in models of disability: understanding disability in the support of self-advocates with learning difficulties, *Disability and Society*, 12(3): 367–79.

Goodley, D. (1998) Supporting people with learning difficulties in self-advocacy groups and models of disability, *Health and Social Care in the Community*, 6(5): 438–46.

Gorz, A. (1989) *Critique of Economic Reason*. London: Verso.

Gould, C. (1988) *Rethinking Democracy: Freedom and Social Co-operation in Politics, Economy, Society*. Cambridge: Cambridge University Press.

Grace, G. (1995) *School Leadership: Beyond Educational Management*. London: Falmer Press.

Grace, G. (1997) Politics, markets and democratic schools: on the transformation of school leadership, in A. Halsey *et al.* (eds) *Education: Culture, Economy, Society*. Oxford: Oxford University Press.

Gramsci, A. (1957) The southern question, in *The Modern Prince and Other Writings*, translated by L. Marks. New York, NY: International Publishers.

Gramsci, A. (1971) *Selections from the Prison Notebooks*, edited and translated by Q. Hoare and G. Nowell Smith. New York, NY: International Publishers.

Gregson, N. and Lowe, M. (1994) *Servicing the Middle Classes*. London: Routledge.

Gregson, N. and Lowe, M. (1995) 'Too much work'? Class, gender and the reconstitution of middle class domestic labour, in T. Butler and M. Savage (eds) *Social Change and the Middle Classes*. London: UCL Press.

Griffith, A. and Smith, D. (1990) 'What did you do in school today?' Mothering, schooling and social class, *Perspectives on Social Problems*, 2: 3–24.

Griffith, A. and Smith, D. (1991) Constructing cultural knowledge: mothering as discourse, in J. Gaskell and A. McLaren (eds) *Women and Education: A Canadian Perspective*. Calgary, Alberta: Detselig Enterprises.

Gulbenkian Foundation (1968) *Community Work and Social Change*. London: Longmans.

Habermas, J. (1987) *The Theory of Communicative Competence, Vol. 2: Lifeworld and System*. Boston, MA: Beacon Press.

Hall, P. (1997) *Social Capital in Britain*. Mimeo, Centre for European Studies, Harvard University.

Hall, S. (1988) *The Hard Road to Renewal*. London: Verso.

Hall, S. (2000) Multicultural citizens, monocultural citizenship?, in N. Peonce and J. Hallgorten (eds) *Tomorrows Citizens*. London: IPPR.

Halpern, D. (1999) *Social Capital: The New Golden Goose?* London: Nexus/IPPR.

Halpin, D. *et al.* (1997) Opting-into the past? Grant-maintained schools and the reinvention of tradition, in R. Glatter, P. Woods and C. Bagley (eds) *Choice and Diversity in Schooling: Perspectives and Prospects*. London: Routledge.

Hammersley, M. and Atkinson, P. (1983) *Ethnography: Principles in Practice*. London: Tavistock Press.

Hanlon, G. (1998) Professionalism as enterprise: service class politics and the redefinition of professionalism, *Sociology*, 32(1): 43–63.

Hatcher, R. (1999) Exclusion, consultation or empowerment? Developing popular democratic participation in decision-making in school education, *Education and Social Justice*, 2(1): 45–57.

Hatcher, R., Troyna, B. and Gewirtz, D. (1993) *Local Management of Schools and Racial Equality*, final report to the Commission for Racial Equality. London: CRE.

Hebdige, D. (1996) Postmodernism and 'the other side', in D. Morley and K-H. Chen (eds) *Stuart Hall, Critical Dialogues in Cultural Studies*. London: Routledge.

Held, D. (1987) *Models of Democracy*. Oxford: Polity Press.

Hewitt, N. (1992) Compounding differences, *Feminist Studies*, 18(2): 313–26.

Hirschman, A. (1970) *Exit, Voice and Loyalty*. Cambridge, MA: Harvard University Press.

Holub, R. (1992) *Antonio Gramsci: Beyond Marxism and Postmodernism*. London: Routledge.

Hughes, M. (1993) Home base: policy on the education of women as adults, in M. David, R. Edwards, M. Hughes and J. Ribbens (eds) *Mothers and Education: Inside Out?* London: Macmillan.

Hughes, M., Wikeley, F. and Nash, T. (1994) *Parents and their Children's Schools*. Oxford: Blackwell.

Jetter, A., Orleck, A. and Taylor, D. (eds) (1997) *The Politics of Motherhood*. Hanover, NH: University Press of New England.

Johnson, R. (1979) 'Really useful knowledge': education and working class culture 1790–1848, in J. Clark, C. Critcher and R. Johnson (eds) *Working Class Culture: Studies in History and Theory*. London: Hutchinson.

Johnson, T. (1972) *Professionals and Power*. London: Macmillan.

Johnston, H. and Klandermans, B. (1995) The cultural analysis of social movements, in H. Johnston and B. Klandermans (eds) *Social Movements and Culture*. London: UCL Press.

Joly, D. (1996) *Haven or Hell? Asylum Policies and Refugees in Europe*. London: Macmillan.

Jones, B. (1996) Political citizenship, activism and socialist beliefs, in J. Demaine and H. Entwhistle (eds) *Beyond Communitarianism: Citizenship, Politics and Education*. London: Macmillan.

Jones, C. (1998) The educational needs of refugee children, in J. Rutter and C. Jones (eds) *Refugee Education: Mapping the Field*. Stoke: Trentham Press.

Jones, C. and Rutter, J. (1998) Mapping the field: current issues in refugee education, in J. Rutter and C. Jones (eds) *Refugee Education: Mapping the Field*. Stoke: Trentham Press.

Jordan, B. (1996) *A Theory of Poverty and Social Exclusion*. Cambridge: Polity Press.

Jordan, B., Redley, M. and James, S. (1994) *Putting the Family First: Identities, Decisions, Citizenship*. London: UCL Press.

Jowell, R. *et al.* (eds) (1998) *British and European Social Attitudes: The 15th BSA Report*. London: Ashgate.

Jowell, R., Curtice, J., Park, A. and Thomson, K. (1999) *Who Shares New Labour Values? British Social Attitudes, 16th Report*. London: Ashgate.

Keane, J. (1988) *Democracy and Civil Society*. London: Verso.

Keane, J. (1992) The modern democratic revolution: reflections on Lyotard's *The Postmodern Condition*, in A. Benjamin (ed.) *Judging Lyotard*. London: Routledge.

Keane, J. (1998) *Civil Society: Old Images, New Visions*. Cambridge: Polity Press.

Kenway, J. (1990) Education and the Right's discursive politics, in S. J. Ball (ed.) *Foucault and Education*. London: Routledge.

Kenway, J. (1995) Having a postmodern turn or postmodernist angst, in R. Smith and P. Wexler (eds) *After Postmodernism*. London: Falmer Press.

Kumar, K. (1993) Civil society: an inquiry into the usefulness of an historical term, *British Journal of Sociology*, 44(3): 375–95.

Landes, J. (1988) *Women and the Public Sphere in the Age of the French Revolution*. Ithaca, NY: Cornell University Press.

Larabee, D. (1999) No exit: public education as a public good. Conference paper presented to the 50th anniversary event of the Japan Society of Educational Sociology, Tokoyo, August.

Lareau, A. (1989) *Home Advantage: Social Class and Parental Intervention in Elementary Education*. London: Falmer Press.

Larson, C. (1997) Re-presenting the subject: problems in personal narrative inquiry, *International Journal of Qualitative Studies in Education*, 10: 455–69.

Larson, M. (1977) *The Rise of Professionalism*. Berkeley, CA: University of California Press.

Lather, P. (1991) *Getting Smart*. London: Routledge.

Lather, P. (1996) Methodology as subversive repetition: practices towards a feminist double science. Paper presented at the American Educational Research Association Annual Conference, New York, April.

Leca, J. (1992) Questions on citizenship, in C. Mouffe (ed.) *The Return of the Political*. London: Verso.

Leonard, P. (1997) *Postmodern Welfare*. London: Sage.

Levitas, R. (1998) *The Inclusive Society? Social Exclusion and New Labour*. Basingstoke: Macmillan.

Lipsky, M. (1980) *Street-level Bureaucrats*. New York, NY: Russell Sage.

Lister, R. (1990) Women, economic dependency and citizenship, *Journal of Social Policy*, 19(4): 445–67.

Lister, R. (1996) Citizenship engendered, in D. Taylor (ed.) *Critical Social Policy*. London: Sage.

Lowe, S. (1986) *Urban Social Movements: The City after Castells*. London: Macmillan.

Lyman, S. (ed.) (1995) *Social Movements: Critiques, Concepts and Case studies*. London: Macmillan.

Lyotard, J-F. (1984) *The Postmodern Condition: A Report on Knowledge*. Manchester: Manchester University Press.

McAuslan, P. (1980) *The Ideologies of Planning Law*. Oxford: Pergamon Press.

McClure, M. and Lindle, J. (eds) (1997) *Expertise versus Responsiveness in Children's Worlds*. London: Falmer Press.

MacLure, M. and Walker, B. (1999) *Secondary School Parents' Evenings*, end of award report to the Economic and Social Research Council.

Maheu, L. (ed.) (1995) *Social Movements and Social Classes: The Future of Collective Action*. London: Sage.

Manicom, A. (1984) Feminist frameworks and teacher education, *Journal of Education*, 166(1): 77–102.

Mansbridge, J. (1990) *Beyond Self Interest*. Chicago, IL: University of Chicago Press.

Mansbridge, J. (1996) Using power/fighting power: the polity, in S. Benhabib (ed.) *Democracy and Difference: Contesting the Boundaries of the Political*. Princeton, NJ: Princeton University Press.

Marfleet, P. (1996) *The Refugee in the Global Era*. London: Centre for the New Ethnicities Research, University of East London.

Marquand, D. (1994) Civic republics and liberal individualists: the case of Britain, in B. Turner and P. Hamilton (eds) *Citizenship: Critical Concepts*, Vol. 1. London: Routledge.

Marshall, T. H. (1981) *The Right to Welfare and other Essays*. London: Heinemann.

Martin, J. and Vincent, C. (1999) Parental voice: an exploration, *International Studies in Sociology of Education*, 9(3): 231–52.

Martin, J., Ranson, S. and Rutherford, D. (1995) The annual parents' meeting: potential for partnership, *Research Papers in Education*, 10(1): 19–49.

Melucci, A. (1985) The symbolic challenge of contemporary movements, *Social Research*, 52(4): 781–816.

Melucci, A. (1988) Social movements and the democratisation of everyday life, in J. Keane (ed.) *Civil Society and the State*. London: Verso.

Melucci, A. (1989) *Nomads of the Present: Social Movements and Individual Needs in Contemporary Society*. London: Hutchinson Radius.

Melucci, A. (1995) The process of collective identity, in H. Johnston and B. Klandermans (eds) *Social Movements and Culture*. London: UCL Press.

Merttens, R. and Vass, J. (1993) *Partnership in Maths*. London: Falmer Press.

Middleton, S. (1993) A post-modern pedagogy for the sociology of women's education, in M. Arnot and K. Weiler (eds) *Feminism and Social Justice in Education: International Perspectives*. London: Falmer Press.

Midwinter, E. (1972) *Priority Education*. London: Longman.

Mirza, H. (1997) Black women in education: a collective movement for social change, in H. Mirza (ed.) *Black British Feminism*. London: Routledge.

Mirza, H. and Reay, D. (1999) Spaces and places of black educational desire: rethinking black supplementary schools as a new social movement. Paper presented at the International Conference in Sociology of Education, Sheffield, January.

Modood, T. *et al.* (1997) *Ethnic Minorities in Britain*. London: Policy Studies Institute.

Moss, P. (1999) Going Critical, in S. Wolfendale and H. Einzig (eds) *Parenting Education and Support*. London: David Fulton.

Mouffe, C. (ed.) (1992) *Dimensions of Radical Democracy*. London: Verso.

Mouffe, C. (1993a) *The Return of the Political*. London: Verso.

Mouffe, C. (1993b) Liberal socialism and pluralism: which citizenship?, in J. Squires (ed.) *Principled Positions*. London: Lawrence and Wishart.

Nagel, T. (1991) *Equality and Partiality*. Oxford: Oxford University Press.

Nazroo, J. (1997) *The Health of Britain's Ethnic Minorities*, Policy Studies Institute Report no. 835. London: Policy Studies Institute.

Neckel, S. (1996) Inferiority: from collective status to deficient individuality, *Sociological Review*, 44(1): 17–34.

Ofsted (Office for Standards in Education) (1999) *Raising the Attainment of Minority Ethnic Pupils: School and LEA Responses*. London: Ofsted.

Oliver, D. (1991) *Government in the United Kingdom*. Buckingham: Open University Press.

Paechter, C. (1996) Power, knowledge and the confessional in qualitative research, *Discourse*, 17(1): 75–83.

Pateman, C. (1989) *The Disorder of Women*. Cambridge: Polity Press.

Pateman, C. (1992) Equality, difference, subordination: the politics of motherhood and women's citizenship, in G. Brock and S. James (eds) *Beyond Equality and Difference*. London: Routledge.

Peters, M. (1994) Individualism and community: education and the politics of difference, *Discourse*, 14(2): 65–78.

Phillips, A. (1993) *Democracy and Difference*. Cambridge: Polity Press.

Phillips, A. (1995) *The Politics of Presence*. Oxford: Oxford University Press.

Phillips, A. (1999) *Which Equalities Matter?* Cambridge: Polity Press.

Pickvance, C. (1995) Social movements in the transition from state socialism: convergence or divergence?, in L. Maheu (ed.) *Social Movements and Social Classes: The Future of Collective Action*. London: Sage.

Plotke, D. (1995) What's so new about New Social Movements?, in S. Lyman (ed.) *Social Movements: Critiques, Concepts and Case Studies*. London: Macmillan.

Power, S. and Gewirtz, S. (1999) Reading Education Action Zones. Paper presented at the British Educational Research Association Annual Conference, Brighton, September.

Power, S., Whitty, G. and Youndell, D. (1995) *No Place to Learn*. London: Shelter.

Power, S., Whitty, G. and Youndell, D. (1998) Refugees, asylum seekers and the housing crisis: no place to learn, in J. Rutter and C. Jones (eds) (1998) *Refugee Education: Mapping the Field*. Stoke: Trentham Press.

Putnam, R. (1993) *Making Democracy Work: Civic Traditions in Modern Italy*. Princeton, NJ: Princeton University Press.

Putnam, R. (1995) Tuning in, tuning out: the strange disappearance of social capital in America, *Political Science and Politics*, 28: 1–20.

Radnor, H., Ball, S. with Vincent, C. and Henshaw, L. (1996) *Local Education Authorities: Accountability and Control*. Stoke: Trentham Press.

Rawls, J. (1971) *A Theory of Justice*. Cambridge, MA: Harvard University Press.

Rawnsley, A. (1999) 'My moral manifesto for the 21st century': an interview with Tony Blair, *Observer*, 5 September.

Reay, D. (1996) Micropolitics in the 1990s: staff relationships in secondary schools. Paper presented at the British Educational Research Association Conference, Lancaster, September.

Reay, D. (1998) *Class Work: Mothers' Involvement in their Children's Primary Schooling*. London: UCL Press.

Reay, D. and Mirza, H. (1997) Uncovering genealogies of the margins: black supplementary schooling, *British Journal of Sociology of Education*, 18(4): 477–99.

Refugee Council (1998a) editorial, *iNexile*, September.

Refugee Council (1998b) Ever decreasing circles, *iNexile*, September: 12–13.

Refugee Council (1998c) editorial, *iNexile*, November: 1.

Refugee Council (1999a) Don't believe the hype, *iNexile*, February: 12–13.

Refugee Council (1999b) What happened to the bill?, *iNexile*, June: 4–5.

Refugee Council (1999c) editorial, *iNexile*, September.

Refugee Council (1999d) All change, *iNexile*, September: 5–8.

Ribbens, J. (1994) *Mothers and their Children*. London: Sage.

Richmond, A. (1994) *Global Apartheid: Refugees, Racism and the New World Order*. Oxford: Oxford University Press.

Roche, M. (1995) Rethinking citizenship and social movements, in L. Maheu (ed.) *Social Movements and Social Classes: The Future of Collective Action*. London: Sage.

Rootes, C. (1995) A new class? The higher educated and the new politics, in L. Maheu (ed.) *Social Movements and Social Classes: The Future of Collective Action*. London: Sage.

Ruddick, S. (1997) Rethinking 'maternal' politics, in A. Jetter, A. Orleck and D. Taylor (eds) *The Politics of Motherhood*. Hanover, NH: University Press of New England.

Rutter, J. and Jones, C. (eds) (1998) *Refugee Education: Mapping the Field*. Stoke: Trentham Press.

Sallis, J. (1991) Home/school contracts: a personal view, parents in a learning society, *Royal Society of Arts News*, 4: 7.

Sandel, M. (1982) *Liberalism and the Limits of Justice*. Cambridge: Cambridge University Press.

Scheurich, J. (1997) *Research Methods in the Postmodern*. London: Falmer Press.

Schuller, T. and Field, J. (1998) Social capital, human capital and the learning society, *International Journal of Lifelong Education*, 17 (4): 226–35.

Scott, J. (1990) *Domination and the Arts of Resistance*. New Haven, CT: Yale University Press.

Showstack Sassoon, A. (1980) *Gramsci's Politics*. London: Croom Helm.

Slee, R. and Weiner, E. with Tomlinson, S. (1998) *School Effectiveness for Whom?* London: Falmer.

Smith, D. (1988) *The Everyday World as Problematic: A Feminist Sociology*. Buckingham: Open University Press.

Smith, D. (1991) Writing women's experiences into social science, *Feminism and Psychology*, 1(1): 155–69.

Sommerville, J. (1997) Social movement theory, women and the questions of interests, *Sociology*, 31(4): 673–95.

Standing, K. (1999) Lone mothers and 'parental involvement': a contradiction in policy? *Journal of Social Policy*, 28(3): 479–96.

Stewart, J. (1997) Towards democratic justice, in J. McCormick and A. Harvey (eds) *Local Routes to Social Justice*. London: Institute for Public Policy Research.

Strauss, A. (1987) *Qualitative Analysis for Social Scientists*. New York, NY: Cambridge University Press.

Strauss, A. and Corbin, J. (1998) *Basics of Qualitative Research*. Thousand Oaks, CA: Sage.

Tassin, E. (1992) Europe: a political community?, in C. Mouffe (ed.) *Dimensions of Radical Democracy*. London: Verso.

Taylor, D. (1996) Citizenship and social power, in D. Taylor (ed.) *Critical Social Policy*. London: Sage.

Taylor, I. (1996) Fear of crime, urban fortunes and suburban social movements: some reflections from Manchester, *Sociology*, 30(2): 317–37.

Taylor, I., Evans, K. and Fraser, P. (1996) *A Tale of Two Cities*. London: Routledge.

Tizard, B. and Hughes, M. (1984) *Young Children Learning*. London: Fontana.

Todd, E. and Higgins, S. (1998) Powerlessness in professional and parent partnerships, *British Journal of Sociology of Education*, 19(2): 227–36.

Tomlinson, S. (1982) *A Sociology of Special Education*. London: Routledge and Kegan Paul.

Tomlinson, S. and Hutchison, S. (1991) *Bangladeshi Parents and Education in Tower Hamlets*. London: Advisory Centre for Education.

Touraine, A. (1985) An introduction to the study of social movements, *Social Research*, 52(4): 749–87.

Troyna, B. and Vincent, C. (1995) The discourses of social justice in education, *Discourse*, 16(2): 149–66.

Troyna, B. and Williams, J. (1986) *Racism, Education and the State*. Beckenham: Croom Helm.

Tooley, J. (1997) On school choice and social class: a response to Ball, Bowe and Gewirtz, *British Journal of Sociology of Education*, 18(2): 217–30.

Turner, B. (1990) Outline of a theory of citizenship, *Sociology* 24(2): 189–217.

Turner, B. (1996) Capitalism, class and citizenship, in D. Lee and B. Turner (eds) *Conflicts about Class: Debating Inequality in Late Industrialism*. London: Longman.

Urry, J. (1995) A middle class countryside?, in T. Butler and M. Savage (eds) *Social Change and the Middle Classes*. London: UCL Press.

Urwin, C. (1985) Constructing motherhood: the persuasion of normal development, in C. Steedman, C. Urwin and V. Walkerdine (eds) *Language, Gender and Childhood*. London: Routledge and Kegan Paul.

Vincent, C. (1992) Tolerating intolerance? Parental choice and race relations – the Cleveland case, *Journal of Education Policy*, 7(5): 429–43.

Vincent, C. (1996) *Parents and Teachers: Power and Participation*. London: Falmer Press.

Vincent, C. and Ball, S. (1999) A market in love? Choosing pre-school child care. Paper presented at the British Educational Research Association Annual Conference, Brighton, September.

Vincent, C. and Martin, J. (2000) School-based parents' groups: a politics of voice and representation?, *Journal of Education Policy*, 15.

Vincent, C. and Tomlinson, S. (1997) Home–school relationships: 'the swarming of disciplinary mechanisms'?, *British Educational Research Journal*, 23(3): 361–77.

Vincent, C. and Tomlinsm, S. (1998) The perils of 'partnership', *Topic*, 20: 1–5.

Vincent, C. and Warren, S. (1997) A 'different kind' of professional? Case studies of the work of parent-centred organisations, *International Journal of Inclusive Education*, 1(2): 271–83.

Vincent, C. and Warren, S. (1998) *Supporting Refugee Children in School: A Focus on Home–School links*, final report to the Nuffield Foundation. Coventry: University of Warwick.

Vincent, C. and Warren, S. (1999) Class, race and collective action, in J. Salisbury and S. Riddell (eds) *Gender, Policy and Educational Change*. London: Routledge.

Vincent, C. and Warren, S. (forthcoming) 'This won't take long . . .' Interviewing, ethics and diversity, *International Journal for Qualitative Studies in Education*, 13.

Vincent, C., Martin, J. and Ranson, S. (1999) 'Little Polities': Schooling, Governance and Parental Participation, end of award report to the ESRC.

Vincent, C., Evans, J., Lunt, I. and Young, P. (1996) Professionals under pressure: the administration of special education in a changing context, *British Educational Research Journal*, 22(4): 475–91.

Walker, B. (1998) Meetings without communication: a study of parents' evenings in secondary schools, *British Educational Research Journal*, 24(2): 163–78.

Walkerdine, V. and Lucey, H. (1989) *Democracy in the Kitchen*. London: Virago.

Weatherley, R. (1979) *Reforming Special Education*. Cambridge, MA: MIT Press.

Westoby, A. (1989) 'Parental choice and voice under the 1988 ERA', in R. Glatter (ed.) *Educational Institutions and their Environments: Managing the Boundaries*. Buckingham: Open University Press.

Whitty, G., Power, S. and Halpin, D. (1998) *Devolution and Choice*. Buckingham: Open University Press.

Wilding, P. (1982) *Professional Power and Social Welfare*. London: Routledge and Kegan Paul.

Williams, R. (1977) *Marxism and Literature*. Oxford: Oxford University Press.

Willmott, H. (1993) Strength is ignorance; slavery is freedom: culture in modern organisations, *Journal of Management Studies*, 30: 215–52.

Witz, A. (1990) Patriarchy and professions: the gendered politics of occupational closure, *Sociology*, 24(4): 675–90.

Woods, P., Bagley, C. and Glatter, R. (1998) *School Choice and Competition*. London: Routledge.

Wyness, M. (1997) Parental responsibilities, social policy and the maintenance of boundaries, *Sociological Review*, 45(2): 304–24.

Yeatman, A. (1993) Corporate managerialism and the shift from the welfare to the competition state, *Discourse*, 13(2): 3–9.

Yeatman, A. (1994) *Postmodern Revisionings of the Political*. London: Routledge.

Young, I. (1989) Polity and group difference: a critique of the ideal of universal citizenship, *Ethics*, 99: 250–74.

Young, I. (1990) *Justice and the Politics of Difference*. Princeton, NJ: Princeton University Press.

Young, I. (1996) Communication and the other: beyond deliberative democracy, in S. Benhabib (ed.), *Democracy and Difference: Contesting the Boundaries of the Political.* Princeton, NJ: Princeton University Press.

Young, I. (1997a) Difference as a resource for democratic communication, in J. Bohman and W. Rehg (eds) *Deliberative Democracy: Essays in Reason and Politics.* Cambridge, Mass: MIT Press.

Young, I. (1997b) Unruly categories: a critique of Nancy Fraser's dual systems theory, *New Left Review*, 222: 147–60.

Yuval Davis, N. (1997) *Gender and Nation.* London: Sage.

Index

CHANGING EDUCATION FOR DIVERSITY

David Corson

Beginning from the premise of the ethical 'principle of equal treatment' – that we should treat everyone equally unless there are relevant reasons for treating them unequally – Corson proceeds not only to show the relevant reasons why 'equal treatment' has not worked in minority education but also to suggest a pragmatic program for change. The book is clearly addressed to educational practitioners – teachers, teacher educators, educational researchers and policy makers – and is clearly intended to serve as a handbook for fostering the change processes he advocates: every chapter includes not only questions for reflection and discussion but also numerous guidelines, stages, steps and checklists for evaluation and goal-setting.

Nancy Hornberger, Goldie Anna Professor of Education,
University of Pennsylvania

- How can schools become more welcoming places for students from backgrounds of diversity?
- How can teachers respond to student diversity and still provide high quality education for all:

Reforms to education for diversity are now getting worldwide attention because of the great population shifts over the last two or three generations. These migrations highlight issues that once went unnoticed, even in countries that always had large minority groups. A climate favouring the more tolerant treatment of students from diverse backgrounds is affecting schools everywhere. Important changes are taking place in the education of:

- girls from immigrant cultures
- indigenous cultural groups
- the urban poor
- language minorities

Using an international and cross-cultural scope, this book presents policies and practices that already work in real schools, and which the world of education can learn from.

Contents

Reforming education for diversity – Building community-based education through critical policy making – Changing the education of aboriginal peoples – Changing the education of girls from immigrant cultures – Changing the education of the urban poor – Changing the education of minority language groups – Making the educational world safe for students from diverse backgrounds – Notes – References – Index.

288pp   0 335 19587 3 (Paperback)   0 335 19588 1 (Hardback)

COLLABORATING FOR EFFECTIVENESS
EMPOWERING SCHOOLS TO BE INCLUSIVE

Jennifer Evans, Ingrid Lunt, Klaus Wedell and Alan Dyson

- How can schools and local education authorities best deploy their available resources to meet a wide range of learning needs efficiently and effectively?
- Is collaboration between schools an effective way of meeting a wide range of learning needs?
- What types of collaboration are possible, and how useful are they?

This book analyses the current context within which schools are required to meet a diverse range of learning needs. Whilst competition and fragmentation appear to be key features of the current system, nevertheless there is growing evidence of widespread collaboration between schools which are working together to support pupils with a range of diverse needs. The authors draw on their recent research to illustrate the variety of collaborative arrangements which exist and make some recommendations for the future organization of schools and services to support a more inclusive education system.

Contents

Introduction – The political and legislative context – Collaboration for special educational needs: a national survey – Collaboration in action – The organization and management of collaboration – Resourcing additional needs – Effective teaching and learning – Sharing expertise – The way forward – References – Index.

160pp   0 335 20228 4 (Paperback)   0 335 20229 2 (Hardback)

STRUGGLES FOR INCLUSIVE EDUCATION

Anastasia D. Vlachou

This is a lucid, authoritative and original study of teachers' views and attitudes towards the integration into mainstream schooling of a particular group of children defined as having special educational needs. It offers one of the clearest and most comprehensive analyses of the socio-political mechanisms by which the 'special' are socially constructed and excluded from the normal education system that has so far been produced.

Sally Tomlinson,
Professor of Educational Policy at Goldsmiths College,
University of London

In its detailed analysis of primary school teachers' and pupils' attitudes towards integration, this book locates the question of inclusive education within the wider educational context. The wealth of original interview material sheds new light on the reality of everyday life in an educational setting, and shows us the nature and intensity of the struggles experienced by both teachers and pupils in their efforts to promote more inclusive school practices. The author's sensitive investigation of the relationship between teachers' contradictory views of the 'special' and their integration, and the wider social structures in which teachers work, adds to our understanding of the inevitable difficulties in promoting inclusive educational practices within a system which functions via exclusive mechanisms.

The book will be of interest to students of education, sociology and disability as well as teachers and policy-makers involved in inclusive education. The original methodologies adopted when working with the children will also appeal to students of attitudinal, disability and educational research.

Contents

Introduction – Part 1: Setting the theoretical scene – Disability, normality and special needs: political concepts and controversies – Towards a better understanding of attitudes – Part 2: Teachers' perspectives – Teachers and the changing culture of teaching – Teachers' attitudes towards integration (with reference to pupils with Down's Syndrome) – Part 3: Children's perspectives – Integration: the children's point of view – Disabled children and children's culture – Conclusion – Appendices – References – Index.

208pp   0 335 19763 9 (Paperback)   0 335 19764 7 (Hardback)